Sustrans'

Circular Day [illegible]H

sustrans

JOIN THE MOVEMENT

Sustrans'
Circular Day Rides SOUTH

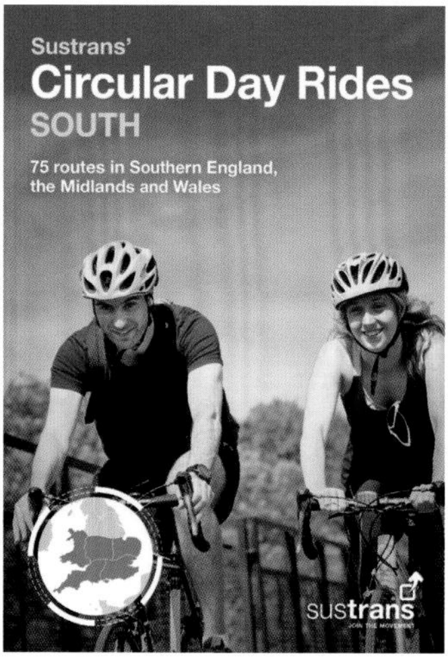

All maps in this publication contain Ordnance Survey data © Crown copyright and database right 2017.

Contains public sector information licensed under the terms of the Open Government Licence v3.0.

Maps © OpenStreetMap contributors

http://www.openstreetmap.org/copyright and http://opendatacommons.org

Cartography © FourPoint Mapping www.fourpointmapping.co.uk

Text Sarah Breaux

Published by
Sustrans,
2 Cathedral Square,
College Green,
Bristol BS1 5DD,
United Kingdom

www.sustrans.org.uk

First published 2017
ISBN: 978-1-910845-44-8

We have taken all responsible steps to ensure that the cycle rides in this book are safe and achievable by people with a reasonable level of fitness. However, all outdoor activities involve a degree of risk and the publisher and author accepts no responsibility for any injuries caused to readers while following these routes.

The contents of this book are believed to be correct at the time of printing. Nevertheless, the publisher and author cannot be held responsible for any errors or omissions or for changes in the details given in this book or for the consequences of any reliance on the information provided by the same. This does not affect your statutory rights.

Download GPX files: www.sustrans.org.uk/cdr-south-gpx

sustrans
JOIN THE MOVEMENT

Registered Charity No. 326550 (England and Wales)
SC039263 (Scotland)

Contents

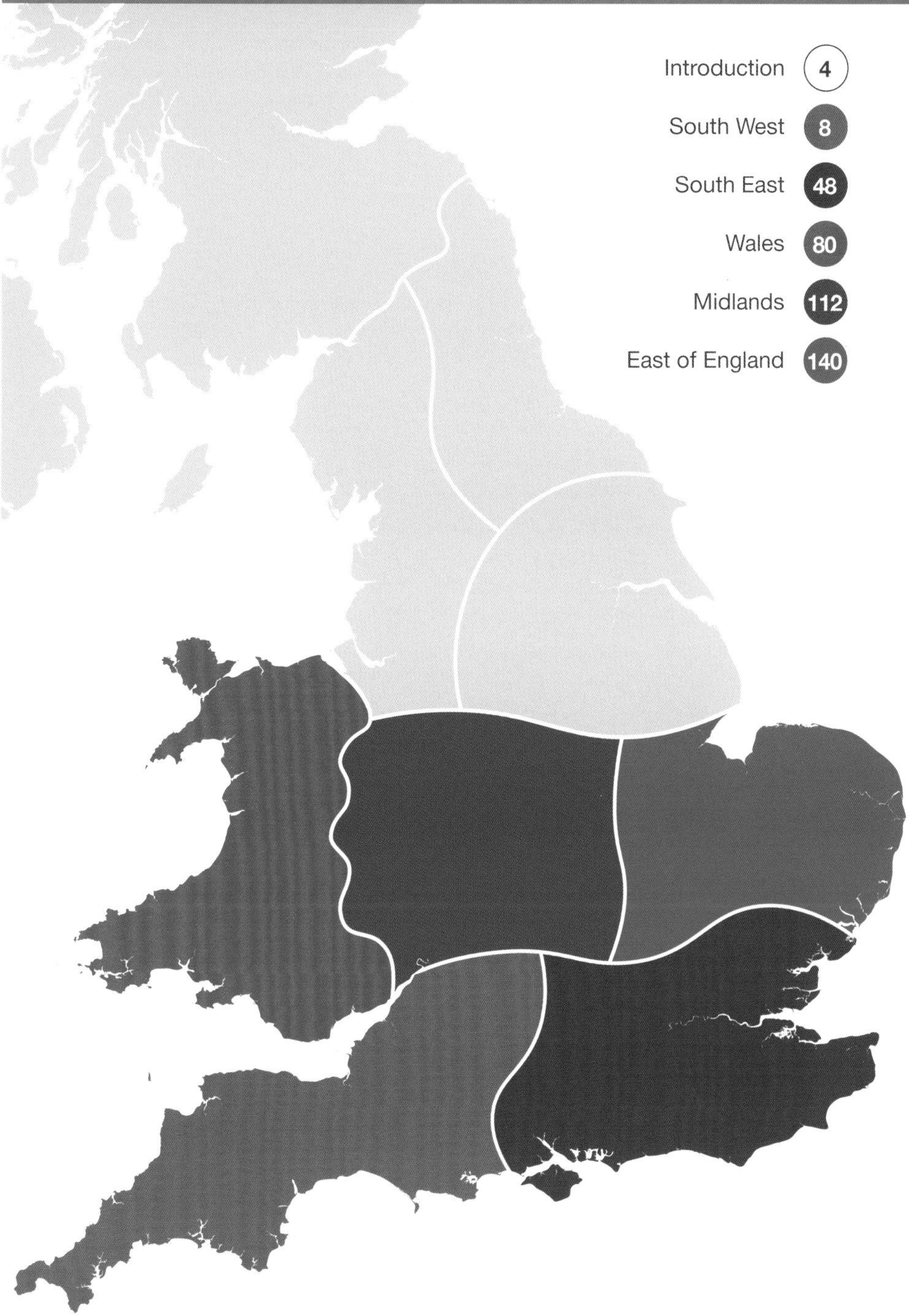

This collection of 75 circular rides has been created by the charity Sustrans to help you explore the southern half of the UK, one day – and one cycle ride - at a time. The rides are mostly between 20 and 30 miles on different terrain across the National Cycle Network, quiet lanes and byways. Suitable for intermediate to experienced cyclists, they have been chosen for their variation and spectacular views of the coast and countryside. This new guide makes it easier than ever to plan exhilarating one-day adventures in the saddle.

Sustrans and the National Cycle Network

Sustrans is the charity making it easier for people to walk and cycle. The charity connects people and places, creates liveable neighbourhoods, transforms the school run and delivers a happier, healthier commute.

The National Cycle Network was launched by Sustrans in 1995 with the aim of giving people safe and pleasant places to walk and cycle. It began with the idea of converting disused railway lines into greenways, starting with the now famous Bristol and Bath Railway Path, which has become the most well-used cycle path in the country.

Today the Network extends to over 14,000 miles, taking in towns and cities, villages and countryside throughout the UK. Some of the routes on the Network have become extremely popular challenge rides for cycle touring, such as the Sea-to-Sea in the North of England, the Devon Coast to Coast in the South West, the Celtic Trail in Wales and the Caledonia Way in Scotland.

Others are much-loved shorter routes that are traffic-free and ideal for leisure and family rides, while some remain hidden gems that take in what must be the most stunning landscapes the UK has to offer.

The complete range of National Cycle Network maps and guidebooks by Sustrans is available at **shop.sustrans.org.uk**

You can find out more about how you can support the charity's work to maintain the National Cycle Network and make it easier for people to walk and cycle at **www.sustrans.org.uk**

You can even sponsor your very own mile of the Network at **www.sustrans.org.uk/mymile**

Sponsor a mile

Signs on the National Cycle Network

National Cycle Network

Regional Cycle Network

When cycling on the National Cycle Network and following a route described in this book, you'll see these signs.

Stay in touch on: **facebook.com/Sustrans** **@sustrans** **@sustrans**

Travel

Most of these Day Rides begin and end at a railway station, and Sustrans fully encourages using public transport to travel to the start-points of these routes.

Cycles are carried free of charge on UK domestic rail services, but spaces are usually limited (maybe only two per train) and reservations are sometimes required. If you know when you are travelling it is advisable to check in advance. Tandems are only carried by exception. There are no restrictions for folding bikes.

Full-size cycles may not be carried on replacement bus services during engineering work or service disruption. For full rail travel information go to **www.nationalrail.co.uk** or call 03457 484950.

For details of all public transport journeys throughout the UK, including local bus services, go to **www.traveline.info** or call 08712 002233 (charges apply).

Practical Information

What kind of bike

The routes utilise a variety of surface types from sealed tarmac roads to fine-compacted gravel tracks and loose stony paths. All-terrain bikes, touring bikes and hybrid bikes are the best choice. We would not recommend using a lightweight racing / road bike for some of the routes.

Preparing for the ride

Before you go, check your bike is in good condition - make sure the tyres are pumped up and the seat and handlebars are set to the right position. Also check brakes and lights are in good working order and tightly secured, gears change smoothly, gear and brake cables aren't rusty or frayed, wheels are tightly secured and the chain is clean and lubricated. See Sustrans' website for details of how to conduct the 'M-Check' - their own 11-step guide.

What to wear

You shouldn't need to invest in lots of specialist clothing or footwear to enjoy the routes. Wear thin layers which you can easily add or remove as you go, and choose light, breathable fabrics. Take waterproof clothing, a hat and gloves. If you are going to be cycling in gloomy conditions, consider a bright reflective top. Padded shorts can be helpful for extra comfort when riding. Wearing a helmet is currently not compulsory in the UK, so the decision is ultimately a question of individual choice. Although helmets don't prevent accidents from happening, they can protect you if an accident does occur. If it's sunny some sun cream might be a good idea as you could be outside all day.

Pannier bags

You shouldn't need to take much with you, but if you want or need to take a lot of equipment we recommend using Ortlieb Pannier Bags. They are reliable, durable and waterproof, and their quick-release mechanism makes them easy to use. Sustrans branded bags are available exclusively from our online shop, so buy yours today from **shop.sustrans.org.uk**

Essentials

There is no definitive list of what you should take with you, but the items below are what we recommend as essential:

- Multi-tool
- Mini-pump
- Tyre levers
- Puncture repair kit
- Spare inner-tube
- Lightweight jacket
- Mobile phone
- Emergency snacks
- Emergency money

Accommodation

There are several organisations that offer accommodation or listing services which may prove useful.

Visit **www.bedsforcyclists.co.uk** for cycle-friendly accommodation listings for the whole of the UK – mapped against the National Cycle Network. Bookings made through **www.fairbookinguk.com** ensure that all your payment goes directly to the accommodation provider.

For information on hostels and bunkhouses visit:
www.yha.org.uk and **www.independenthostels.co.uk**

Find camping and caravan sites at **www.campingandcaravanningclub.co.uk**
Facilities may vary, so check before you arrive.

For more information about places to visit, where to stay and attractions go to:
www.visitbritain.com, **www.visitengland.com**, **www.visitwales.com**, **www.visitscotland.com** and **www.discovernorthernireland.com**

Cycle shops

Where available, we have provided some details of bike shops and bike hire for each route. Further information for bike shops in the area can be found at:
www.thecyclingexperts.co.uk

Tarka Trail, National Route 3, Westleigh, Devon.

Good Cycling Code

Please follow this simple Good Cycling Code and do your bit to keep the National Cycle Network a friendly, safe network that's accessible for all users.

- Cycle at a safe and responsible speed and cycle slowly where there is limited space and / or when you cannot see clearly ahead.
- Remember shared-use paths are for sharing not for speeding. Do not use the paths for recording times with challenge apps or for fitness training.
- Give way and be courteous to pedestrians and wheelchair users, and take care around horse-riders leaving them plenty of room.
- Have a bell on your bike and use it gently to try and avoid surprising people and horses. If you've no bell, a friendly greeting works just as well. Remember many people are hard of hearing or visually impaired.
- Take care when pulling out to overtake other cyclists, and learn the technique of looking over your shoulder - there may be another cyclist overtaking YOU.
- Keep to your side of any dividing line and keep to the left where there isn't one.
- Be particularly careful at junctions, bends, access points and any other blind spots.
- Take extra care going downhill and on loose surfaces. Cover your brakes and ride within your own limits, not those of others.
- In dark or dull conditions make sure you have bike lights and consider wearing bright clothing or hi-vis.
- Do not cycle whilst using your mobile phone or listening to MP3 players.
- Do not cycle on pavements unless they are designated for shared-use.
- When cycling beside waterways, give consideration to anglers and boat users, and watch out for obstacles such as fishing lines and mooring ropes.

National Route 4 between Bath and Bristol.

South West

South West

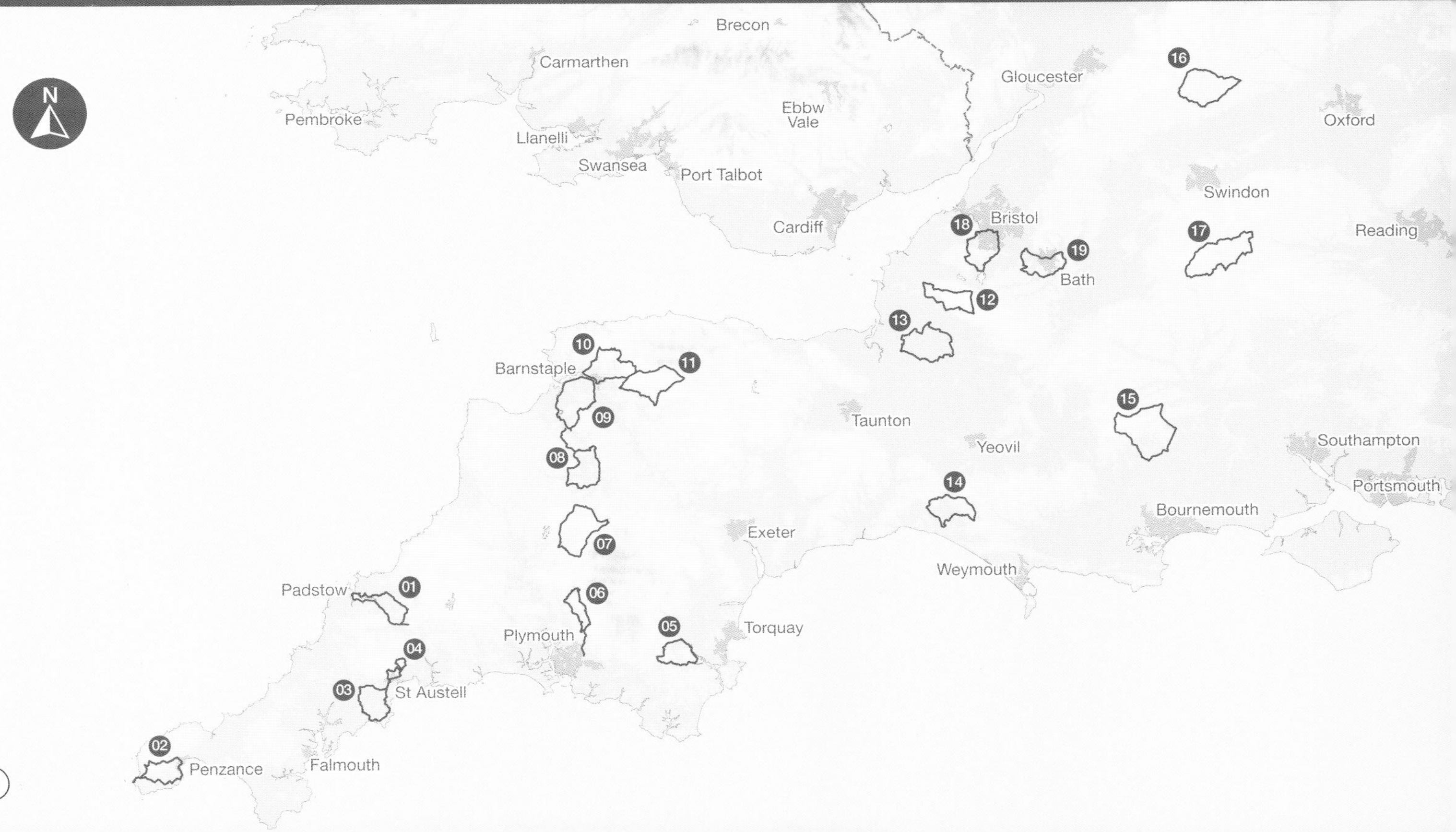
N
Brecon
Carmarthen
Gloucester
Oxford
Pembroke
Ebbw Vale
Llanelli
Swansea
Port Talbot
Swindon
Cardiff
Bristol
Reading
Bath
Barnstaple
Taunton
Yeovil
Southampton
Portsmouth
Bournemouth
Exeter
Weymouth
Padstow
Plymouth
Torquay
St Austell
Penzance
Falmouth
01
02
03
04
05
06
07
08
09
10
11
12
13
14
15
16
17
18
19

From Bodmin head west on Berrycoombe Rd / Route 32 / Camel Trail (near Bodmin Gaol). Follow the traffic-free path along the River Camel to Wadebridge, continue **straight** on Guineapost Rd, then turn **right** at The Regal cinema. Stay **straight** at The Swan Hotel and then at the Lidl roundabout take the path straight ahead. Follow the trail to where it ends in Padstow and continue **straight** along the water – the ferry to Rock will be on your right. From Rock ferry go **right** on Rock Rd, then hard **right** on Porthilly Ln. At the T-junction go **right**. At the B3314 turn **right** and then keep **straight** (don't turn right) towards Chapel Amble. At the T-junction turn **right** and then **left** at the Maltster's Arms. At the next junction turn **right** towards St Mabyn. Continue **straight** over the A39, then after St Mabyn turn **right** towards Helland and Bodmin. At the B3266 turn **right** for Bodmin and then **left** for Helland. Cross over the bridge, then turn **right** at the small white house and you will see the entrance to the Camel Trail / Route 3. Follow the trail all the way back to where you started in Bodmin.

Alternatively, you can start and end the route in Padstow or Rock.

Bike shops

Bodmin Bikes
PL31 2LL Tel: 01208 73192

The Wadebridge Bike Shop
PL27 7NS Tel: 01208 815262

Camel Trail Cycle Hire
PL27 7AL Tel: 01208 814104

Bridge Bike Hire
PL27 7AL Tel: 01208 813050

Padstow Cycle Hire Ltd
PL28 8BL Tel: 01841 533533

Trail Bike Hire
PL28 8BL Tel: 01841 532594

Eat & drink

The Camel Trail Tea Garden
PL30 5LG Tel: 01208 74291

The Swan Hotel
PL27 7DD Tel: 01208 812526

The Old Custom House
PL28 8BL Tel: 01841 532359

The Harbour Inn
PL28 8BU Tel: 01841 533148

The Rock Inn
PL27 6LD Tel: 01208 863498

Mariner's Rock
PL27 6LD Tel: 01208 863679

Maltster's Arms
PL27 6EU Tel: 01208 812473

The St Mabyn Inn
PL30 3BA Tel: 01208 841266

The Borough Arms
PL31 2RD Tel: 01208 73118

Various in Bodmin

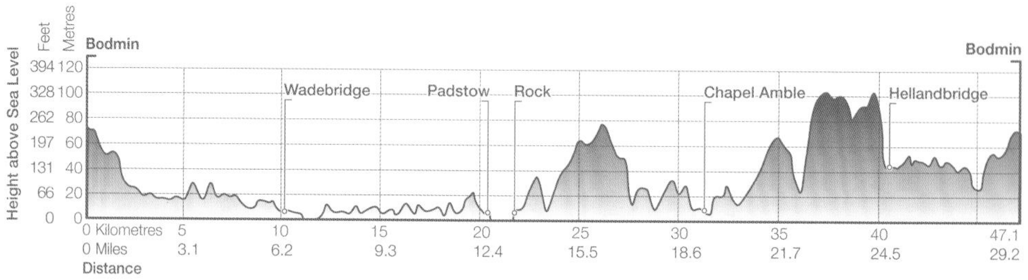

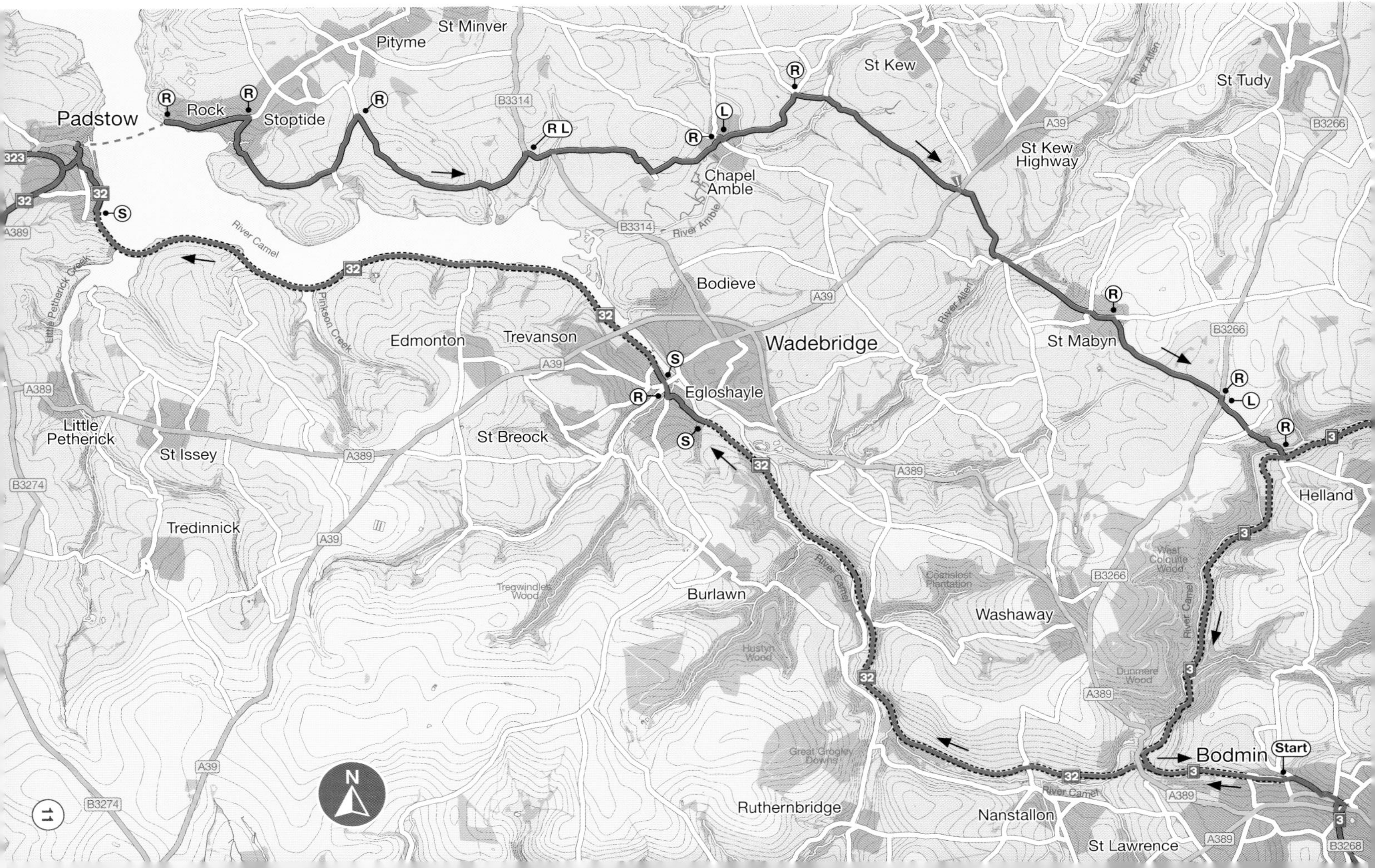
Padstow
Rock
Stoptide
Pityme
St Minver
B3314
Chapel
Amble
River Amble
St Kew
St Kew
Highway
River Allen
St Tudy
A39
B3266
River Camel
Little Petherick Creek
Pinkson Creek
Bodieve
Edmonton
Trevanson
Wadebridge
Egloshayle
St Mabyn
Little
Petherick
St Issey
St Breock
A389
B3274
Tredinnick
Helland
West
Colquite
Wood
Costislost
Plantation
Washaway
Tregwindles
Wood
Burlawn
Hustyn
Wood
Dunmere
Wood
Great Grogley
Downs
Rutherbridge
Nanstallon
Bodmin
Start
St Lawrence
B3268
32
3
R
L
S
N

From Penzance Station take Route 3 south along the coast through Newlyn and Mousehole, then west through Castallack, Lamorna, St Buryan and Sennen Cove to Land's End. On the return journey follow Route 3 back to the A30 and turn **left** towards Penzance, leaving Route 3. Exit **left** for the B3306 towards St Just. After passing Land's End Airport turn **right** towards Dowran. At the next T-junction turn **right** towards Grumbla. Turn **left** towards Tremethick Cross. At the A3071 turn **jink right left** towards Madron and Heamoor. Go **right** twice towards Penzance. At the A30 go **straight** and continue on Nancealverne. After The Fountain Tavern turn **left** on Taroveor Rd. At the T-junction turn **left** on Alverton St, then curve **left** on Morrab Rd. At the coast turn **left** on Route 3 and follow back to the station.

Bike shops

The Cycle Centre
TR18 2LZ Tel: 01736 351671

Penzance Bike Hire Torwood
TR18 4LZ Tel: 01736 360063

Eat & drink

The Fisherman's Arms
TR18 5JR Tel: 01736 363399

The Ship Inn
TR19 6QX Tel: 01736 731234

Lamorna Wink
TR19 6XQ Tel: 01736 731566

St Buryan Inn
TR19 6BA Tel: 01736 810385

The Old Success Inn
TR19 7DG Tel: 01736 871232

First & Last House
TR19 7AA

Land's End Visitors Centre
TR19 7AA Tel: 0871 720 0044

Trengwainton Tea Room & Garden
TR20 8RZ Tel: 01736 331717

The Fountain Tavern
TR18 2PD Tel: 01736 369340

Various in Penzance

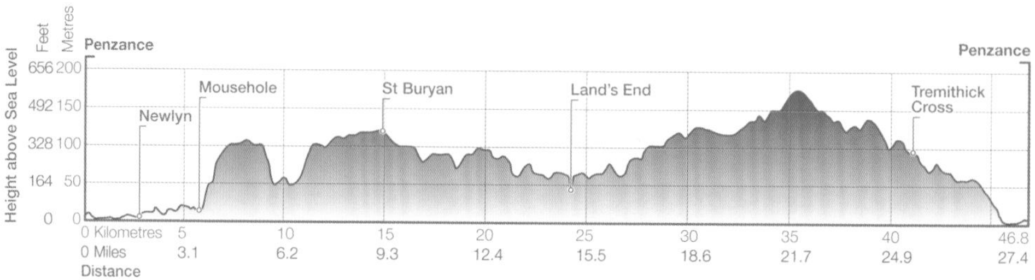

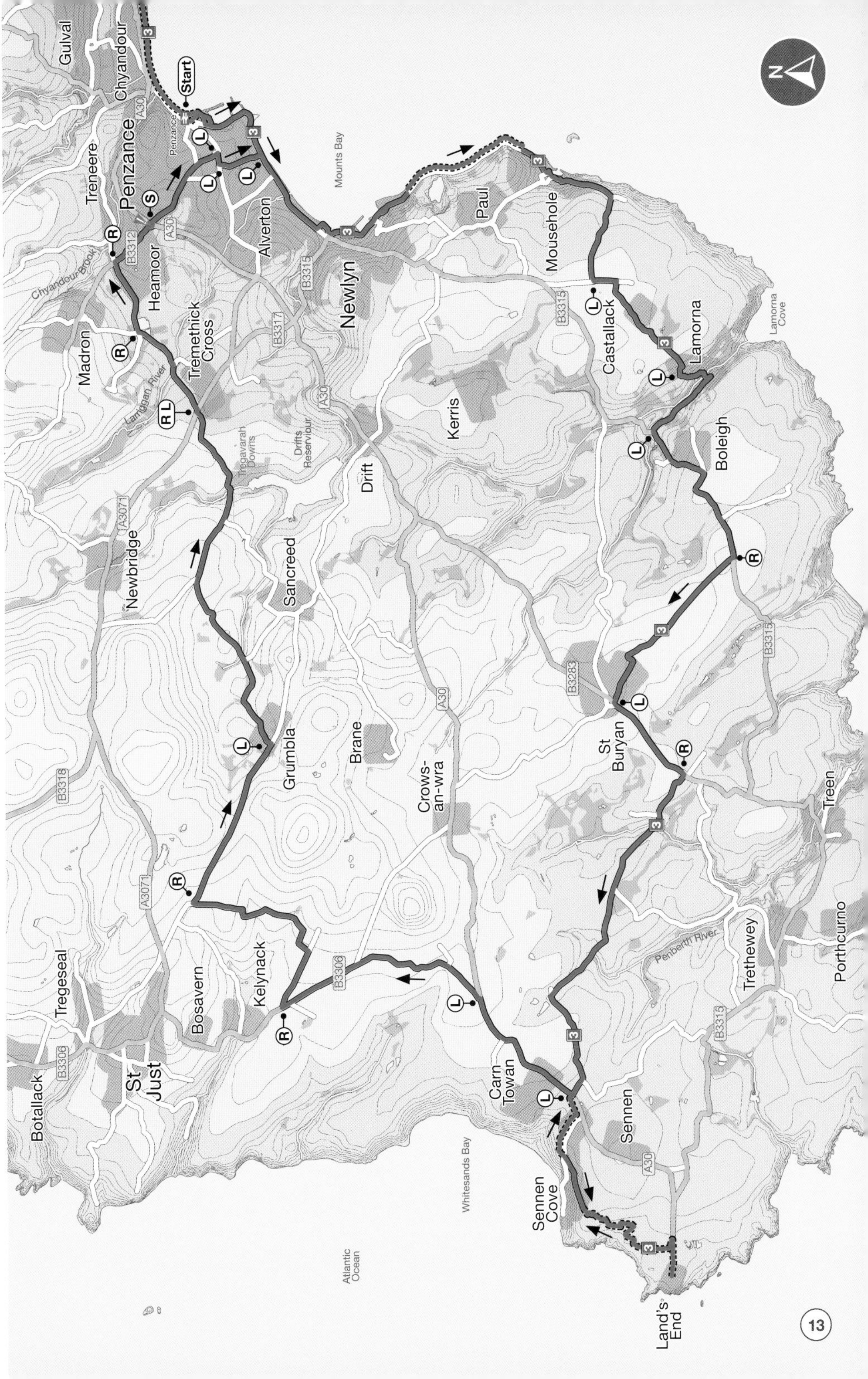
Start
Penzance
Gulval
Chyandour
Treneere
Heamoor
Madron
Chyandour Brook
Lariggan River
Tremethick Cross
Alverton
Newlyn
Mounts Bay
Paul
Mousehole
Castallack
Lamorna
Lamorna Cove
Kerris
Drift
Drifts Reservoir
Tregavarah Downs
Newbridge
Sancreed
Boleigh
Grumbla
Brane
Crows-an-wra
St Buryan
Treen
Trethewey
Porthcurno
Penberth River
Kelynack
Bosavern
Tregeseal
St Just
Botallack
Carn Towan
Sennen
Sennen Cove
Whitesands Bay
Atlantic Ocean
Land's End
A30
A3071
B3312
B3315
B3317
B3283
B3306
B3318

From St Austell Station follow Route 3 south along Eastbourne Rd and Sawles Rd, then join the traffic-free path. There is an optional detour to Pentewan, and be sure to visit the Lost Gardens of Heligan before continuing on to Mevagissey. We also recommend a visit to Caerhays Castle & Gardens (open Feb-June). Follow Route 3 passing through St Michael Caerhays, then when the route goes left towards St Mawes stay **right**, leaving Route 3. At the next T-junction turn **left**, then at the fork go **right** towards Tregony. Take the next **right** towards Grampound. At the B3287 turn **right** and then take the next **left** towards Creed. At the A390 **jink right left** onto Pepo Ln. At the T-junction turn **right**. Continue **straight** at the next junction and then **left** at the unsigned T-junction. At the next junction turn **right** towards Sticker. At The Hewas Inn turn **left** and then **right** on Chapel Hill towards Mevagissey. At the junction take the second **left** towards London Apprentice. When the road ends turn **right**, then turn **left** on the B3273 towards St Austell. Turn **right** into the River Valley Holiday Park and join Route 3 heading north back to St Austell. Before you depart you may want to visit the St Austell Brewery just north of the station.

Bike shops

Pavé Velo
PL25 5AA Tel: 01726 64950

Halfords
PL25 5BU Tel: 01726 68981

Eat & drink

Ship Inn
PL26 6BX Tel: 01726 842855

Various in Mevagissey Harbour

The Rising Sun Inn
PL26 6PL Tel: 01726 843235

The Barley Sheaf
PL26 6HN Tel: 01726 843330

Caerhays Beach Restaurant
PL26 6LX Tel: 01872 501115

Dolphin Inn
TR2 4RR Tel: 01726 882435

The Hewas Inn
PL26 7HB Tel: 01726 73497

The Polgooth Inn
PL26 7DA Tel: 01726 74089

Kingswood Bar & Restaurant
PL26 7AP Tel: 01726 63780

Various in St Austell

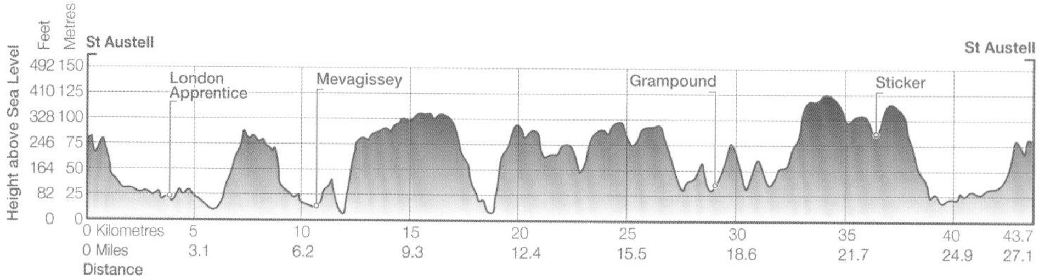

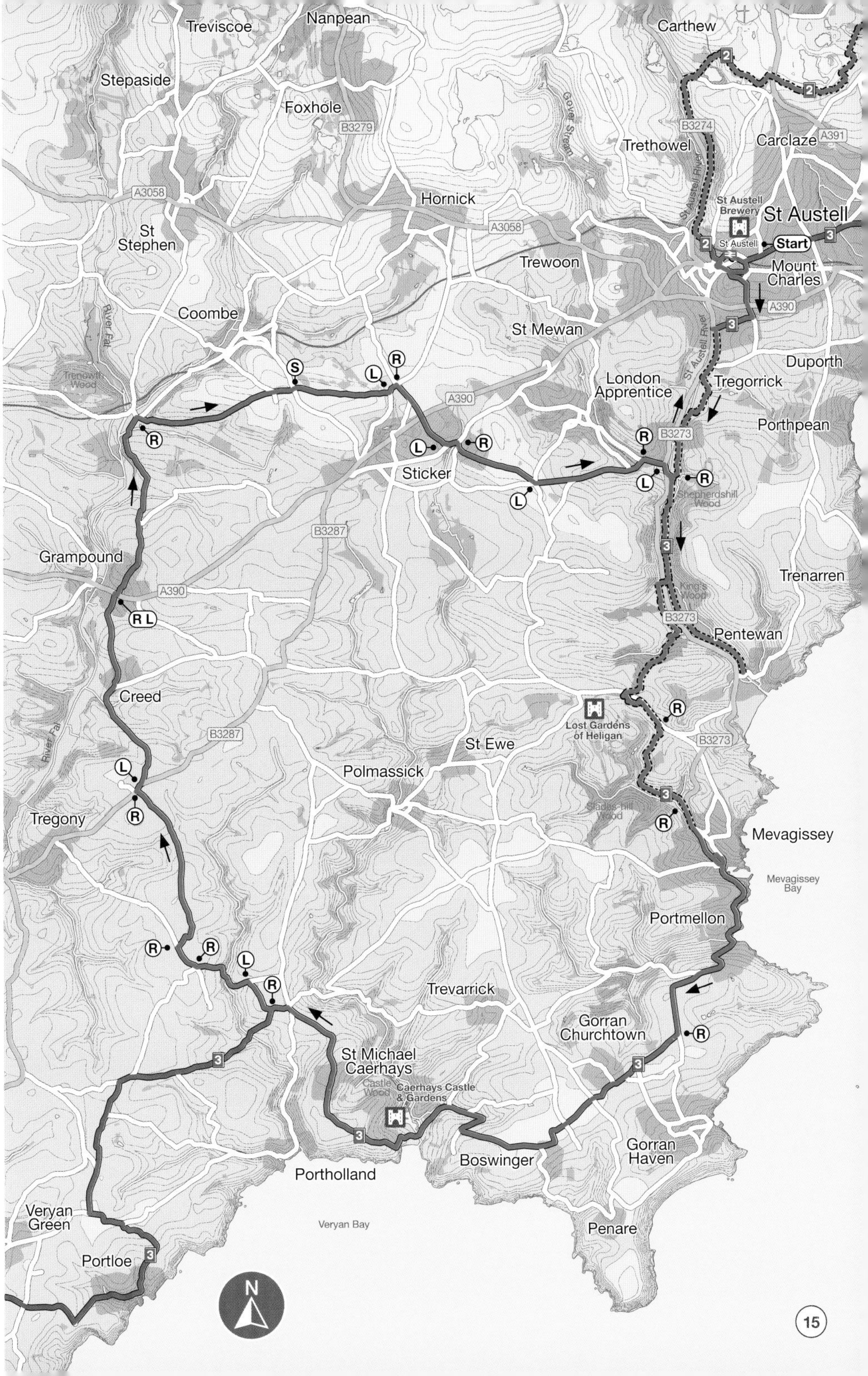
Treviscoe
Nanpean
Carthew
Stepaside
Foxhole
B3279
Gover Stream
B3274
Trethowel
Carclaze
A391
A3058
Hornick
St Austell River
St Austell Brewery
St Austell
St
Stephen
A3058
St Austell
Start
Trewoon
Mount
Charles
River Fal
Coombe
A390
St Mewan
Duporth
St Austell River
Trenowth
Wood
London
Apprentice
Tregorrick
A390
Porthpean
B3273
Sticker
Shepherdshill
Wood
B3287
Grampound
Trenarren
A390
King's
Wood
B3273
Pentewan
Creed
Lost Gardens
of Heligan
B3273
B3287
St Ewe
River Fal
Polmassick
Tregony
Mevagissey
Mevagissey
Bay
Portmellon
Trevarrick
Gorran
Churchtown
St Michael
Caerhays
Castle
Wood
Caerhays Castle
& Gardens
Boswinger
Gorran
Haven
Portholland
Veryan
Green
Veryan Bay
Penare
Portloe
N

Clay Trails & the Eden Project

15.7 miles / 25.3 km

From St Austell Station turn **left** on Trevarthian Rd, **right** on North St and **left** on Tremena Rd to join Route 2. Follow Route 2 all the way to where it meets Route 3 at the Eden Project. You can stop for a visit now if you wish, or wait for the return loop. To continue, take Route 3 north and then turn **left** on Route 305. Follow Route 305 until you come to a road T-junction signed Clay Trails / Bugle left. Turn **right** here leaving Route 305. At The King's Arms turn **left**, then turn **right** towards Lavery – you are now on Route 3. Follow the route south, pass under the rail tracks, then turn **right** to continue on Route 3 back to the Eden Project. You can visit now if you did not before. To continue, take Route 3 south and follow all the way back to St Austell Station. Before you depart you may want to visit the St Austell Brewery just north of the station.

Bike shops

Pavé Velo
PL25 5AA Tel: 01726 64950

Halfords
PL25 5BU Tel: 01726 68981

Eat & drink

Knightor Winery
PL26 8YQ Tel: 01726 851101

Eden Project Coffee House / Med Terrace
PL24 2SG Tel: 01726 811911

The Innis Inn
PL26 8YH Tel: 01726 851162

King's Arms
PL30 5EF Tel: 01726 850202

Various in St Austell

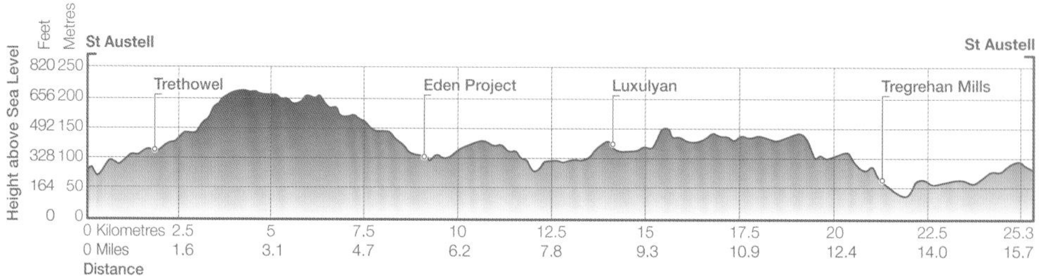

Bilberry
A391
305
Bugle
Bugle
305
Luxulyan
R
Luxulyan
L
305
R
Bridges
3
A391
B3374
B3274
305
Trevanney Wood
Stenalees
R
Penwithick
A391
B3374
B3274
Carthew
Pengall Plantation
Trethurgy
Warren Wood
305
Cornish Wood
L
3
Tremains Wood
St Austell River
Trelawney
2
Eden Project
2
2
2
2
B3274
Carclaze
A391
3
Trethowel
A390
Boscoppa
St Austell River
Bethel
A390
St Blazey Gate
3
St Austell Brewery
St Austell
L
L
Start
2
R
St Austell
3
Sandy Bottom
Holmbush
A390
Cuddra Plantation
A3082
Crinnis Wood
B3274
3
Mount Charles
A390
A390
Carlyon Bay
B3273
St Austell River
Charlestown
St Austell Bay
3
Tregorrick
Duporth

From Totnes Station exit **left** through the car park to the riverside Route 2 path. Go under the rail tracks and along the river. The route is traffic-free until the A384. There turn **left** and **left** to follow the route towards Rattery. Descend into Rattery, leaving Route 2 (don't follow right). Cross under the rail tracks, **straight** over the A385 and keep **straight** ahead. Turn **right** towards Avonwick then at the T-junction turn **left**. Turn **left** at the River Avon and follow the road to Diptford. Turn **right** towards Moreleigh and Kingsbridge. Turn **right** again for the same and then turn **left** for Beenleigh. Turn **right** towards Murtwell and then **left** towards Harbertonford. When the road ends turn **left**, then turn **right** to Harbertonford. **Jink right left** at The Maltster's Arms then turn **right** on Bow Rd. Turn **right** towards Bow Bridge. **Jink right left** towards Ashprington. When you reach a pillar with 'Sharpham', turn slight **left** onto the Route 28 off-road path towards Totnes. When the path ends turn **left** towards Totnes. At the roundabout keep **straight**, then join the shared-use path on your right. Follow the path over the rail tracks and back to the station.

Bike shops

Hot Pursuit Cycles
TQ9 5LQ Tel: 01803 865174

Eat & drink

The Church House Inn
TQ10 9LD Tel: 01364 642220

The Avon Inn
TQ10 9NB Tel: 01364 73475

The Maltster's Arms
TQ9 7SZ Tel: 01803 732630

The Waterman's Arms Inn
TQ9 7EG Tel: 01803 732214

Durant Arms
TQ9 7UP Tel: 01803 732240

Sharpham Vineyard
TQ9 7UT Tel: 01803 732203

The Steam Packet Inn
TQ9 5EW Tel: 01803 863880

The Dartmouth Inn
TQ9 5EL Tel: 01803 863252

Various in Totnes

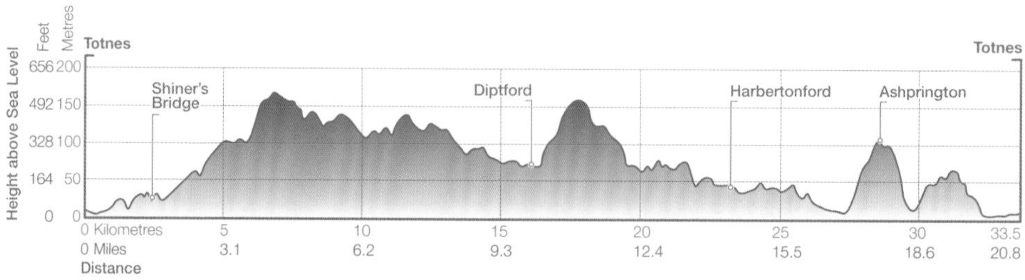

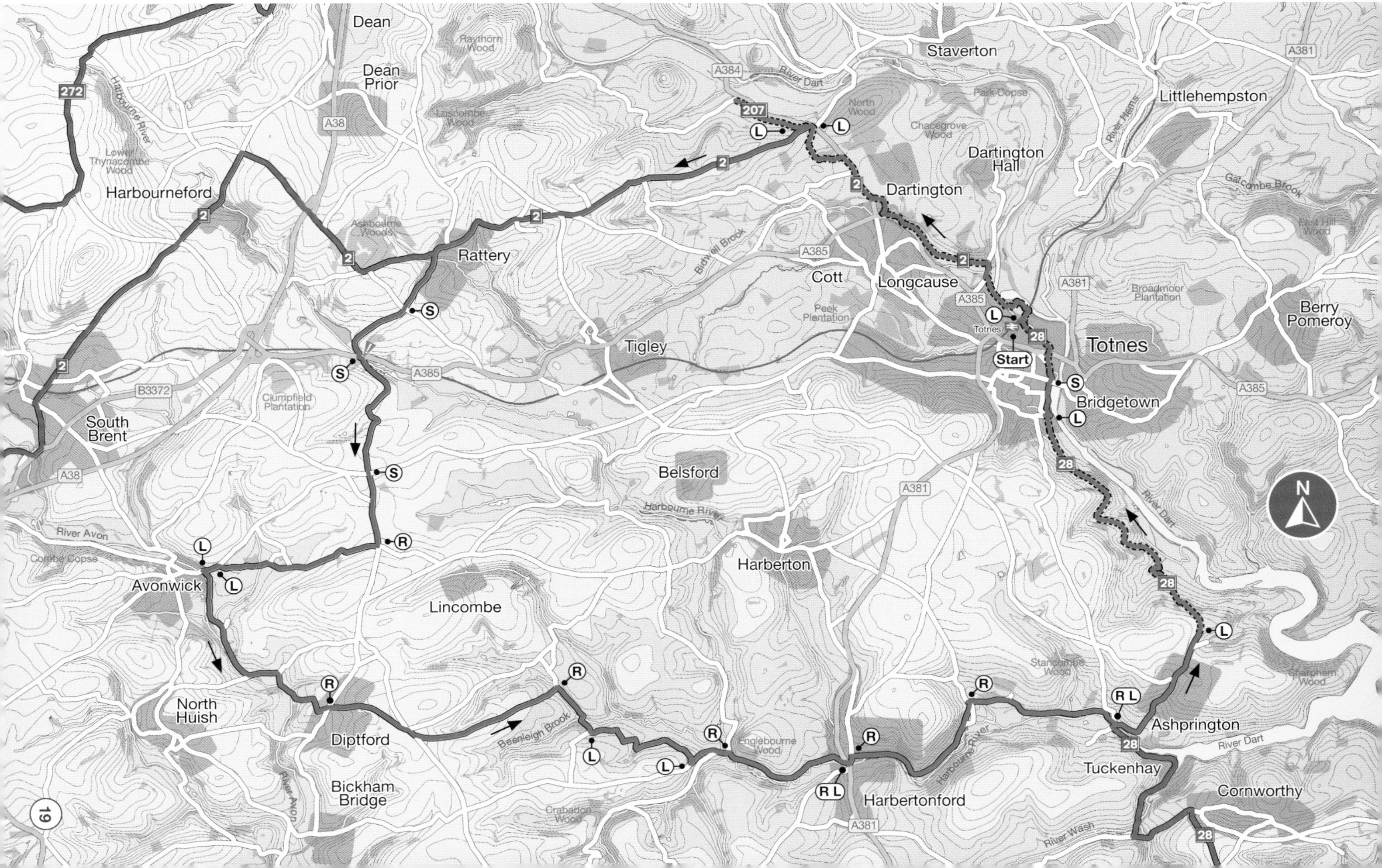
Dean
Dean Prior
Raythorn Wood
Staverton
Littlehempston
Luscombe Wood
Harbourne River
Lower Thynacombe Wood
Harbourneford
Ashbourne Woods
Rattery
Park Copse
North Wood
Chacegrove Wood
Dartington Hall
Dartington
River Dart
River Hems
Galcombe Brook
East Hill Wood
Bidwell Brook
Cott
Longcause
Peek Plantation
Broadmoor Plantation
Berry Pomeroy
Totnes
Start
Bridgetown
Tigley
Clumpfield Plantation
South Brent
Belsford
Harbourne River
River Avon
Combe Copse
Harberton
Avonwick
Lincombe
North Huish
Diptford
Bickham Bridge
Beenleigh Brook
Englebourne Wood
Crabadon Wood
Harbertonford
Stancombe Wood
Sharpham Wood
Ashprington
Tuckenhay
Cornworthy
River Wash
A38
A381
A384
A385
B3372
2
28
207
272
S
L
R
R L
N

06 Plymouth to Tavistock (Drake's Trail) 30.7 miles / 49.4 km

The mapped route begins from Plym Bridge car park, but you can also start from Plymouth.

From Plymouth Station: Take Route 2 east, then follow Route 27 to cross the River Plym on the bridge north of Laira Bridge. Continue left (north) on traffic-free Route 27.

From Plym Bridge car park follow signs for Tavistock and Route 27. Go up to the railway path and head north on traffic-free Route 27 to Clearbrook. When the path ends turn **right**, then after crossing the river turn **left** towards Meavy. Continue to follow signs for Route 27 / 274 north. Before reaching Peter Tavy turn **left** on Langsford Rd. At the A386 turn **left** towards Tavistock, joining the shared-use path. At the triangle cycle sign turn **right**, then turn **left** after passing under the bridge. The route will go off-road for a bit, then continue **left** on Old Exeter Rd. Go left on Route 270 if you want to avoid the town centre, or continue **straight** on Route 27 to pass through Tavistock. If you opt for Route 270 it will re-join 27 after crossing the A390. Continue south on Route 27 back to the start. For a visit to National Trust property Buckland Abbey, please go left at the Yelverton roundabout and follow the signs.

Returning to Plymouth: Where Route 27 splits at Plymouth Rd / B3416, keep straight towards the city centre if you want to return to the train station, otherwise go left to follow Route 27 which will take you past Saltram House & Garden, the National Marine Aquarium and the Tinside Lido.

Bike shops

Red Brick Cycles
PL3 4NU Tel: 01752 603526

Evans Cycles Plymouth
PL4 0BG Tel: 01752 444100

Tavistock Cycles Ltd
PL19 0HF Tel: 01822 617630

Rockin Bikes Ltd
PL20 6DJ Tel: 01822 258022

Eat & drink

The Royal Oak
PL20 6PJ
Tel: 01822 852944

The Burrator Inn
PL20 6PE
Tel: 01822 853121

The Trout 'n' Tipple
PL19 0JS
Tel: 01822 618886

Various in Tavistock

The Whitchurch
PL19 9ED
Tel: 01822 612181

Drake's Café
PL19 9ER
Tel: 01822 617697

The London Inn
PL20 7ST
Tel: 01822 853567

The Rock Inn Yelverton
PL20 6DS
Tel: 01822 852022

Skylark Inn
PL20 6JD
Tel: 01822 853258

Various in Plymouth

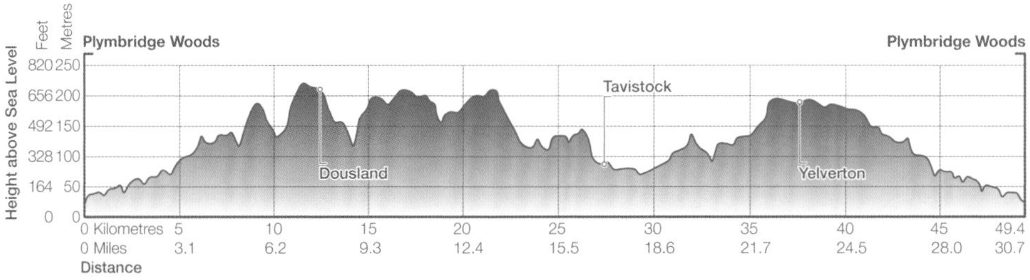

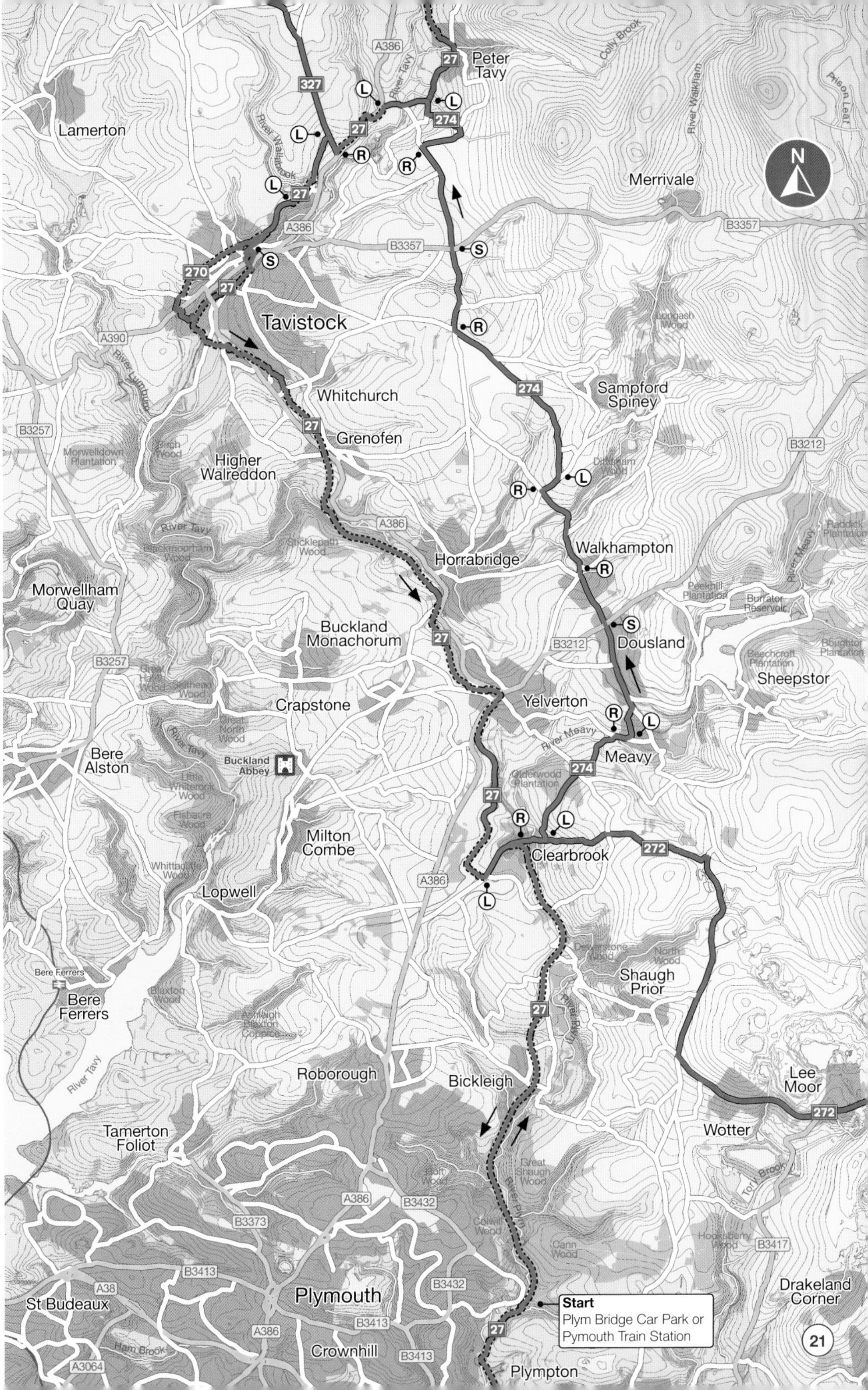
Peter Tavy
Lamerton
Merrivale
Tavistock
Whitchurch
Grenofen
Sampford Spiney
Higher Walreddon
Walkhampton
Horrabridge
Morwellham Quay
Buckland Monachorum
Dousland
Sheepstor
Crapstone
Yelverton
Bere Alston
Buckland Abbey
Meavy
Milton Combe
Clearbrook
Lopwell
Shaugh Prior
Bere Ferrers
Roborough
Bickleigh
Lee Moor
Tamerton Foliot
Wotter
Plymouth
St Budeaux
Drakeland Corner
Crownhill
Plympton
Start
Plym Bridge Car Park or Pymouth Train Station
River Tavy
River Walkham
River Meavy
Colly Brook
River Wallabrook
River Lumburn
Tory Brook
Ham Brook
Longash Wood
Ditsworthy Wood
Peekhill Plantation
Burrator Reservoir
Beechcroft Plantation
Morwelldown Plantation
Birch Wood
Sticklepath Wood
Olderwood Plantation
Great Shaugh Wood
Cann Wood
A386
A390
A38
A3064
B3357
B3257
B3212
B3432
B3373
B3413
B3417
327
27
274
270
272

07 Okehampton to Lydford (Granite Way) **28.7 miles / 46.3 km**

From Okehampton Station take Route 27 north towards the town centre. At the church turn **left** on Fore St. Turn **right** on High St and then **right** on Old Rd. Take the second **right**, then first **right**. Turn **right** at the T-junction. Stay **right** towards Northlew then **straight** ahead at the A386. Pass through Northlew and then continue south towards Bratton Clovelly crossing the A3079. Once you've reached Bratton Clovelly continue following signs for Lewdown, passing under the A30. At the crossroads turn **left** towards Axworthy, then stay **right** towards Alder. Turn **left** then **right** towards Lydford. At the next T-junction turn **left** and continue on to Lydford. At the war memorial turn **left** towards Okehampton. Turn **left** off the road onto Route 27 / Granite Way towards Okehampton. Follow the traffic-free route all the way back to Okehampton, enjoying the views from the Lake and Meldon Viaducts. Before leaving you can visit the Okehampton Castle ruins.

Bike shops

Okehampton Cycles
EX20 1BQ Tel: 01837 53811

Granite Way Cycles
EX20 1EW Tel: 01837 650907

Eat & drink

The Green Dragon Inn
EX20 3NN Tel: 01409 221228

Clovelly Inn
EX20 4JZ Tel: 01837 871447

Castle Inn
EX20 4BH Tel: 01822 820242

Bearslake Inn
EX20 4HQ Tel: 01837 861334

The Dartmoor Inn
EX20 4AY Tel: 01822 820221

The Highwayman Inn
EX20 4HN Tel: 01837 861243

Various in Okehampton

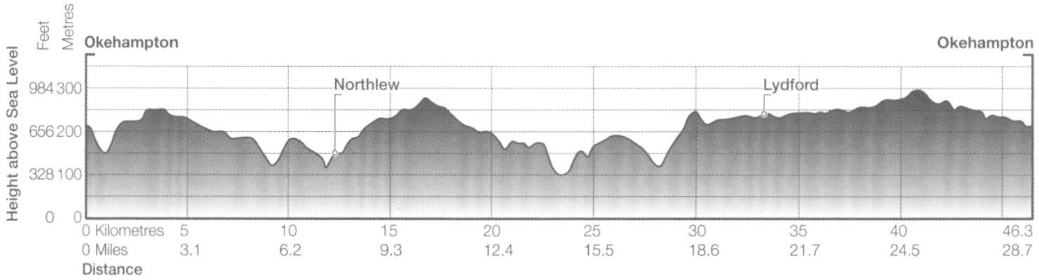

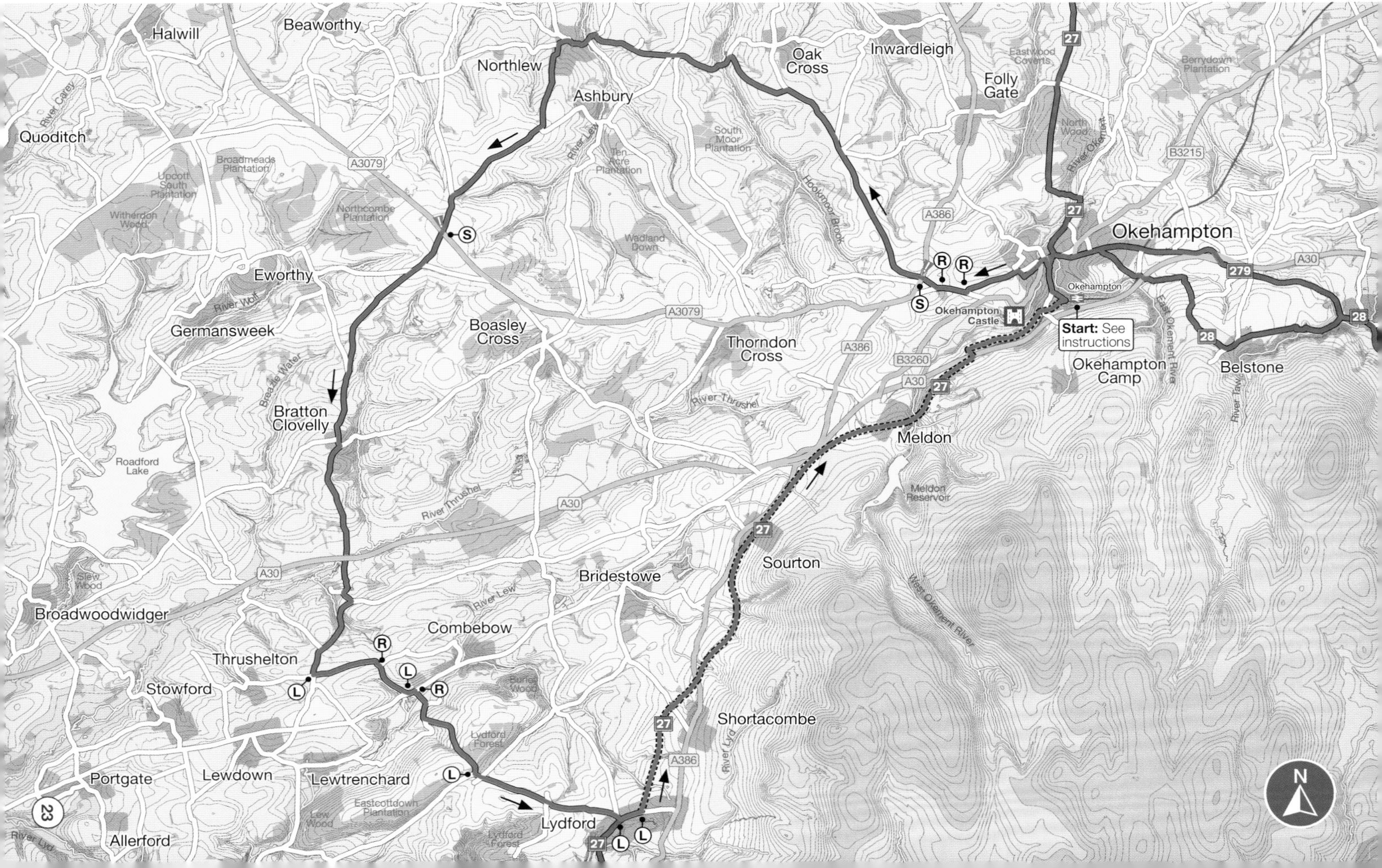

Halwill
Beaworthy
Northlew
Ashbury
Oak Cross
Inwardleigh
Folly Gate
Eastwood Coverts
Berrydown Plantation
North Wood
River Okement
B3215
Quoditch
River Carey
Broadmeads Plantation
Upcott South Plantation
Witherdon Wood
Northcombe Plantation
A3079
River Lew
Ten Acre Plantation
South Moor Plantation
Hookmoor Brook
A386
Okehampton
A30
279
Wadland Down
Eworthy
River Wolf
Germansweek
Boasley Cross
Thorndon Cross
Okehampton Castle
Start: See instructions
Okehampton Camp
East Okement River
Belstone
River Taw
28
27
B3260
Breazle Water
Bratton Clovelly
River Thrushel
Meldon
Roadford Lake
Meldon Reservoir
Sourton
West Okement River
Slew Wood
Bridestowe
Broadwoodwidger
Combebow
Thrushelton
Stowford
Burley Wood
Shortacombe
River Lyd
Lydford Forest
Portgate
Lewdown
Lewtrenchard
Eastcottdown Plantation
Lew Wood
Lydford
Allerford
N

Hatherleigh, Sheepwash (Tarka Trail South)

36.6 miles / 59.0 km

From the Puffing Billy head south on the traffic-free Tarka Trail / Route 3 / 27. When you come to the tarmac junction, continue **straight** ahead on the road towards Petrockstowe leaving the Tarka Trail (don't continue on off-road path). Keep following Route 3 towards Sheepwash. There keep **straight** ahead on Route 27 towards Highampton (don't follow Route 3 right). There turn **left** to follow Route 27 towards Hatherleigh. After passing through Hatherleigh stay **straight** on Victoria Rd, leaving Route 27. At the fork go **left** towards Iddesleigh. At the church go **left** towards Dolton. Continue **straight** until the road ends in a T-junction, then go **left** and **left** towards Beaford. Turn **left** on Green Ln. At the A386 turn **right**. Take the second **left** off the A386. When you come to the Route 3 path turn **right**. Follow the path back to where you started.

Bike shops

Torrington Cycle Hire
EX38 8JD Tel: 01805 622633

Eat & drink

The Laurels Inn
EX20 3HJ Tel: 01837 810578

The Half Moon Inn
EX21 5NE Tel: 01409 231376

The Golden Inn
EX21 5LT Tel: 01409 231200

The George in Hatherleigh
EX20 3JN Tel: 01837 811755

Duke of York
EX19 8BG Tel: 01837 810253

The Royal Oak
EX19 8QF Tel: 01805 804288

Puffing Billy
EX38 8JD Tel: 01805 623050

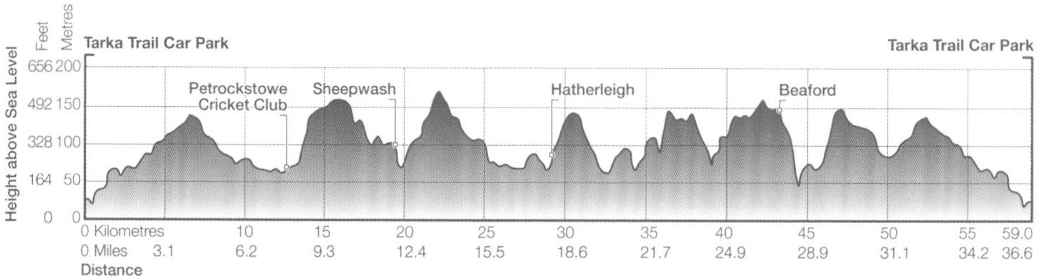

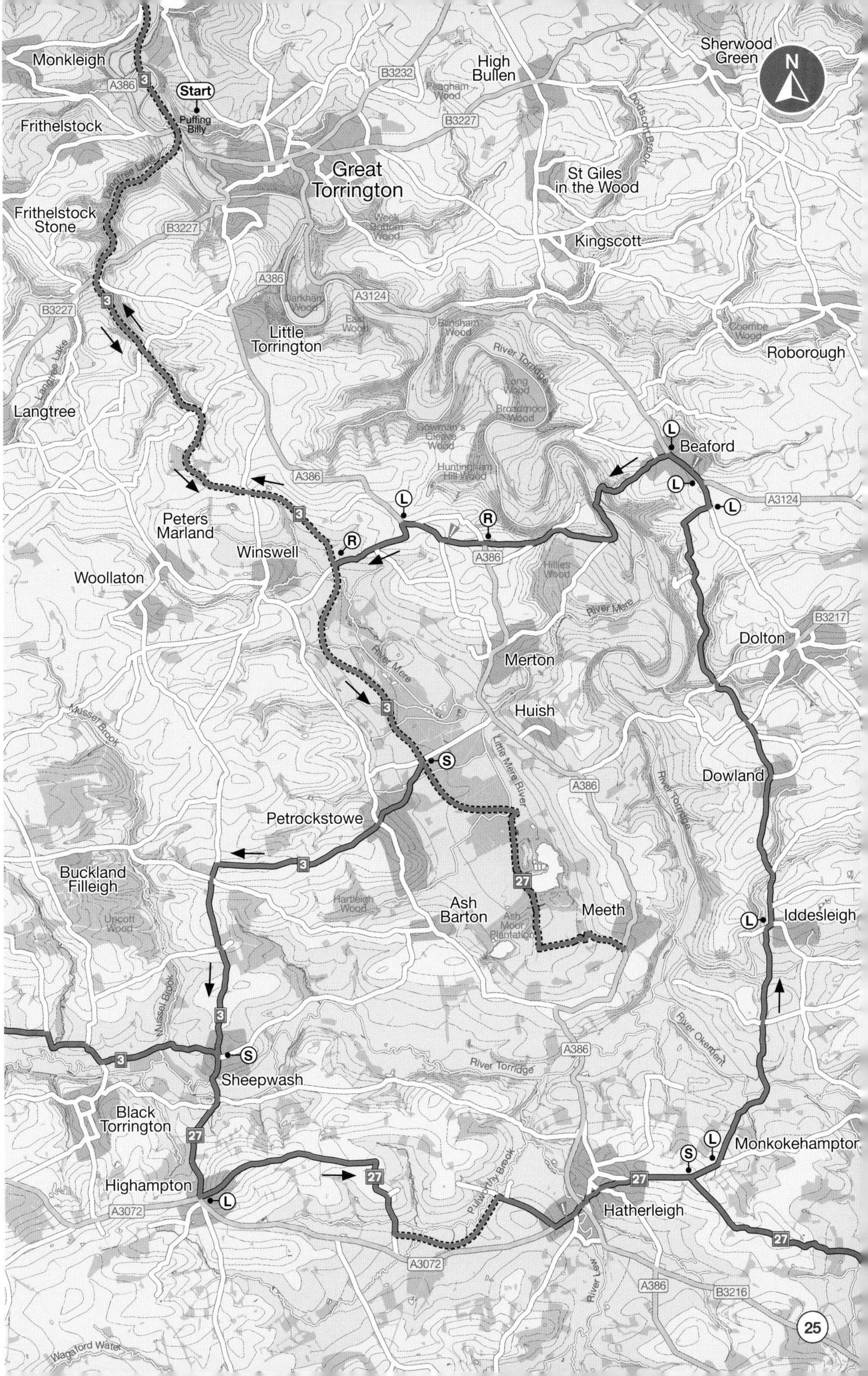

Start
Puffing Billy
Monkleigh
Frithelstock
Frithelstock Stone
Langtree
Great Torrington
Little Torrington
High Bullen
Sherwood Green
St Giles in the Wood
Kingscott
Roborough
Beaford
Peters Marland
Winswell
Woollaton
Merton
Huish
Dolton
Iddesleigh
Dowland
Petrockstowe
Buckland Filleigh
Ash Barton
Meeth
Sheepwash
Black Torrington
Highampton
Hatherleigh
Monkokehampton
River Torridge
River Mere
Little Mere River
River Okement
River Lew
Mussel Brook
Langtree Lake
Dodscott Brook
Pulworthy Brook
Wagaford Water
A386
A3124
A3072
B3227
B3232
B3217
B3216

09 Great Torrington to Barnstaple (Tarka Trail North)

27.2 miles / 43.7 km

Option 1: From St Michael Church in Great Torrington head north on School Ln. At the three-way fork go **left**. Follow the road to Weare Giffard. After the road turns right in front of the church, keep **left** towards Bideford. Pass under the bridge and then turn **right** onto the Tarka Trail / Route 3 / 27 heading north.

Option 2: From Great Torrington take the A386 to the Puffing Billy and join the Tarka Trail there.

Follow the Tarka Trail all the way to Barnstaple. On the way you can visit Tapeley Park & Gardens. To go into Barnstaple follow Route 3 to Long Bridge. You can visit the Museum of Barnstaple & North Devon and the Pannier Market.

Cross under the A3125 and the path ends at Sticklepath Hill – turn **left** and go through the mini roundabout heading up the hill. Continue **straight** on the road crossing the A39. In Tawstock turn **left** towards Uppacott. Turn **right** towards Smemington and Harracott. At the T-junction turn **right** towards Hiscott. Keep **straight** and follow the road to the B3232 – turn **right**. Turn **left** towards Huntshaw and stay **straight** on Darracott Rd. When the road ends in a T-junction turn **left** for Torrington – School Ln takes you back to the centre.

You can also begin and end the route at Barnstaple Station.

Bike shops

Torrington Cycle Hire
EX38 8JD Tel: 01805 622633

Bideford Bicycle Hire
EX39 4DR Tel: 01237 424123

Cycles Scuderia
EX39 2PF Tel: 01237 476509

Tarka Trail Cycle Hire
EX31 2AU Tel: 01271 324202

Bike It
EX32 8LS Tel: 01271 323873

Carb Cycles
EX32 7AA Tel: 01271 346316

The Bike Shed
EX32 8LS Tel: 01271 328628

Halfords
EX31 2AY Tel: 01271 344490

Eat & drink

Puffing Billy
EX38 8JD
Tel: 01805 623050

Cyder Presse
EX39 4QR
Tel: 01237 425517

Blacksmiths
EX39 4DP
Tel: 01237 477747

Various in Bideford

The Westleigh Inn
EX39 4NL
Tel: 01271 860867

Instow Arms
EX39 4JJ
Tel: 01271 860608

Yelland Manor Brewery
EX31 3EN
Tel: 07770267592

Fremington Quay Café
EX31 2NH
Tel: 01271 268720

Various in Barnstaple

Various in Great Torrington

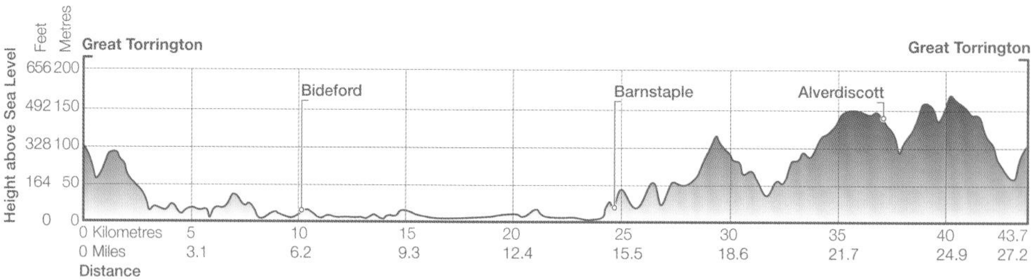

N
Braunton
Pudnor Wood
B3230
27
A361
Ashford
A39
Chivenor
A361
Barnstaple
B3149
27
Museum of Barnstaple & North Devon
River Taw
3
River Taw
3
Fremington
B3233
A3125
L
Bickington
3
B3233
Yelland
Brake Plantations
Lake
A39
S
Appledore
Little Pill
Instow
Bickleton
A39
A377
River Torridge
L
Tawstock
River Taw
St John's Chapel
Tapeley Park & Gardens
R
3
A386
B3233
Westleigh
B3232
Northam
A39
A39
Horwood
Eastleigh
Bideford
Newton Tracey
A386
R
East-the-Water
Ensis
Woodtown
3
Hiscott
L
Alverdiscott
R
River Torridge
Landcross
Yarnscombe
River Yeo
3
L
Huntshaw
B3232
A388
R
Weare Giffard
Huntshaw Wood
B3227
Monkleigh
3
Sherwood Green
High Bullen
A386
Peagham Wood
B3232
Frithelstock
Puffing Billy
L
L
St Giles in the Wood
Dodscott Brook
A388
B3227
Start
Great Torrington
River Torridge
A386
Frithelstock Stone
B3227
Week Bottom Wood
3
A3124
Kingscott

Starting from Barnstaple Station: Turn left on Station Rd. At the roundabout join the shared-use path to go right and join Route 3. Don't cross the river – turn right on the path just before the bridge and follow Route 3.

Mapped start: From the clock tower in the centre of Barnstaple follow the shared-use path and Route 27 signs alongside the river, with the water to your right. At the obelisk keep **right** to follow the path through the park. Turn **left** on Route 3.

Follow the traffic-free section of Route 3, then when the path ends at Ivy Cross turn **right** on the road towards Willesleigh. Continue to follow signs for Route 3. When you reach the A399 join the shared-use path to your **left** and stay **left** when the path ends. At the next T-junction leave Route 3 and go **left** towards Barnstaple on Route 276. Continue **right** on Mill Ln, then **right** towards Loxhore. Turn **left** towards Arlington where you have the option to visit National Trust property Arlington Court & Carriage Museum. At the A39 turn **left** for Barnstaple, leaving Route 276. Take the next **right** towards East Down and Pyne Arms. Turn **left** towards Churchill, then at the fork stay **right**. At the T-junction turn **left** then **right** towards Berry Down. Turn **left** towards Muddiford. At the B3230 turn **left** for Barnstaple, then turn **right** at the church over the bridge. Turn **left** towards Guineaford, then **right** towards Ashford and Heanton. Turn **left** into Ashford, then **left** on Strand Ln towards Barnstaple. At the A361 junction turn **right** then **left** to descend to the Tarka Trail / Route 27. Head **left** along the river back to Barnstaple where you can visit the Museum of Barnstaple & North Devon and the Pannier Market. To return to the station, cross Long Bridge and take Station Rd back.

Returning to the station without visiting the centre: Cross the A361 bridge over the River Taw and follow the shared-use path on the right for Town Centre on Route 3 / 27. The path will take you back to the first roundabout where you turn right on Station Rd to return to the train station.

Bike shops

The Bike Shed	
EX32 8LS	Tel: 01271 328628
Halfords	
EX31 2AY	Tel: 01271 344490
Bike It	
EX32 8LS	Tel: 01271 323873
Carb Cycles	
EX32 7AA	Tel: 01271 346316

Eat & drink

The New Inn	
EX32 7LX	Tel: 01271 342488
Arlington Court & Carriage Museum Tea Room	
EX31 4LP	Tel: 01271 850296
Pyne Arms	
EX31 4LX	Tel: 01271 850055
The Muddiford Inn	
EX31 4EY	Tel: 01271 850243
Various in Barnstaple	

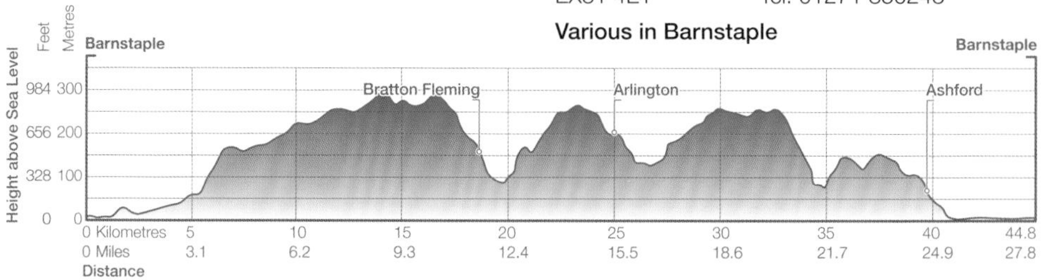

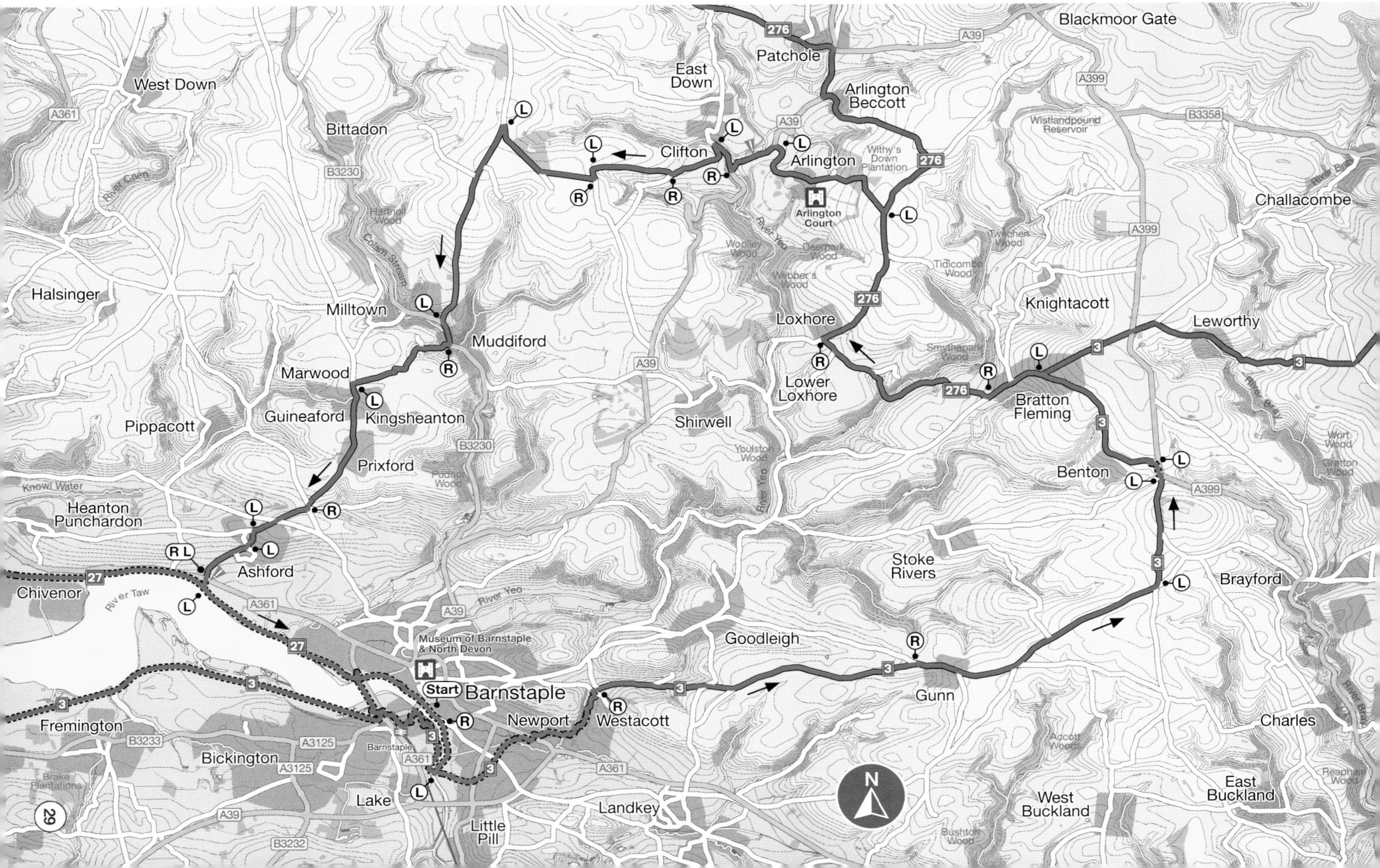

Blackmoor Gate
Patchole
East Down
Arlington Beccott
West Down
Bittadon
Clifton
Arlington
Withy's Down Plantation
Arlington Court
Challacombe
Wistlandpound Reservoir
Halsinger
Milltown
Muddiford
Loxhore
Lower Loxhore
Knightacott
Leworthy
Marwood
Guineaford
Kingsheanton
Shirwell
Bratton Fleming
Pippacott
Prixford
Benton
Heanton Punchardon
Knowl Water
Ashford
Stoke Rivers
Brayford
Chivenor
River Taw
River Yeo
Goodleigh
Museum of Barnstaple & North Devon
Start
Barnstaple
Gunn
Newport
Westacott
Fremington
Bickington
Lake
Landkey
Little Pill
West Buckland
East Buckland
Charles
Colam Stream
Harnell Wood
River Caen
Woolley Wood
Deerpark Wood
Webber's Wood
Twitchen Wood
Tidicombe Wood
Smythapark Wood
Youlston Wood
Pudicott Wood
Wort Wood
Gratton Wood
Acott Woods
Bushton Wood
Reapham Wood
Brake Plantations
River Bray
A39
A399
A361
A3125
B3358
B3230
B3233
B3232
276
3
27
N

With your back to the museum clock tower go **left** past the post office towards Barnstaple. Follow the road to the right, then at the roundabout turn **left** towards Barnstaple. Before reaching the A361 turn **left** towards Shallowford. Continue **straight** towards East and West Buckland. Cross over the A361 and follow the road **left**. Just outside Swimbridge turn **right** towards Gunn. At the fork stay **right** towards Stone Cross. Turn **right** towards Brayford.

To do the longer version of the route, turn left to follow Route 3 through Benton, Bratton Fleming and east, joining the shorter route at Sandyway.

To continue on the shorter route, follow the road to Brayford. Continue **straight** at the A399. After you pass the Poltimore Arms turn **left**. Take the third **right** on Route 3.

At Sandyway turn **right** towards North Molton, leaving Route 3. Pass through North Molton and curve south, **jink right left** to cross the A361. Continue on Station Rd to the B3227 then turn **right** to return to the start.

Bike shops

Freedom to Cycle
EX36 4EJ Tel: 01769 579907

Eat & drink

The North Gate Inn
EX36 3RG
Tel: 01769 579555

Stag's Head Inn
EX32 0RN
Tel: 01598 760250

The Jack Russell
EX32 0PN
Tel: 01271 830366

Poltimore Arms
EX36 3HA
Tel: 01598 710381

The Sportsman's Inn
EX36 3LU
Tel: 01643 831109

The Miner's Arms
EX36 3HT
Tel: 01598 740316

Poltimore Inn
EX36 3HR
Tel: 01598 740338

The George Hotel
EX36 3AB
Tel: 01769 572514

The Coaching Inn
EX36 3BJ
Tel: 01769 572526

King's Arms
EX36 3BL
Tel: 01769 572679

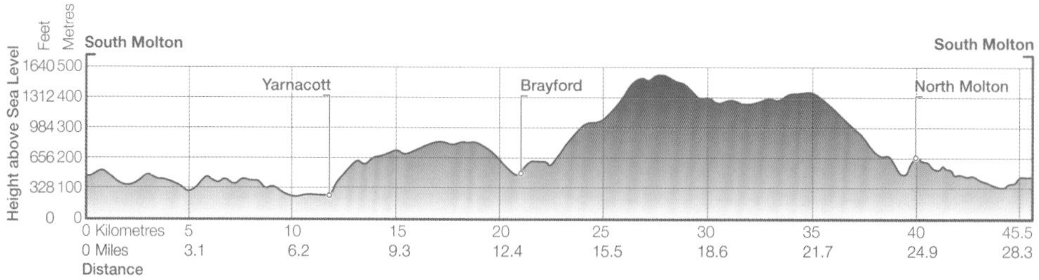

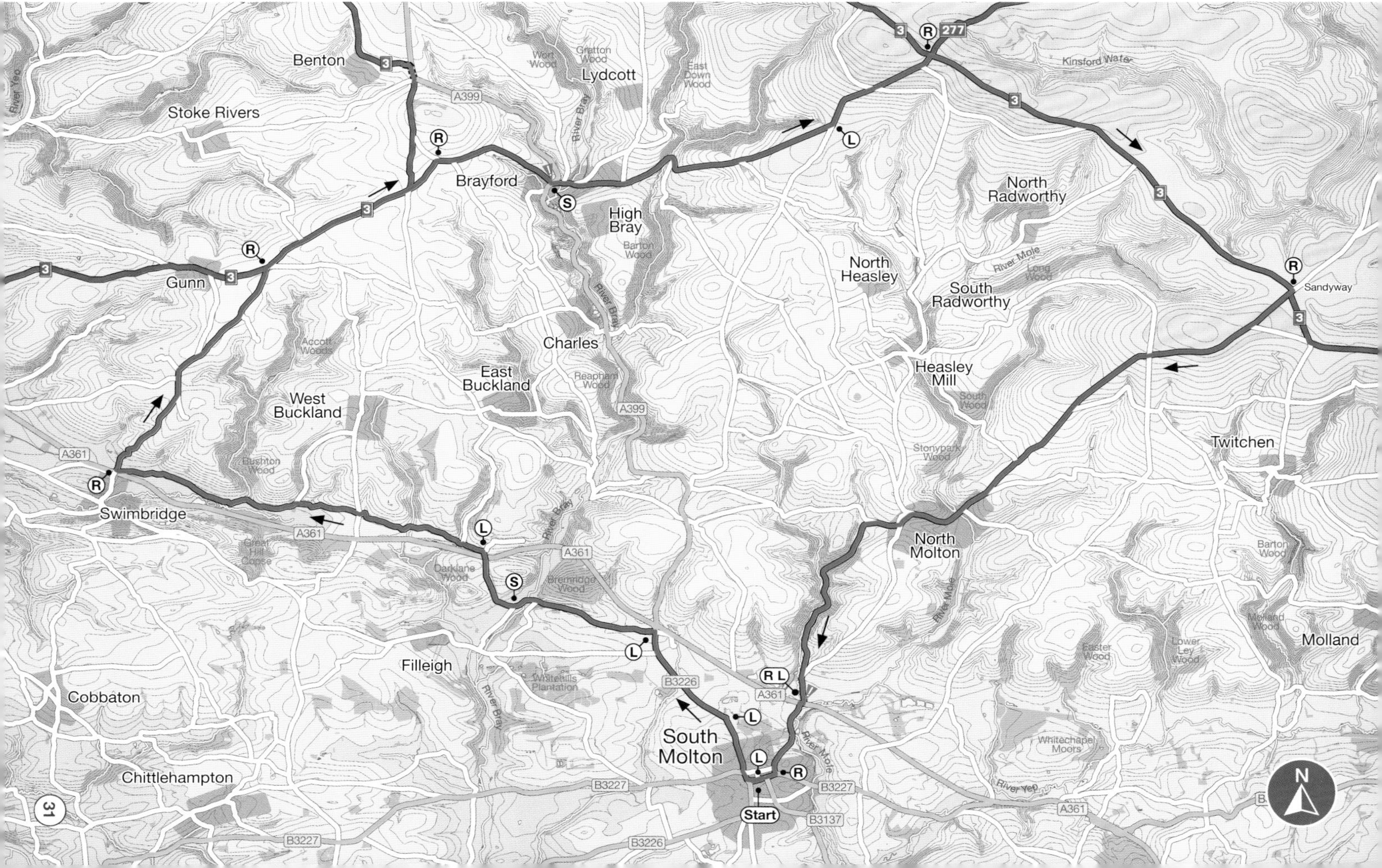
Benton
Lydcott
Stoke Rivers
Brayford
High Bray
Gunn
Charles
East Buckland
West Buckland
Swimbridge
North Radworthy
North Heasley
South Radworthy
Heasley Mill
Sandyway
Twitchen
North Molton
Molland
South Molton
Filleigh
Cobbaton
Chittlehampton
Start
River Bray
River Mole
River Yeo
A399
A361
B3226
B3227
B3137
277
Whitechapel Moors
Bremridge Wood
Darklane Wood
Whitehills Plantation
Stonypark Wood
Reapham Wood
Barton Wood
East Down Wood
Gratton Wood
Wort Wood
Accott Woods
Bushton Wood
Great Hill Copse
South Wood
Long Wood
Easter Wood
Lower Ley Wood
Molland Wood
N

From Axbridge head west on High St / Route 26. At the A371 junction turn **left** onto the signed shared-use path, then turn **right** towards Weston-super-Mare. If you'd like to visit Thatchers Cider Shop, head all the way to the A368 and turn right. Otherwise, exit the path (you will see a graveyard on your left) and turn **right** over the bridge. At New Rd in Shipham turn **right** towards Cheddar, then turn **left** towards Charterhouse. Turn **left** to continue towards Charterhouse and Compton Martin. After crossing the B3134, take the second **right** away from Route 3. At the Castle of Comfort bear **left**. At the second cross roads turn **right** towards Priddy. When the road comes to a T-junction turn **right**, then turn **left** and **left** towards Cheddar. When you reach Draycott, turn **right** on the A371 and then immediate slight **right** on Top Road towards Cheddar. To take the optional detour to Cheddar Gorge and Caves stay right at the fork and turn right at the car park. To continue back to Axbridge stay **left** at the fork, then when Redcliffe St ends turn **left**, then turn **right** on the A371. Bear **left** at the war memorial. Turn **right** signed Valley Line Industrial Park and follow Route 26 back to Axbridge.

Bike shops

Cheddar Cycle Store
BS27 3EE Tel: 01934 741300

Gorge-Us-Bikes
BS27 3EJ Tel: 07786 722155

Eat & drink

Thatchers Cider Shop
BS25 5RA
Tel: 01934 822862

The Cider Shed Wilcox Farm
BS25 1UG
Tel: 01934 842812

Miner's Arms
BS25 1TW
Tel: 01934 842146

Castle of Comfort
BS40 6DD
Tel: 01761 221321

The Hunter's Lodge Inn
BA5 3AR
Tel: 01749 672275

The Queen Victoria Inn
BA5 3BA
Tel: 01749 676385

The Cider Barn
BS27 3RU
Tel: 01934 741837

Detour to Cheddar Gorge area for various options

The Bath Arms
BS27 3AA
Tel: 01934 742425

The Crown Inn
BS26 2BN
Tel: 01934 732518

The Lamb Inn
BS26 2AP
Tel: 01934 732253

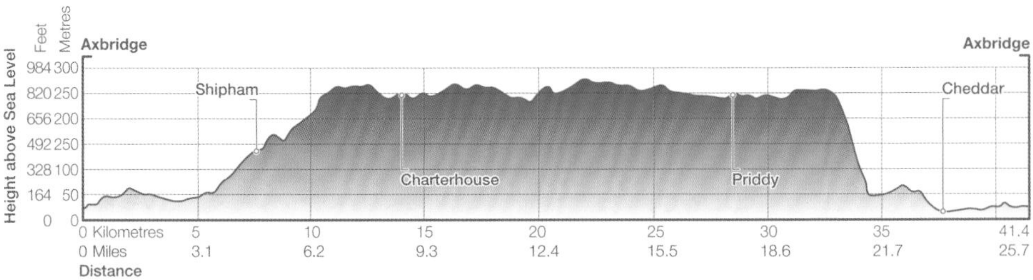

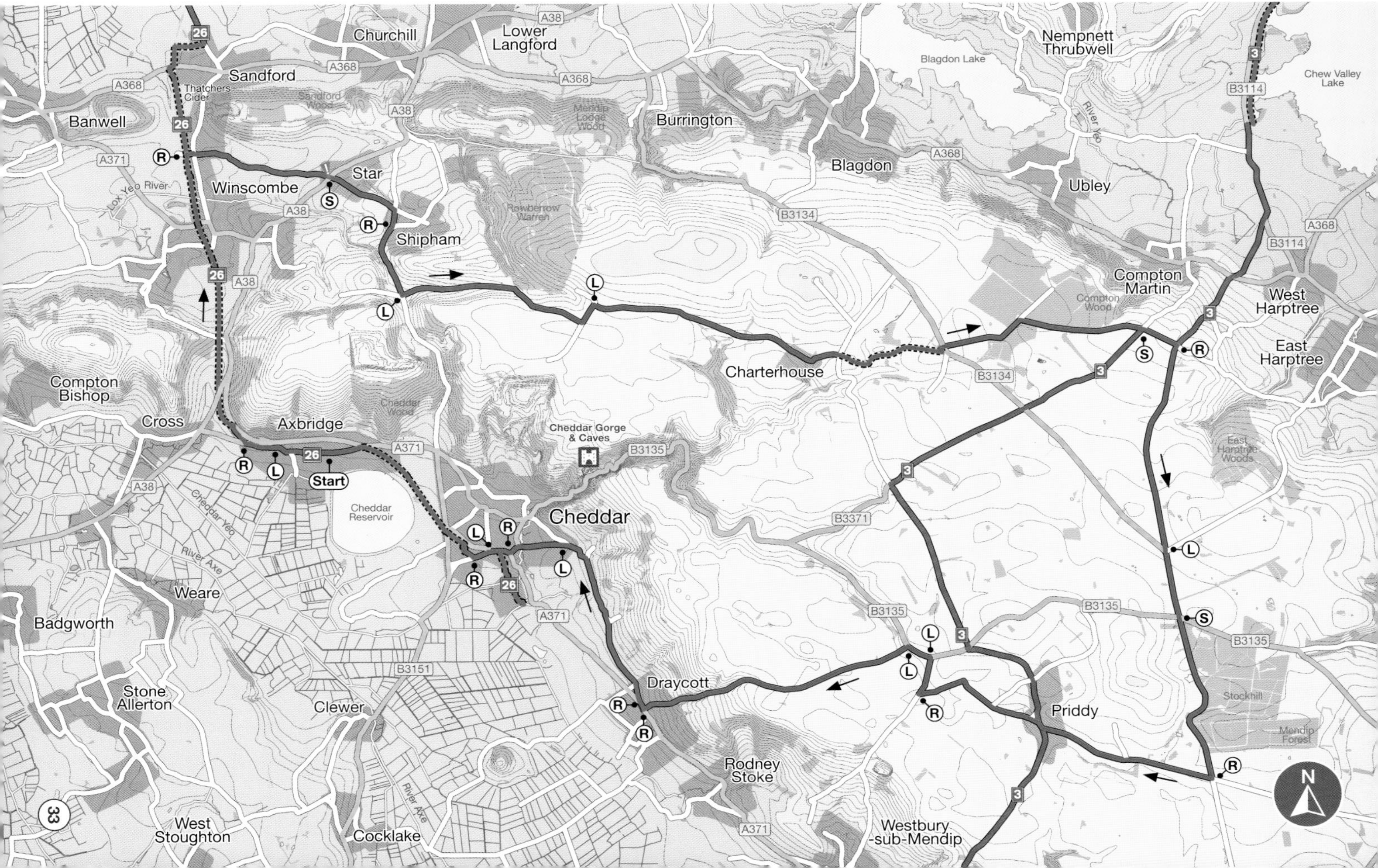

Churchill
Lower Langford
Nempnett Thrubwell
Blagdon Lake
Chew Valley Lake
Sandford
Thatchers Cider
Sandford Wood
Banwell
Mendip Lodge Wood
Burrington
Blagdon
Ubley
River Yeo
Winscombe
Star
Lox Yeo River
Shipham
Rowberrow Warren
Compton Martin
Compton Wood
West Harptree
East Harptree
Charterhouse
Compton Bishop
Cross
Axbridge
Cheddar Wood
Cheddar Gorge & Caves
Start
Cheddar Reservoir
Cheddar
Cheddar Yeo
River Axe
Weare
Badgworth
East Harptree Woods
Draycott
Stone Allerton
Clewer
Priddy
Stockhill
Mendip Forest
Rodney Stoke
West Stoughton
Cocklake
Westbury -sub-Mendip
A38
A368
A371
B3114
B3134
B3135
B3151
B3371
N

From The Swan Wedmore follow Church St past the church. After the school turn **left** on Kelson's Ln, then turn **right**. Pass through Heath House and then at the first paved crossroads turn **right**. Follow the road **right** and then turn **left** and **left**. At the next road turn **left** and then turn **right** towards Cossington. Follow the road as it bends back and forth. When you reach Cossington turn **left** on Middle Rd / Route 3. Follow Route 3 all the way to Glastonbury. If you have the time, you can turn left onto the off-road Glastonbury Canal path which will take you to the Avalon Marshes Centre. Otherwise cycle on to visit Glastonbury Abbey, Glastonbury Tor and the White Spring of Avalon. To head back to Wedmore, leave Route 3 and go north on Northload St. At the A39 roundabout go **straight**, then turn **right** on Godney Rd. Follow the road as it curves northwest, criss-crossing the rhines (waterways) typical of the area. Turn **right** on Dagg's Ln at a weak bridge sign, then when the road ends turn **left** on Snake Ln. Take the third **right** on Sand Rd and end with a gentle climb back to Wedmore. To return to The Swan Wedmore turn **left** on Glanville Rd and **right** at the church.

Bike shops

Cog & Sprocket Cycles
BA16 0ER Tel: 01458 441752

Eat & drink

The Red Tile Inn
TA7 8LN Tel: 01278 722333

White Hart Inn
TA7 9EW Tel: 01278 722723

King William Inne
TA7 9HU Tel: 01278 722933

Ring o' Bells
TA7 9PZ Tel: 01458 210232

Various in Glastonbury

The Sheppey Inn
BA5 1RZ Tel: 01458 831594

The Panborough Inn
BA5 1PN Tel: 01934 712554

The George Inn
BS28 4AB Tel: 01934 712124

The Swan Wedmore
BS28 4EQ Tel: 01934 710337

The New Inn
BS28 4DU Tel: 01934 712009

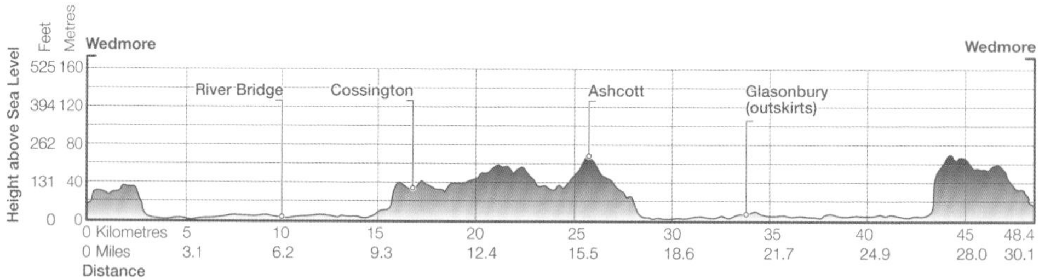

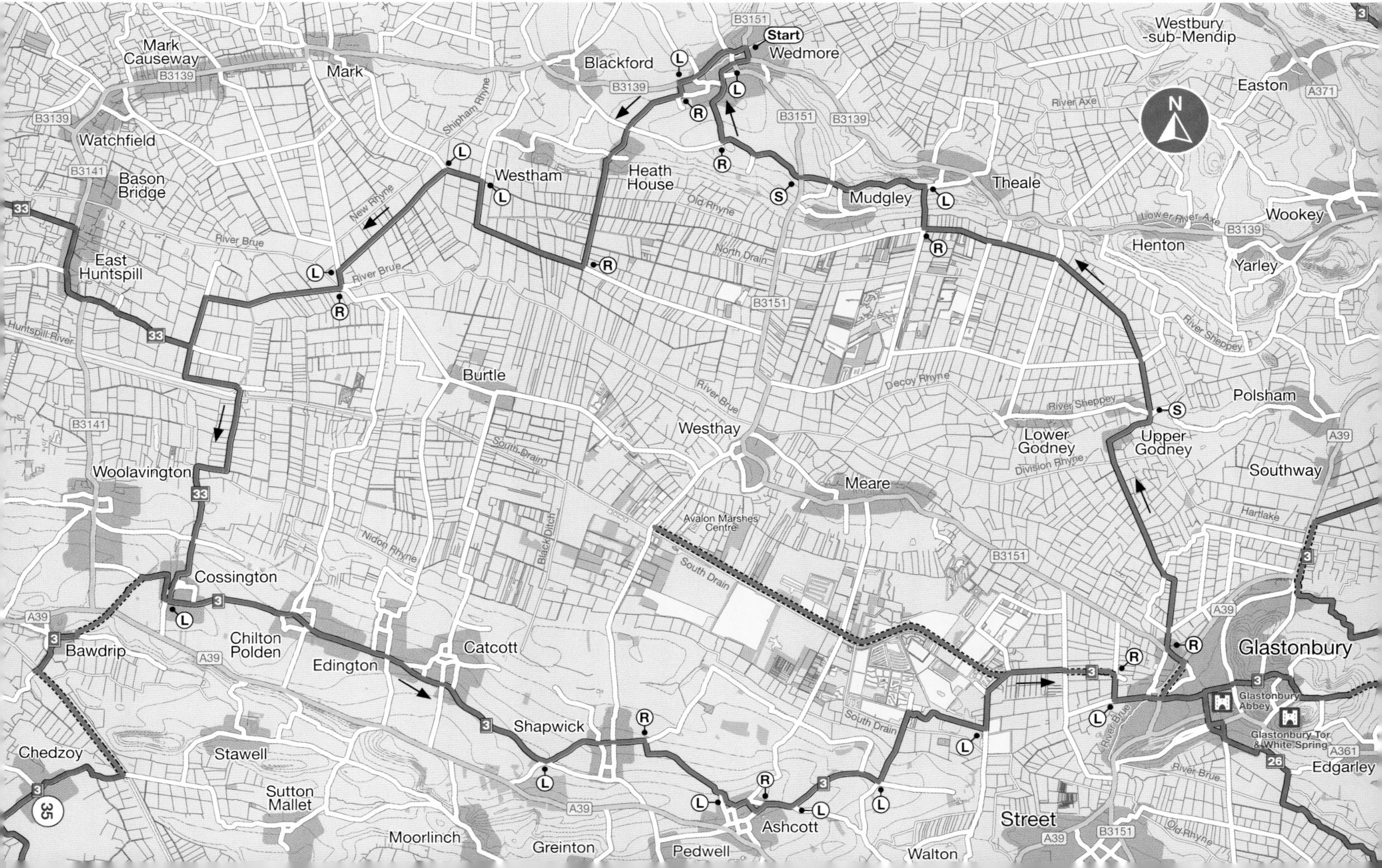
Start
Wedmore
Westbury
-sub-Mendip
Easton
A371
Mark
Causeway
B3139
Mark
Blackford
B3151
River Axe
Watchfield
B3141
Bason
Bridge
Shipham Rhyne
Westham
Heath
House
Mudgley
Theale
Wookey
Lower River Axe
Henton
Yarley
New Rhyne
River Brue
East
Huntspill
Old Rhyne
North Drain
Huntspill River
Burtle
River Sheppey
Decoy Rhyne
Polsham
Westhay
Lower
Godney
Upper
Godney
Division Rhyne
Southway
Woolavington
South Drain
Meare
Hartlake
Avalon Marshes
Centre
Nidon Rhyne
Black Ditch
Cossington
A39
Bawdrip
Chilton
Polden
Edington
Catcott
Glastonbury
Glastonbury
Abbey
Glastonbury Tor
& White Spring
A361
Edgarley
Shapwick
Stawell
Chedzoy
Sutton
Mallet
Moorlinch
Greinton
Pedwell
Ashcott
Walton
Street
Old Rhyne
3
26
33
N
S
R
L

14 Bridport & Beaminster

25.2 miles / 40.6 km

The ride begins in Bridport, famous for its weekly Wednesday and Saturday markets. From the Bridport Tourist Information Centre turn **left** on West St. Turn **right** on Victoria Grove. Turn **right** on Watford Ln towards Loders and Beaminster. At the A3066 **jink right left** to cross, then keep **left** towards Mangerton Mill. Follow the road through West Milton, then turn **left** downhill towards Powerstock and **right** in front of the church. At the crossroads turn **left** towards Toller Porcorum. At the T-junction bear **left** and continue to follow signs for Beaminster. At the B3163 turn **left**. At the A3066 turn **right** and pass through Beaminster. At the mini roundabout bear **left** on the B3163 and then turn **left** on Stoke Rd towards Stoke Abbott. Continue through Stoke Abbott and across the B3162. Turn **left** onto Blackney Lane, then **left** on Monkwood Lane. This road ends at the T-junction with Route 2. Turn **left** and follow the route to Dottery, then turn **right** onto B3162 to return to Bridport. If you have time, you can cycle 2 miles south to West Bay on Dorset's Jurassic Coast.

Bike shops

Bridport Cycles
DT6 6HG Tel: 01308 808595

Eat & drink

The Pyemore Inn
DT6 5PN Tel: 01308 422625

Three Horses Inn
DT6 3TF Tel: 01308 485328

The Marquis of Lorne
DT6 3SY Tel: 01308 485236

The Red Lion
DT8 3AX Tel: 01308 862364

The Greyhound
DT8 3AW Tel: 01308 862496

The New Inn
DT8 3JW Tel: 01308 868333

The Oddfellow's Arms
DT6 5EB Tel: 01308 422665

Various in Bridport & West Bay

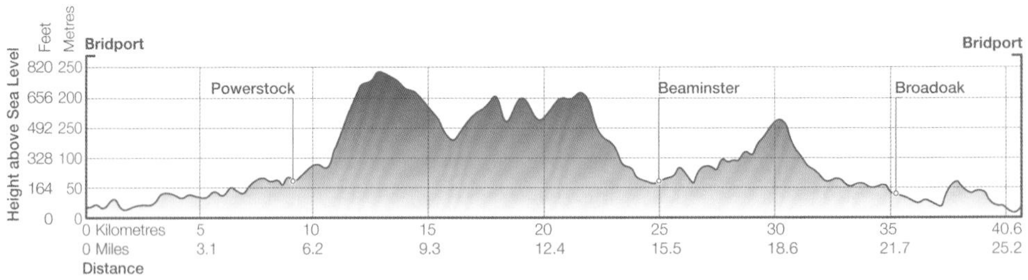

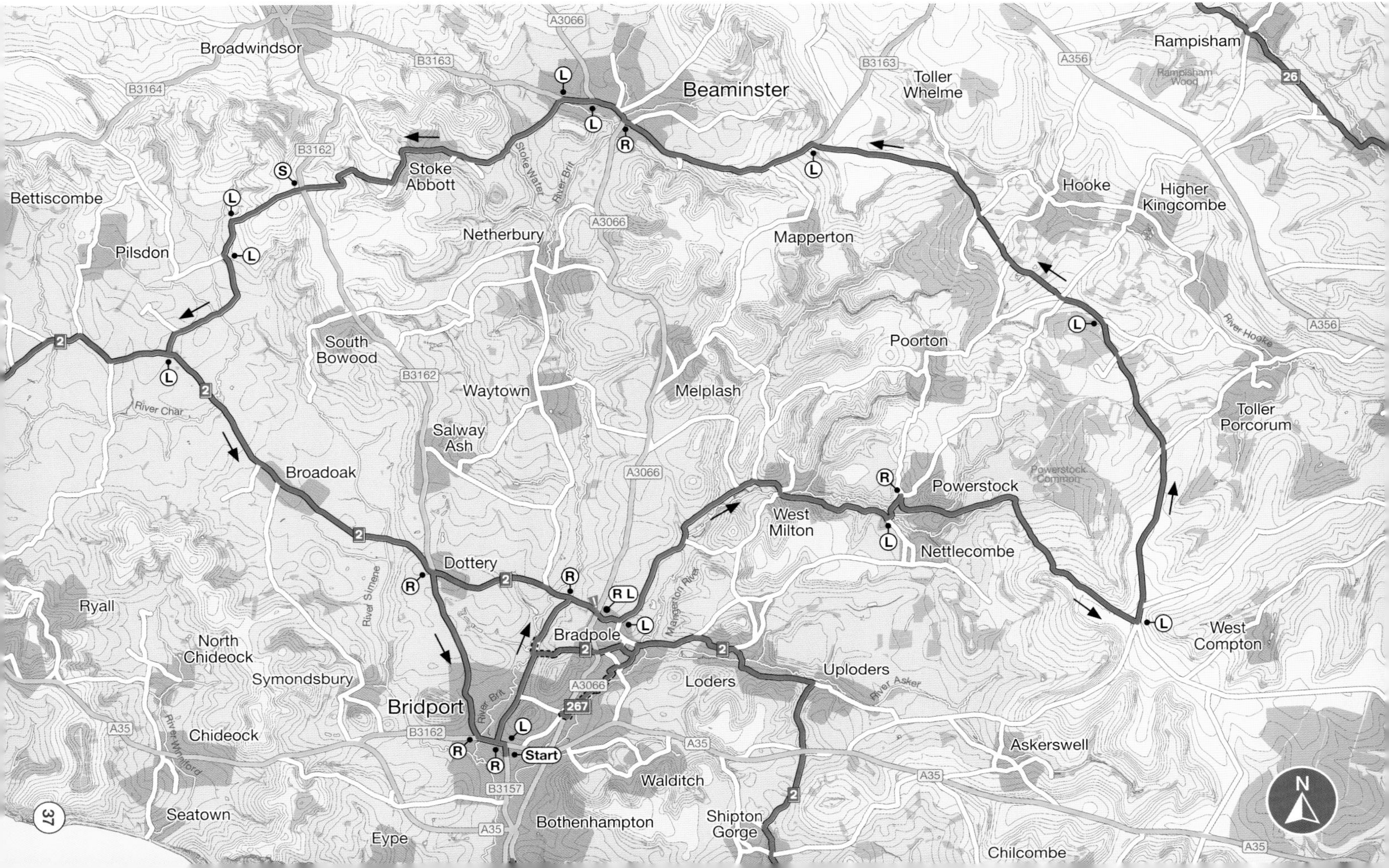
Broadwindsor
Beaminster
Rampisham
Rampisham Wood
Toller Whelme
Hooke
Higher Kingcombe
Bettiscombe
Stoke Abbott
Pilsdon
Netherbury
Mapperton
South Bowood
Poorton
Waytown
Melplash
Toller Porcorum
Salway Ash
Broadoak
Powerstock
Powerstock Common
West Milton
Nettlecombe
Dottery
Ryall
Bradpole
West Compton
North Chideock
Symondsbury
Loders
Uploders
Bridport
Chideock
Askerswell
Walditch
Seatown
Bothenhampton
Shipton Gorge
Eype
Chilcombe
Start
River Char
River Simene
River Brit
Stoke Water
Mangerton River
River Asker
River Hooke
River Winniford
A3066
B3163
B3164
B3162
A356
A35
B3157
267
26
2

With your back to the Sheaf of Arrows, turn **left** on High St heading north out of Cranborne to Boveridge and Tidpit. Turn **left** onto Martin Drove End and keep **straight** until Broad Chalke. After crossing the River Ebble, turn **left** onto High Road / Route 254 and keep following the route through lush, green fields. Just before the A30 turn **left** to head south towards Ashmore. Continue south, keeping left and following B3081. When you see the sign for Farnham turn slight **right** onto Oakley Ln. Turn **left** onto Route 253 towards Minchington and continue on until Gussage All Saints. After you pass The Drover's Inn, take the next **left** for Wimborne St Giles and Cranborne. Turn **right** between the two brick houses towards Cranborne. Turn **left** at the T-junction to return to Cranborne.

Bike shops

No bike shops

Eat & drink

The Queen's Head
SP5 5EN Tel: 01722 780344

The Horseshoe Inn
SP5 5JF Tel: 01722 780474

The Crown Inn
SP5 5JY Tel: 01722 780335

The Talbot Inn
SP7 0HA Tel: 01747 828222

The King John Inn
SP5 5PS Tel: 01725 516207

Museum Inn
DT11 8DE Tel: 01725 516261

Cashmoor Inn
DT11 8DN Tel: 01725 552230

The Drover's Inn
BH21 5ET Tel: 01258 840550

The Inn at Cranborne
BH21 5PP Tel: 01725 551249

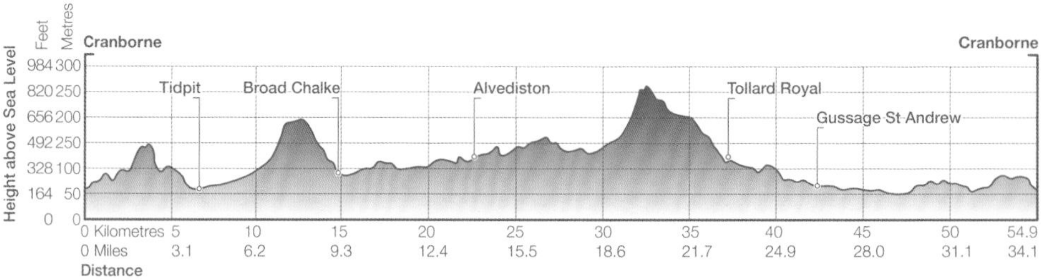

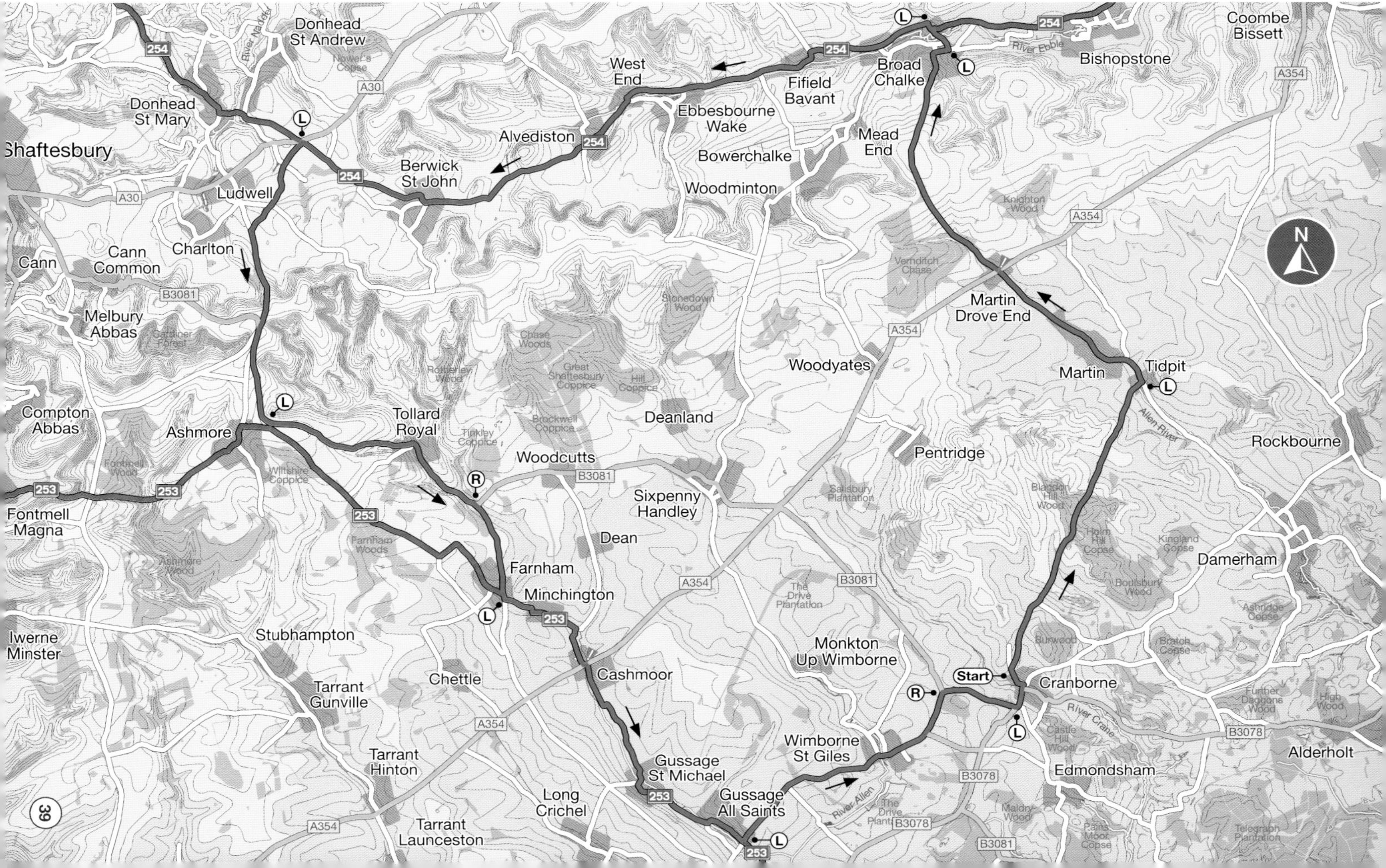

Coombe Bissett
Bishopstone
Broad Chalke
Fifield Bavant
West End
Ebbesbourne Wake
Mead End
Bowerchalke
Woodminton
Alvediston
Berwick St John
Donhead St Andrew
Donhead St Mary
Shaftesbury
Ludwell
Charlton
Cann
Cann Common
Melbury Abbas
Compton Abbas
Ashmore
Fontmell Magna
Iwerne Minster
Stubhampton
Tarrant Gunville
Tarrant Hinton
Tarrant Launceston
Long Crichel
Chettle
Tollard Royal
Woodcutts
Farnham
Minchington
Dean
Sixpenny Handley
Deanland
Woodyates
Martin Drove End
Martin
Tidpit
Rockbourne
Pentridge
Damerham
Cashmoor
Gussage St Michael
Gussage All Saints
Wimborne St Giles
Monkton Up Wimborne
Cranborne
Start
Edmondsham
Alderholt
River Allen
Allen River
River Crane
River Ebble
River Nadder
A30
A354
B3081
B3078
254
253
N

16 Cotswold Lanes around Burford & Northleach

27.7 miles / 44.6 km

From the Tolsey Museum in Burford head west on Route 57 / Sheep St. Follow the route all the way to Northleach. When you reach the T-junction at High St, turn **right** towards Cirencester. Here we recommend a visit to the very unique and entertaining Mechanical Music Museum. To continue turn **left** into the square, then immediately **left** and **right** through the second square. You are now on Route 48. When you reach the River Coln turn **left**, leaving Route 48, and continue following the signs for Winson and Bibury. Stay **left** passing through Winson and continue to follow the river through Ablington and Arlington. After passing through Arlington on the B4425 turn **right** on Salt Way towards Coln St Aldwyns. When the road ends in a T-junction turn **right**, then turn **left** at the Post Office. When the road comes to a T-junction at Hatherop turn **left**. Stay **left** twice to continue towards Westwell. In Westwell turn **left** towards Burford. At the A40 **jink right left** on Tanners Lane, then turn **right** on Sheep St to return to where you started.

Bike shops

No bike shops

Eat & drink

The Fox Inn
OX18 4TB Tel: 01451 844385

Sherborne Village Tea Room
GL54 3DH Tel: 01451 844668

The Wheatsheaf Inn
GL54 3EZ Tel: 01451 860244

The Swan Hotel
GL7 5NW Tel: 01285 740695

The Catherine Wheel
GL7 5ND Tel: 01285 740250

The William Morris Tea Room
GL7 5NP Tel: 01285 740555

The New Inn
GL7 5AN Tel: 01285 750651

Various in Burford

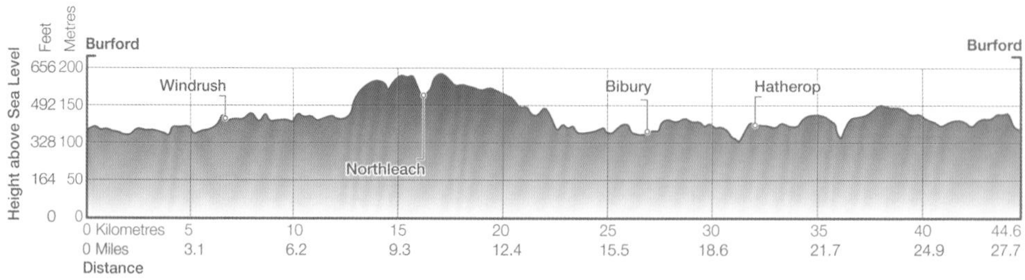

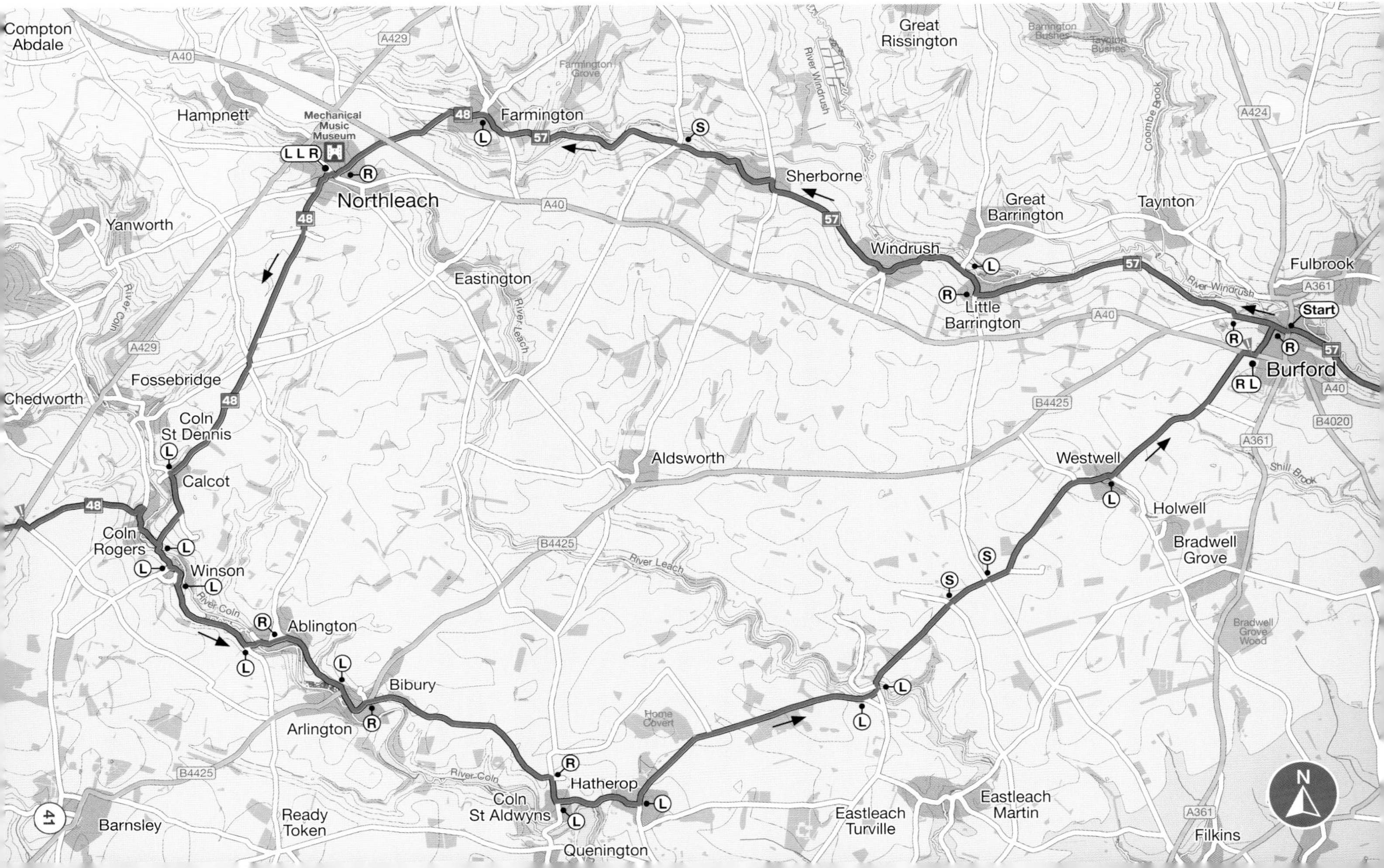

Compton Abdale
A429
A40
Farmington Grove
Great Rissington
Barrington Bushes
Taynton Bushes
River Windrush
Coombe Brook
A424
Hampnett
Mechanical Music Museum
L L R
48
Farmington
57
S
R
L
Northleach
Sherborne
A40
Great Barrington
Taynton
Yanworth
Windrush
Fulbrook
Eastington
River Windrush
A361
River Coln
River Leach
Little Barrington
Start
A429
A40
Burford
R L
Fossebridge
Chedworth
B4425
A40
Coln St Dennis
B4020
A361
Aldsworth
Westwell
Shill Brook
Calcot
Holwell
Coln Rogers
Bradwell Grove
Winson
B4425
River Leach
River Coln
Ablington
Bradwell Grove Wood
Bibury
Home Covert
Arlington
B4425
River Coln
Hatherop
Coln St Aldwyns
Eastleach Martin
Ready Token
Eastleach Turville
A361
Barnsley
Filkins
Quenington
N

Starting in front of Castle & Ball on High St, go through the opposite archway onto Hilliers Yard. Follow the road through the industrial estate and then turn **right** on George Ln / Route 403. At the roundabout continue **straight** on Granham Close which will turn into a traffic-free path and then Preshute Ln. When you reach the T-junction with The Outside Chance on your right, turn **left** on Manton Rd leaving Route 403. Continue **straight** on, crossing the Kennet & Avon Canal, until you reach Woodborough. Turn **left** onto the road signed Village Centre, Church and Garden Centre – this is Route 4. At the fork in the road go **left** and follow Route 4 to Pewsey. Follow the route **left** on Vale Rd then **right** on Old Hospital Rd, then at the T-junction go **right** on the A345. Go **right** at the Royal Oak, then turn **left** at the statue. Continue to follow Route 4, then after crossing the A346 turn **left** at the T-junction for Hungerford and Durley, leaving Route 4. When the road ends in a forked T-junction go **right**. Take the next hard **left**, then turn **right** for Chisbury. At the triangle go **left** for Ramsbury and continue straight on this road. At the T-junction turn **left** for Ramsbury – this is Route 254. At the next T-junction turn **left** towards Marlborough and follow Route 254 all the way back. When Silverless St ends, turn **left** on Kingsbury St which takes you back to High St on your right.

You can also start and end the route in Pewsey if you take the train.

Bike shops

Fixthebike
SN8 1PW Tel: 07785 926021

Pewsey Velo
SN9 5AQ Tel: 01672 562264

Eat & drink

The Outside Chance
SN8 4HW
Tel: 01672 512352

Who'd a Thought It
SN8 4EL
Tel: 01672 861255

The Barge Inn
SN9 5PS
Tel: 01672 851705

The Seven Stars Inn
SN9 6LT
Tel: 01672 851325

The Royal Oak Pewsey
SN9 5ES
Tel: 01672 563426

The Royal Oak
SN8 4NQ
Tel: 01672 810322

The Three Horseshoes
SN8 3AE
Tel: 01672 810324

The Bell Ramsbury
SN8 2PE
Tel: 01672 520230

Red Lion Axford
SN8 2HA
Tel: 01672 520271

The Horseshoe Inn
SN8 2LR
Tel: 01672 514725

Various in Marlborough

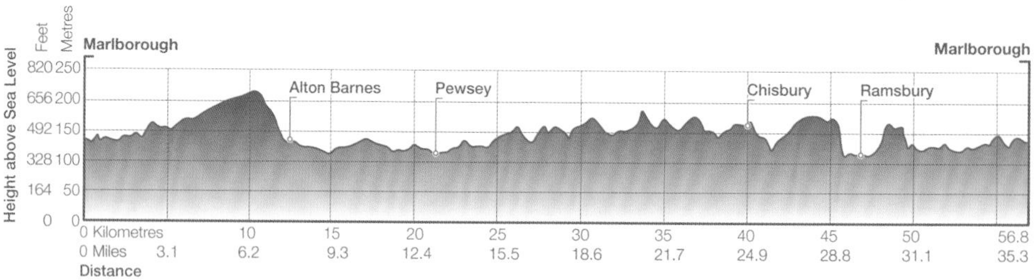

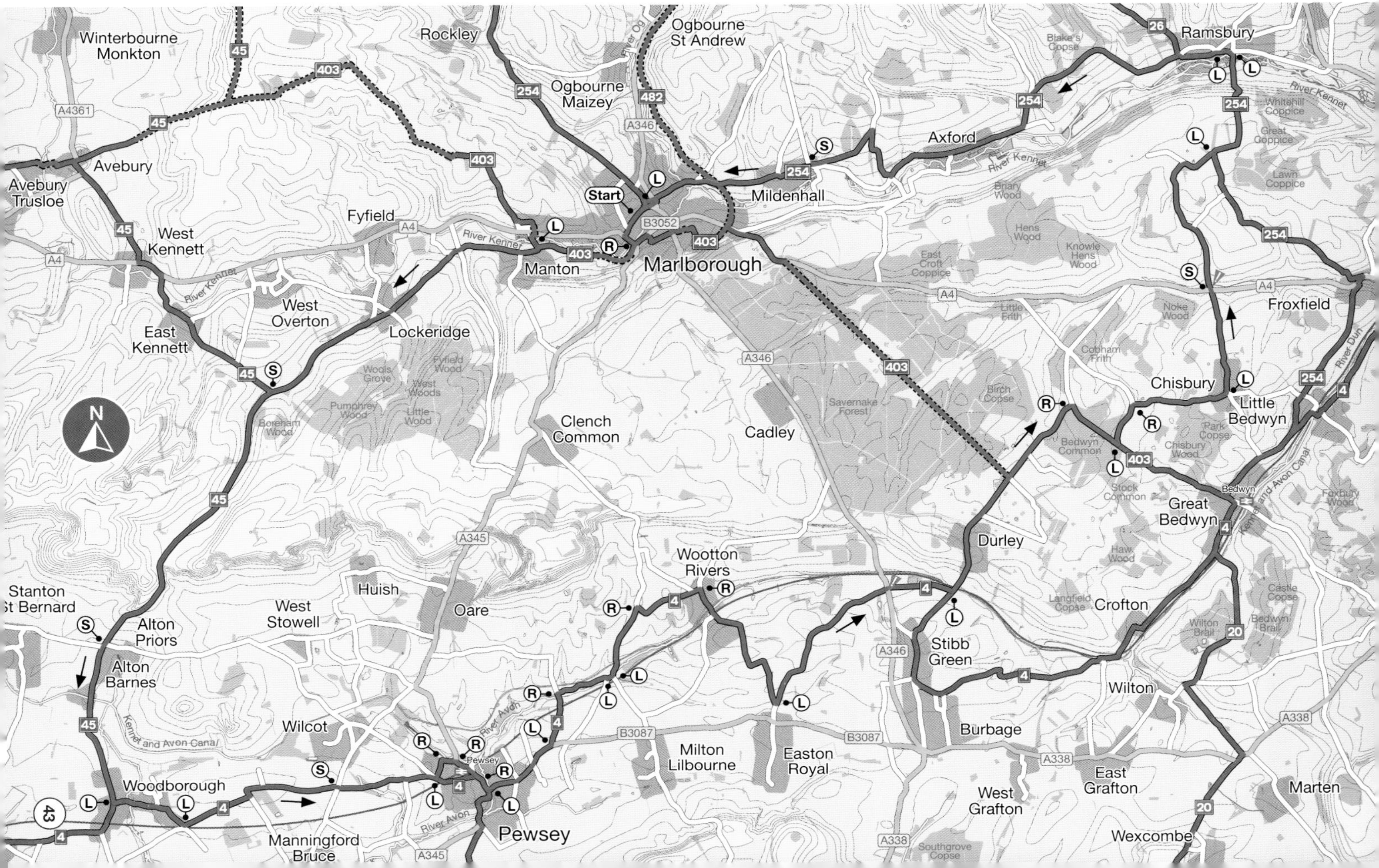
Winterbourne Monkton
Rockley
Ogbourne St Andrew
Ramsbury
Ogbourne Maizey
Avebury
Avebury Trusloe
Axford
Mildenhall
Start
Fyfield
West Kennett
Manton
Marlborough
River Kennet
River Og
West Overton
Lockeridge
East Kennett
Froxfield
Chisbury
Little Bedwyn
Clench Common
Cadley
Savernake Forest
Great Bedwyn
Durley
Wootton Rivers
Huish
Oare
West Stowell
Stanton St Bernard
Alton Priors
Alton Barnes
Crofton
Stibb Green
Wilton
Wilcot
Burbage
Milton Lilbourne
Easton Royal
East Grafton
West Grafton
Marten
Woodborough
Pewsey
Manningford Bruce
Wexcombe
River Avon
River Dun
Kennet and Avon Canal
N

From Temple Meads Station exit **left** along the shared-use path, then turn **left** following the path along Cattle Market Rd. Pass through the tunnel and turn **right** to follow Route 3. Keep following the mainly traffic-free path called Whitchurch Way. You can detour to visit Arnos Vale Cemetery Park by turning right on Bath Rd. The entrance will be on your left. From Whitchurch keep following Route 3 towards Chew Magna, taking care to use the path to cross the A37. To visit the Stanton Drew Stone Circles, turn left to leave the route, then take Route 410 to Chew Stoke to continue on the route. Follow Silver St through Chew Magna and continue on Route 3 towards Chew Stoke (the entrance to the Chew Valley Lake area will be on your left). At Chew Stoke turn **right** on Bristol Rd to join Route 410 / 10 / Avon Cycleway all the way to Felton. At Felton turn **right** at the junction signed Route 334 / Clifton Link towards Long Ashton. When you see the sign for Route 33 / Festival Way towards Long Ashton and Bristol turn **right**. The route is well signed through Long Ashton and Ashton Court Estate. When you reach the River Avon go **left** across the old train bridge and **right** to follow the route along the river. Pass behind the M Shed Museum and turn **left** to cross the Prince St Bridge. Turn **right** into Queens Square and follow the Route 3 path to cross the bridge and continue along Portwall Ln. You will see St Mary Redcliffe Church on your right, which is well worth a visit. Before reaching the large roundabout use the crossings to follow the shared-use path slight **right** back to the station entrance.

Bike shops

Brompton Bike Hire dock next to Temple Meads

Bristol Cycle Shack (repair & hire)
BS2 0QT Tel: 01179 551017

Cycle the City Bike Hire
BS1 5UH Tel: 07873 387167

Bristol Electric Bike Hire
BS1 5UW Tel: 01179 252218

BW Cycling
BS1 6SE Tel: 01179 272947

Mud Dock Cycleworks
BS1 4RB Tel: 01179 292151

Chaos Cycles
BS1 1JQ Tel: 01179 300030

Eat & drink

Arnos Vale Cemetery Park & Café
BS4 3EW
Tel: 0117 971 4850

Whitehall Garden Centre Café
BS14 0BT
Tel: 01275 832296

Bear & Swan
BS40 8PR
Tel: 01275 331100

The Pelican Inn
BS40 8SL
Tel: 01275 331777

Salt & Malt
BS40 8XS
Tel: 01275 333345

Stoke Inn
BS40 8XE
Tel: 01275 332120

The Crown
BS40 8AY
Tel: 01275 472388

Fox & Goose
BS48 3SL
Tel: 01275 472202

The Prince's Motto
BS48 3RY
Tel: 01275 474608

The Ashton
BS41 9LX
Tel: 01275 392245

The Cottage Inn
BS1 6XG
Tel: 0117 921 5256

The Ostrich
BS1 6TJ
Tel: 0117 927 3774

Various in Bristol

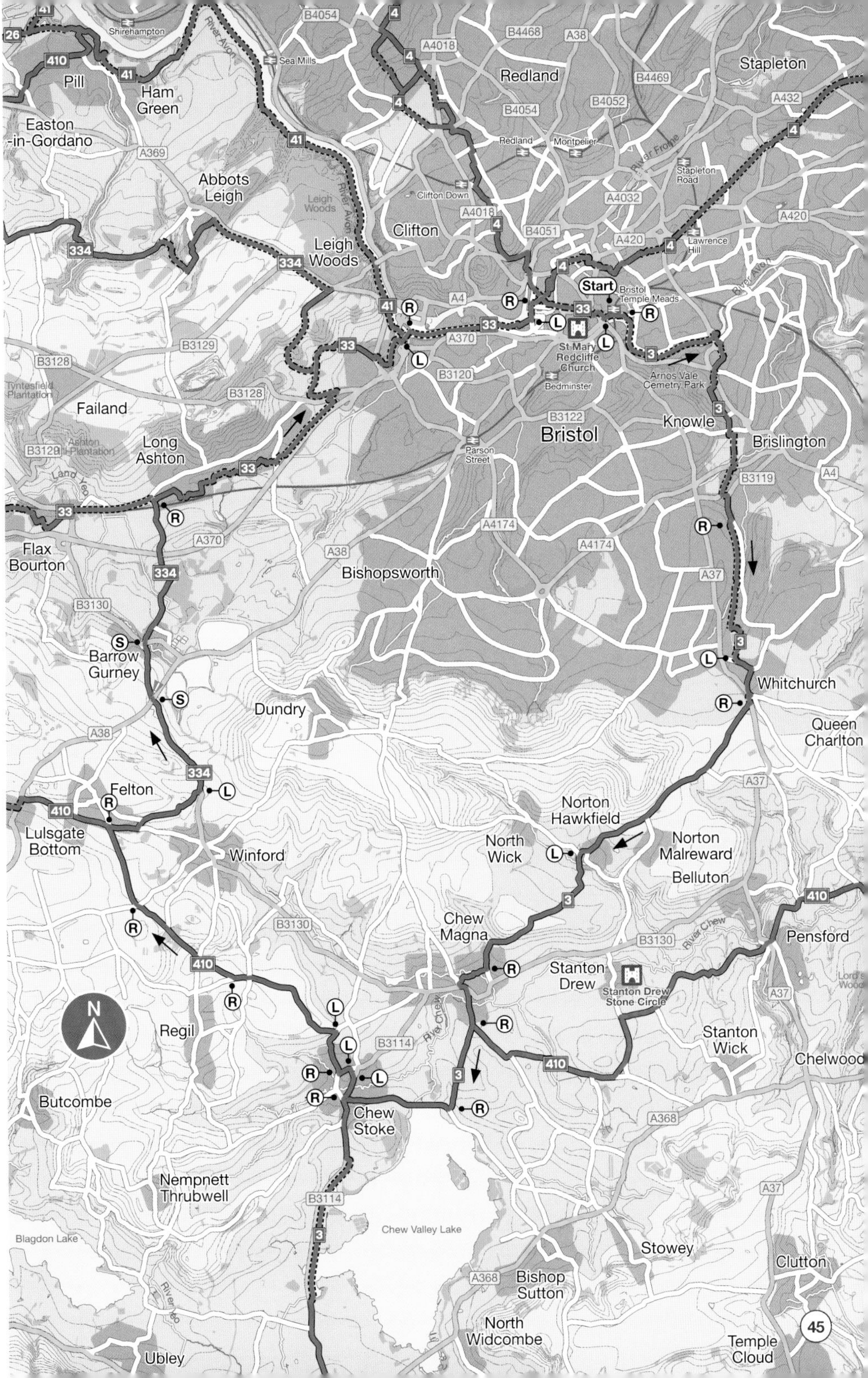
Shirehampton
River Avon
Sea Mills
B4054
A4018
B4468
A38
Stapleton
Redland
B4469
Pill
Ham Green
B4054
B4052
A432
Easton -in-Gordano
Redland
Montpelier
River Frome
A369
Stapleton Road
Abbots Leigh
Leigh Woods
Clifton Down
A4032
A4018
Clifton
B4051
A420
Lawrence Hill
A420
Leigh Woods
Start
Bristol Temple Meads
River Avon
A4
A370
St Mary Redcliffe Church
B3129
B3128
Tyntesfield Plantation
B3120
Arnos Vale Cemetery Park
Bedminster
B3128
Failand
Knowle
B3122
Bristol
Brislington
Long Ashton
Ashton Hill Plantation
B3128
Parson Street
Land Yeo
B3119
A4
Flax Bourton
A370
A4174
A4174
A38
Bishopsworth
A37
B3130
Barrow Gurney
Whitchurch
Dundry
Queen Charlton
A38
Felton
A37
Lulsgate Bottom
Norton Hawkfield
North Wick
Norton Malreward
Winford
Belluton
Chew Magna
B3130
B3130
River Chew
Pensford
Stanton Drew
Stanton Drew Stone Circle
A37
Regil
River Chew
B3114
Stanton Wick
Chelwood
Butcombe
Chew Stoke
A368
Nempnett Thrubwell
B3114
A37
Blagdon Lake
Chew Valley Lake
Stowey
A368
Bishop Sutton
Clutton
River Yeo
North Widcombe
Temple Cloud
Ubley
Start
R
L
S
3
4
26
33
41
334
410

From Bath Spa Station, follow signs straight ahead towards Bath Abbey. Turn **left** onto Cheap St and follow the signs west for Route 4 until you reach the entrance for the traffic-free Bristol and Bath Railway Path. Take the path along the river until you pass the Bird in Hand car park on your left. Cross the bridge and turn **right** off the path on Avon Ln. Turn **right** on Mead Ln, going under the bridge and past the pub. Turn **left** on Beech Rd signed Route 410 and cross the A4 carefully. Follow Manor Rd and keep **left** to follow Route 410 south. Stay **straight** towards Stanton Prior, don't follow Route 410 right. Cross the A39, then take the next **left** (unsigned). Take the next **right** towards Marksbury, then next **left** towards Priston. Pass through Priston and continue **straight** towards Englishcombe. At the crossroads turn **right** towards Bath and continue through Combe Hay. When you reach a T-junction signed Monkton Combe turn **right**. Turn **right** onto Route 24 towards Bath and follow to join Route 4. Follow Route 4 all the way back to Bath Abbey, and take time to explore the many sites and shops of Bath.

Bike shops

nextbike bike share dock next to Bath Spa Station

Avon Valley Cyclery
BA1 1SX Tel: 01225 442442

Julian House Bike Workshop
BA1 1UF Tel: 01225 463350

Halfords
BA1 1EB Tel: 01225 445255

Cadence Bike Shop
BA1 3PP Tel: 01225 446887

Eat & drink

Bird in Hand
BS31 3EJ Tel: 01225 873335

The Wheatsheaf
BA2 9HB Tel: 01225 872915

Ring O'Bells
BA2 9EF Tel: 01761 471467

The Wheatsheaf
BA2 7EG Tel: 01225 833504

The Hope & Anchor Inn
BA2 7DD Tel: 01225 832296

The Wheelwright's Arms
BA2 7HB Tel: 01225 722287

The Angelfish
BA2 7JD Tel: 01225 723483

George Inn
BA2 6TR Tel: 01225 425079

Various in Bath

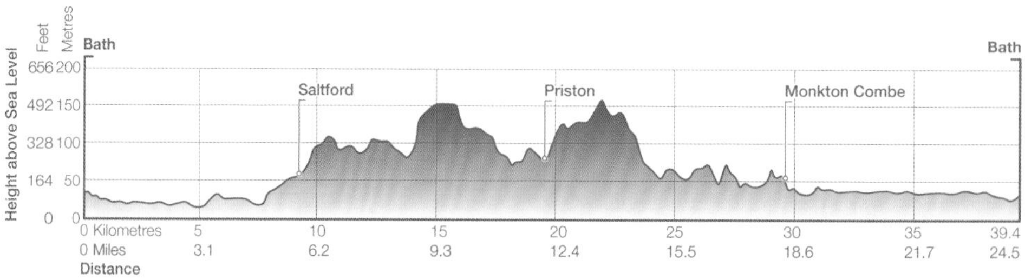

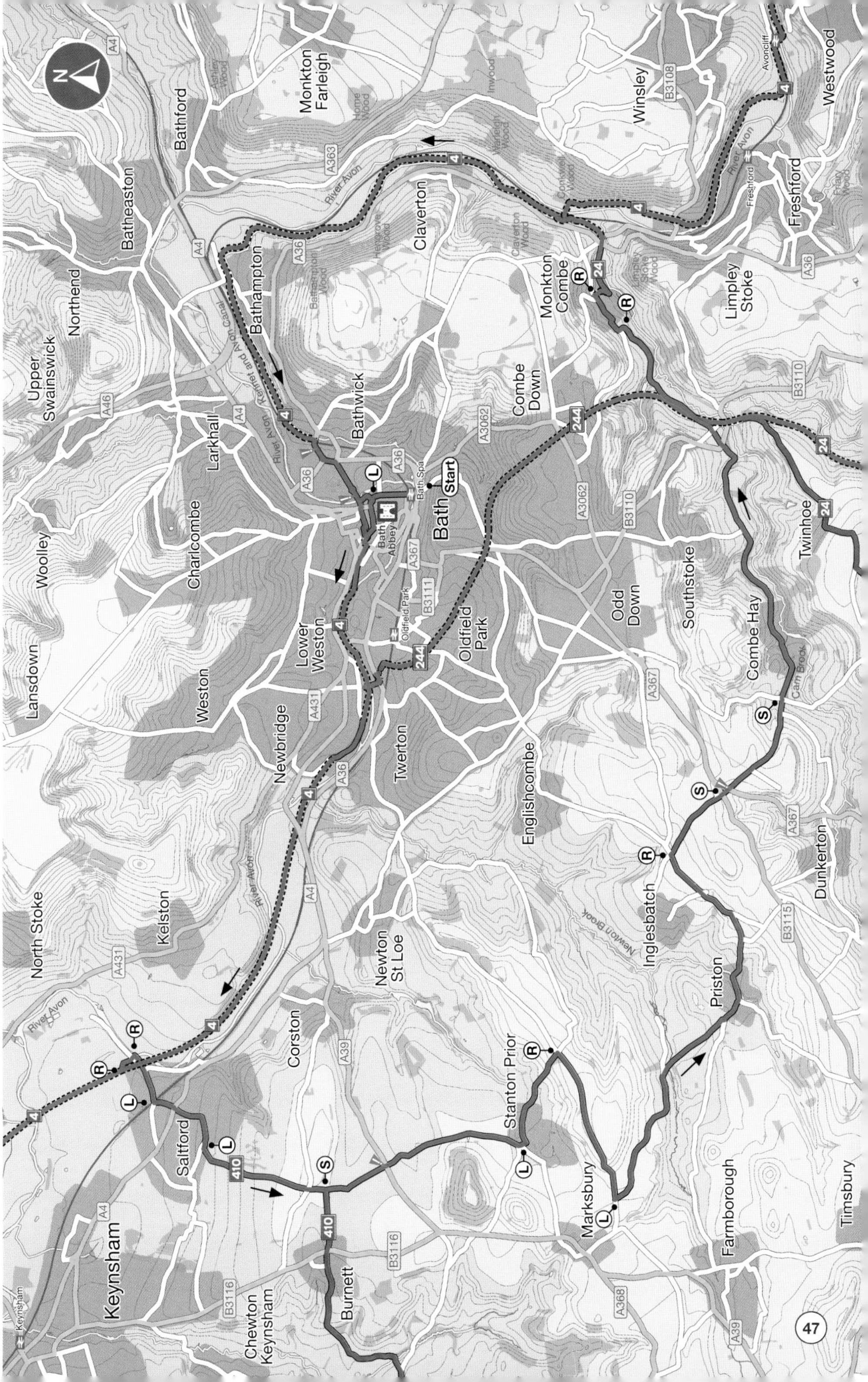
Keynsham
Saltford
Chewton Keynsham
Burnett
Corston
Newton St Loe
Stanton Prior
Marksbury
Priston
Farmborough
Timsbury
Inglesbatch
Englishcombe
Dunkerton
Twerton
Newbridge
Lower Weston
Weston
Kelston
North Stoke
Lansdown
Woolley
Charlcombe
Larkhall
Upper Swainswick
Northend
Batheaston
Bathford
Bathampton
Bathwick
Bath
Start
Bath Abbey
Bath Spa
Oldfield Park
Odd Down
Southstoke
Combe Hay
Combe Down
Claverton
Monkton Combe
Limpley Stoke
Freshford
Westwood
Winsley
Monkton Farleigh
Twinhoe
Cam Brook
Newton Brook
River Avon
Kennet and Avon Canal
Bathampton Wood
Claverton Wood
Conkwell Wood
Warleigh Wood
Home Wood
Ashley Wood
Inwood
Limpley Stoke Wood
Friary Wood
Avoncliff
A4
A36
A46
A363
A431
A3062
A367
A39
A368
B3108
B3110
B3111
B3115
B3116
4
24
244
410

South East

South East

Kidderminster
Coventry
Northampton
Worcester
Hereford
Cambridge
Bedford
Ipswich
10
12
13
Luton
Gloucester
15
14
Chelmsford
Oxford
Swindon
11
Southend-on-Sea
London
Bristol
Reading
Bath
08
Canterbury
Aldershot
Maidstone
06
09
02
Ashford
Crawley
01
04
07
Folkestone
03
Taunton
Yeovil
Southampton
05
Brighton
Portsmouth
Eastbourne
Bournemouth
Weymouth
N

From Dean Station go **left**, then turn **left** on E Dean Rd / Route 24 toward Romsey and Lockerley. After passing Mottisfont and Dunbridge Station turn **left** to continue on Route 24. You have the option to stop and visit the National Trust property Mottisfont – a romantic house and gallery set in beautiful riverside gardens. When you reach the A3057, turn **left** onto the traffic-free cycle path that runs along the road – Route 246. Follow this path until you come to the first road crossing where you will turn **left** onto Horsebridge Rd. Follow the road as it curves left, then turn **right** at the sign for Broughton. At The Greyhound Inn turn **left** towards Tytherley. Turn **left** on the B3084, then fork **right**. Turn **right** at the crossroads. At the T-junction turn **right** towards Winterslow. Turn **right** on West Dean Rd. At The Lion's Head turn **left**. After passing Winterslow Baptist Church, turn **left** onto Livery Rd. Turn **left** at the T-junction towards West Dean. Follow the road left after passing through East Grimstead. Here it becomes Dean Rd / Route 24 and returns to West Dean.

Bike shops

No bike shops

Eat & drink

The Old Brewers
SP5 1HU Tel: 01794 341596

Bear & Ragged Staff
SO51 0LB Tel: 01794 368602

John of Gaunt Inn
SO20 6PU Tel: 01794 388644

The Tally Ho
SO20 8AA Tel: 01794 301280

The Greyhound Inn
SO20 8AA Tel: 01794 301992

The Lion's Head
SP5 1PJ Tel: 01980 862234

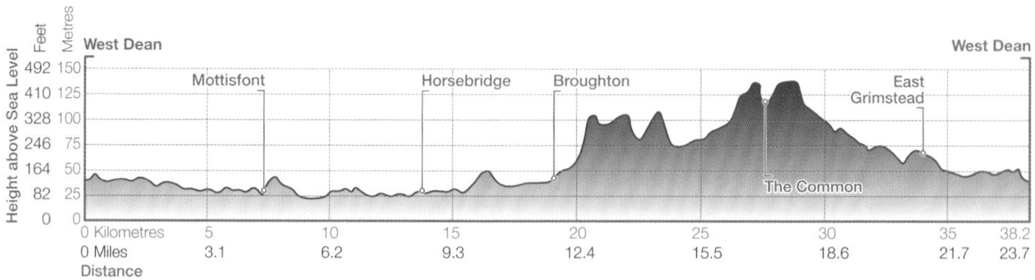

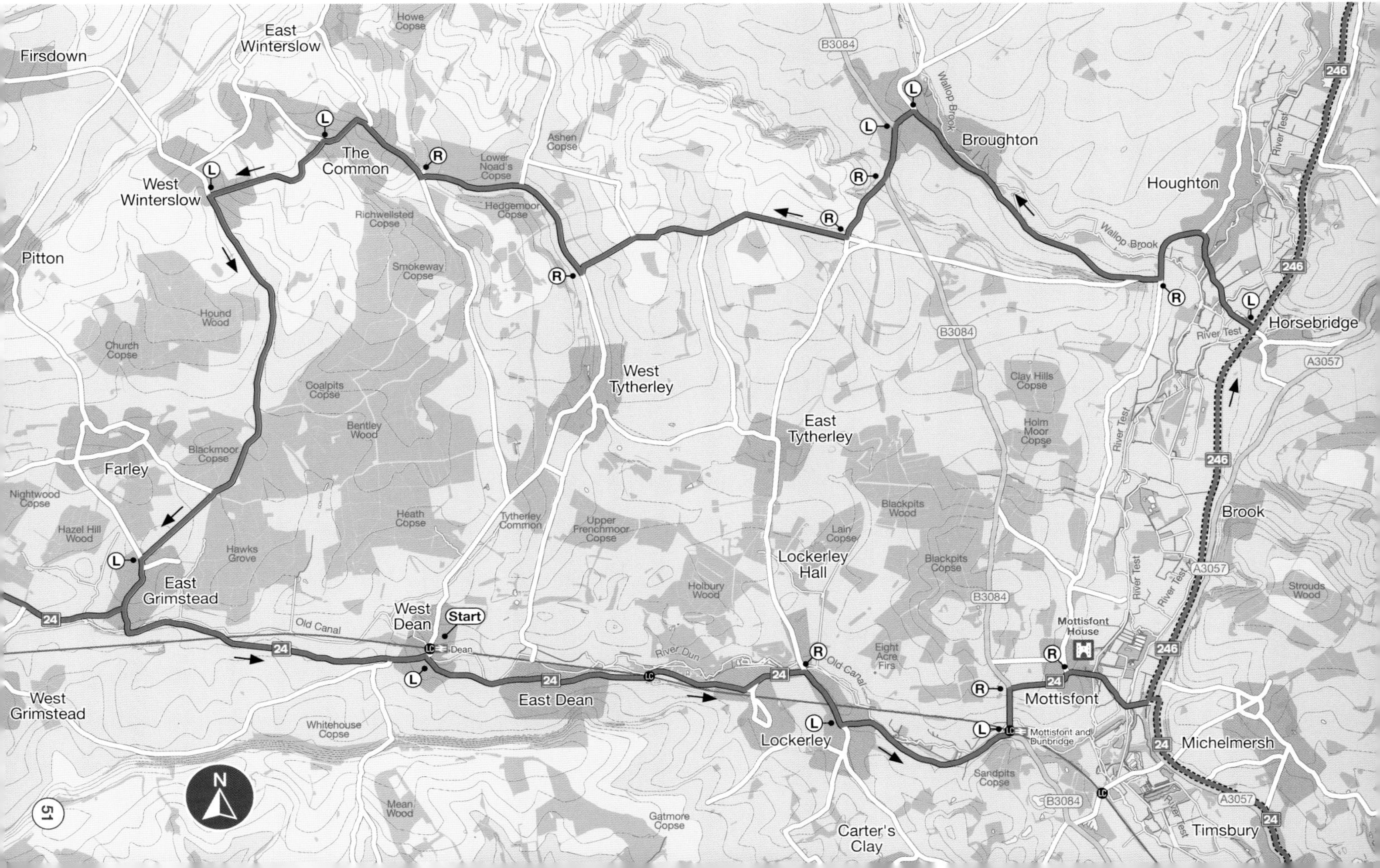
Firsdown
East Winterslow
Howe Copse
West Winterslow
The Common
Lower Noad's Copse
Ashen Copse
Broughton
Houghton
Wallop Brook
River Test
Horsebridge
Richwellsted Copse
Hedgemoor Copse
Smokeway Copse
Pitton
Hound Wood
Church Copse
Coalpits Copse
Bentley Wood
West Tytherley
East Tytherley
Clay Hills Copse
Holm Moor Copse
Blackmoor Copse
Farley
Nightwood Copse
Hazel Hill Wood
Heath Copse
Tytherley Common
Upper Frenchmoor Copse
Blackpits Wood
Lain Copse
Lockerley Hall
Blackpits Copse
Brook
Strouds Wood
Hawks Grove
East Grimstead
Holbury Wood
West Dean
Start
Dean
Old Canal
River Dun
Eight Acre Firs
Mottisfont House
Mottisfont
East Dean
West Grimstead
Whitehouse Copse
Lockerley
Mottisfont and Dunbridge
Michelmersh
Sandpits Copse
Mean Wood
Gatmore Copse
Carter's Clay
Timsbury
B3084
A3057
246
24
N

Head out from Alton Station and turn **right** onto Anstey Rd. Continue **straight** crossing the A31 and River Wey, then turn **left** towards Isington. Follow the road around to cross back under the A31, then turn **left** at the T-junction. Follow the road around to the **right** and continue northwest through Lower Froyle and South Warnborough. At Upton Grey turn **left** onto Weston Rd. Follow this road all the way to the **left** turn signed Route 23 towards Moundsmere. Continue south on Route 23, and after passing through Medstead turn **left** on Red Hill. Follow the Route 23 sign to turn **left** onto the off-road path. Follow the route, which will become Chawton Park Rd, straight on back to Alton. If you'd like to visit Jane Austen's House Museum before returning, turn right onto Northfield Ln just before the playing fields and take the 2nd exit at the A31 roundabout (signed).

Bike shops

1st Gear Cycles
GU34 1EN Tel: 01420 543922

Eat & drink

The Anchor Inn
GU34 4NA Tel: 01420 23261

The Poacher Inn
RG29 1RP Tel: 01256 636518

The Hoddington Arms
RG25 2RL Tel: 01256 862371

The Fur & Feathers
RG25 2PN Tel: 01256 510510

The Yew Tree
SO24 9RX Tel: 01256 389224

The Castle of Comfort
GU34 5LU Tel: 01420 562112

Various in Alton

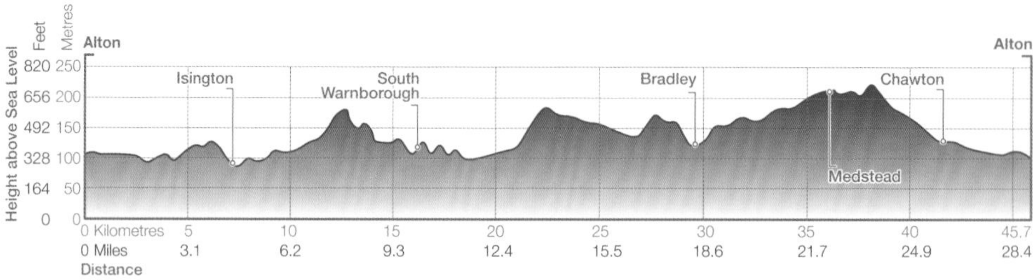

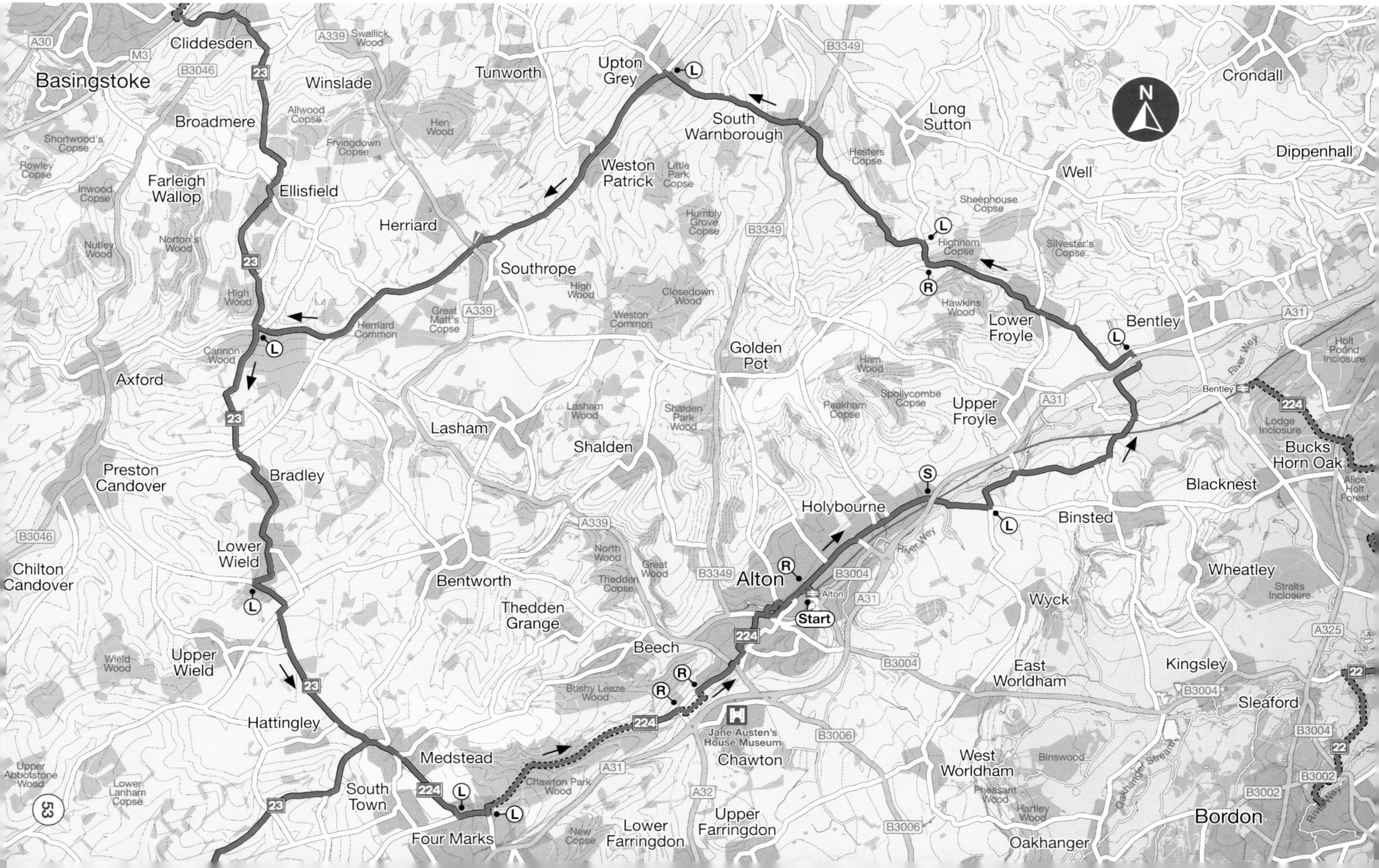
Basingstoke
Cliddesden
Broadmere
Farleigh Wallop
Ellisfield
Winslade
Tunworth
Upton Grey
South Warnborough
Long Sutton
Crondall
Dippenhall
Well
Weston Patrick
Herriard
Southrope
Axford
Lasham
Shalden
Golden Pot
Lower Froyle
Upper Froyle
Bentley
Holt Pound Inclosure
Bucks Horn Oak
Lodge Inclosure
Alice Holt Forest
Blacknest
Binsted
Holybourne
Alton
Start
Preston Candover
Bradley
Lower Wield
Chilton Candover
Bentworth
Thedden Grange
Beech
Upper Wield
Hattingley
Medstead
South Town
Four Marks
Lower Farringdon
Upper Farringdon
Chawton
Jane Austen's House Museum
West Worldham
East Worldham
Wyck
Wheatley
Kingsley
Sleaford
Bordon
Oakhanger
Binswood
Straits Inclosure
Oakhanger Stream
River Wey
A30
M3
B3046
A339
B3349
A31
A32
B3004
B3006
B3002
A325
23
224
22
Swallick Wood
Allwood Copse
Fryingdown Copse
Hen Wood
Shortwood's Copse
Rowley Copse
Inwood Copse
Norton's Wood
Nutley Wood
High Wood
Cannon Wood
Herriard Common
Great Matt's Copse
Weston Common
Closedown Wood
Humbly Grove Copse
Little Park Copse
Hesters Copse
Sheephouse Copse
Highnam Copse
Silvester's Copse
Hawkins Wood
Ham Wood
Peakham Copse
Spollycombe Copse
Lasham Wood
Shalden Park Wood
North Wood
Great Wood
Thedden Copse
Bushy Leaze Wood
Chawton Park Wood
New Copse
Wield Wood
Upper Abbotstone Wood
Lower Lanham Copse
Pheasant Wood
Hartley Wood
Bentley
Alton
N
L
R
S

Turn **right** out of the station on North St. After crossing the tracks, turn hard **right** onto the B2180. Turn **left** onto Depot Rd, then when the road ends at the little roundabout turn **right** on Comptons Ln. Turn **left** onto Hammerpond Rd, then **right** onto Doomsday Ln which becomes Sedgwick Ln. The road curves to the left, then at the T-junction turn **left** on Broadwater Lane and follow to Copsale. Turn **right** following sign for Southwater, then turn **right** again onto the off-road path signed Southwater / Downs Link. After passing Rudgwick turn **right** off the Downs Link heading towards the B2128. When you reach it turn **right** towards Ellen's Green. In Ellen's Green turn **left** on Furzen Ln, then **right** on Horsham Rd which becomes Rowhook Rd. Briefly join the A281 before turning **left** on Strood Ln. Stay right until the road ends in a T-junction at Broadbridge Heath Rd, turn **left** and then take first **right** onto Robin Hood Ln. Pass under the A24 and then turn **left** onto the shared-use path signed for Horsham. When the shared-use path ends **jink right left** onto Spencers Pl, turn **left** on Trafalgar Rd, then **right** on the B2237. Turn **left** on Hurst Rd to go back to the station, or continue straight on if you'd like to stop in central Horsham.

Bike shops

The Cycle Room
RH12 1HR Tel: 01403 252744

A D Cycles
RH13 5AA Tel: 01403 258391

Eat & drink

Bax Castle
RH13 0LA Tel: 01403 730369

The Fox Inn
RH12 3JP Tel: 01403 822386

The King's Head
RH12 3EB Tel: 01403 822200

Firebird Brewing Co
RH12 3UW Tel: 01403 823180

The Chequers Inn
RH12 3PY Tel: 01403 790480

The Greets Inn
RH12 3QY Tel: 01403 265047

The Shelley Arms
RH12 3JU Tel: 01403 253406

Dog & Bacon Inn
RH12 2QR Tel: 01403 252176

Various in Horsham

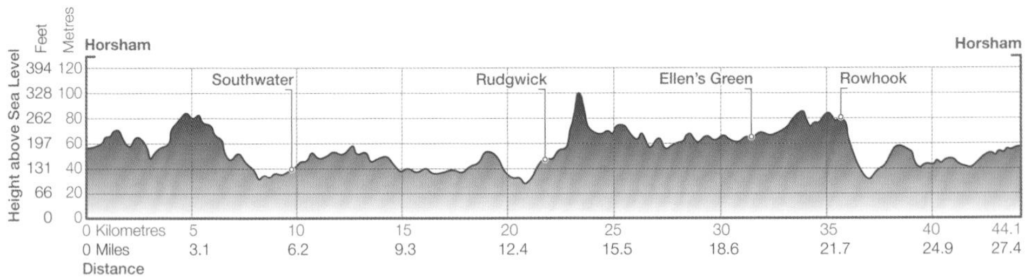

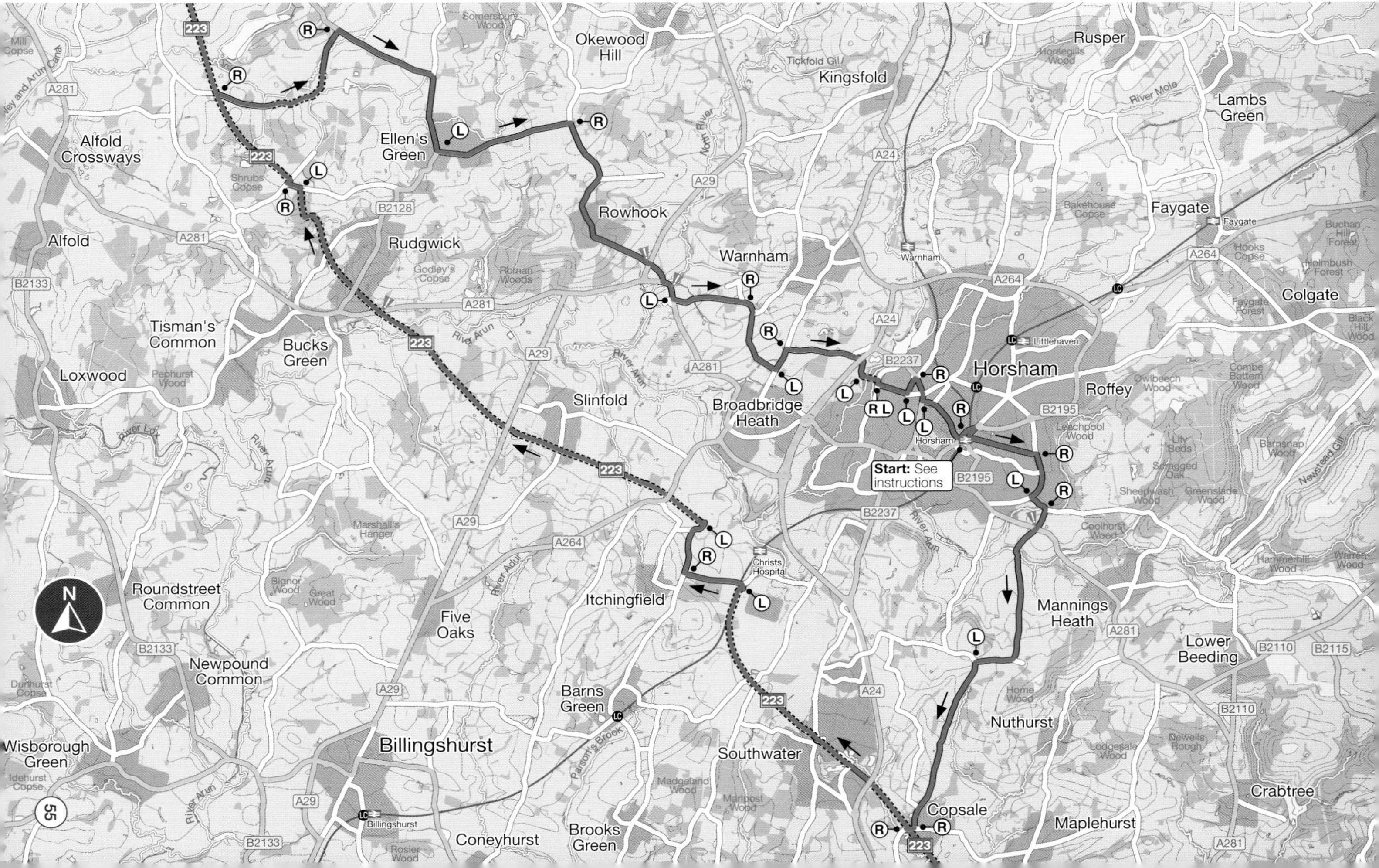
Start: See instructions
Horsham
Roffey
Littlehaven
Warnham
Broadbridge Heath
Rowhook
Okewood Hill
Ellen's Green
Rudgwick
Alfold Crossways
Alfold
Tisman's Common
Bucks Green
Loxwood
Slinfold
Itchingfield
Christs Hospital
Five Oaks
Roundstreet Common
Newpound Common
Barns Green
Billingshurst
Southwater
Coneyhurst
Brooks Green
Wisborough Green
Copsale
Nuthurst
Maplehurst
Mannings Heath
Lower Beeding
Crabtree
Kingsfold
Rusper
Lambs Green
Faygate
Colgate
River Arun
River Mole
North River
River Lox
River Adur
223
A281
A29
A24
A264
B2237
B2195
B2128
B2133
B2110
B2115

Turn **right** out of Crowborough Station and then **right** on Western Rd. Turn **left** on Hadlow Down Rd and then **left** on Steep Rd. Follow the road until it ends, turn **right** on Castle Hill. When this road ends, turn **right** on Dewlands Hill. Turn **left** on Stonehurst Ln towards Mayfield. When you reach a crossroads with a school road sign, turn **left** away from the sign. When you reach the A267 turn **left** and then immediately **left** again onto Horleigh Green Rd. Keep **right** – the road becomes Fir Toll Rd / Route 21. Cross the A267 onto the signed shared-use path, then turn **right** onto Station Rd following the sign for the Cuckoo Trail. Continue following the signs for Route 21 until you reach a **right** turn onto an off-road path signed Heathfield. This becomes Marklye Ln. Cross the A265 onto Tower St and then turn **right** onto Downsview. At the end of the road **zig zig left right left** onto Highcroft Cres, then turn **left** on Gibraltar Rise and **left** onto Station Rd. On your right you will see a car park with a Cuckoo Trail sign, please enter the trail here. Continue on the trail until near Maynard's Green – you will come to a small green bridge with a path to your **left** going down to the road under the bridge. Take this and turn **right** onto the road passing under the bridge. When you reach West Street Ln turn **left**. Continue straight and cross the A267, then turn **right** when the road ends at a T-junction (no sign). Stay **left** at the road triangle, then turn **right** following Hanging Birch Ln towards Cross in Hand and Heathfield. Take the next **left** towards Cross in Hand, then turn **right** on Back Ln. Turn **left** in front of the gated property, then turn **left** on Whitehouse Ln. Follow the road until you reach the memorial cross and turn **right**. Continue **straight** on crossing the B2102, then when the road ends turn **right** following the sign for Hadlow Down. Bear **left** towards Hadlow Down. At the fork stay **left**, then continue straight on. Turn **left** onto Fordbrook Hill, then **right** onto Burnt Oak Rd. When this road reaches a five-way junction, turn **right** towards Crowborough. Turn **right** on Walshes Rd, cross over the tracks and turn **left** on the B2100 / Crowborough Hill. The train station entrance is on your left.

Bike shops

Wealden Cycles
TN6 2QN Tel: 01892 653736

Bikegoo
TN6 2NQ Tel: 01892 668800

Cycle Revival
TN21 8AA Tel: 01435 866118

Eat & drink

The Middle House
TN20 6AB
Tel: 01435 872146

Rose & Crown
TN20 6TE
Tel: 01435 872200

Various in Heathfield

The Runt in Tun
TN21 0DJ
Tel: 01435 864284

The Star Inn
TN21 0RA
Tel: 01435 812495

New Inn Hadlow
TN22 4HJ
Tel: 01825 830939

The Wheatsheaf
TN6 2NF
Tel: 01892 663756

Various in Crowborough

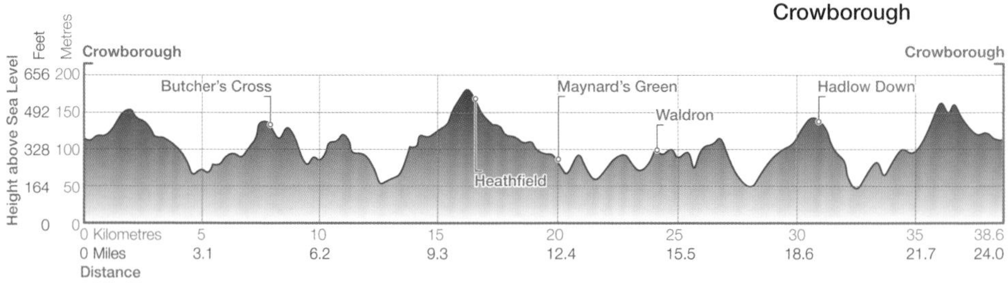

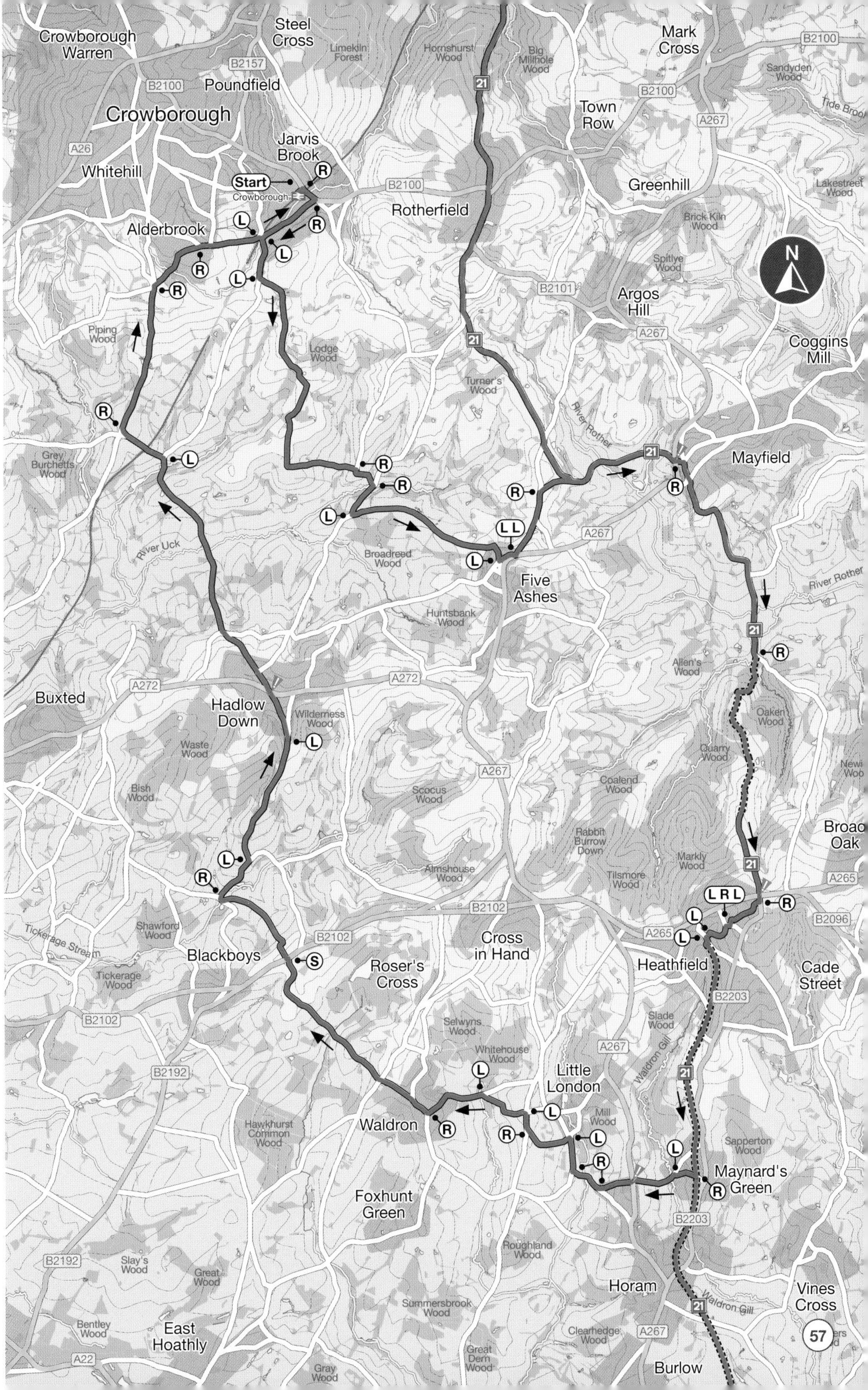
Crowborough Warren
Steel Cross
Limekiln Forest
Hornshurst Wood
Big Millhole Wood
Mark Cross
B2100
Sandyden Wood
B2157
Poundfield
B2100
Crowborough
B2100
Town Row
Tide Brook
A267
A26
Jarvis Brook
Whitehill
Start
Crowborough
B2100
Rotherfield
Greenhill
Lakestreet Wood
Alderbrook
Brick Kiln Wood
Spitlye Wood
B2101
Argos Hill
A267
Piping Wood
Lodge Wood
Coggins Mill
Turner's Wood
River Rother
Mayfield
Grey Burchetts Wood
River Uck
Broadreed Wood
A267
Five Ashes
River Rother
Huntsbank Wood
Allen's Wood
A272
A272
Buxted
Hadlow Down
Wilderness Wood
Oaken Wood
Waste Wood
Quarry Wood
A267
Coalend Wood
Scocus Wood
Bish Wood
Rabbit Burrow Down
Broad Oak
Markly Wood
Almshouse Wood
Tilsmore Wood
A265
B2102
B2096
Shawford Wood
Tickerage Stream
B2102
Cross in Hand
A265
Blackboys
Roser's Cross
Heathfield
Cade Street
Tickerage Wood
B2203
B2102
Slade Wood
Selwyns Wood
A267
Whitehouse Wood
Waldron Gill
B2192
Little London
Mill Wood
Hawkhurst Common Wood
Waldron
Sapperton Wood
Maynard's Green
Foxhunt Green
B2203
Roughland Wood
B2192
Slay's Wood
Great Wood
Horam
Summersbrook Wood
Vines Cross
Waldron Gill
Bentley Wood
East Hoathly
Clearhedge Wood
A267
A22
Great Dern Wood
Gray Wood
Burlow
21
L
R
S
N

Turn **right** out of the station on High St, **right** onto the B2247, then **left** onto School Ln. Join the shared-use path Route 2 to your right. Follow the path, turning **left** after crossing over the A27, until it ends at Robin Post Ln, turn **left**. Turn **right** and then **right** onto Bayley's Ln, then **left** towards Berwick Station and Arlington. Turn **left** at the Yew Tree Inn. Follow the road as it bends right and left, and turn **right** when you reach Station Rd. Turn **left** on Lower Wick St, follow the road as it zig zags, then turn **left** on Church Ln towards Ripe. Bear **right** towards Golden Cross and continue straight, crossing the A22. Turn **left** towards Chiddingly then **left** again at the Six Bells. Turn **right** on Parsonage Ln towards Horam then **left** on Smithlands Ln. At the fork in the road stay **right** towards Waldron and continue until the road ends. Turn **right** towards Horam and Hailsham, then **left** towards Little London. At the four-way crossing turn **right** towards Horam, stay **right** at the triangle, then bear **left** onto Sandy Ln. Turn **right** on Tubwell Ln, then when you reach a small green bridge join the shared-use path to your right just under the bridge signed for Hailsham and Polegate. You are now on the Cuckoo Trail / Route 21. Follow the route all the way to Polegate – the path ends where you first joined. To return to the station turn **right** on the B2247 then **left** on High St and the station will be on your left.

Bike shops

Kontour Cycles
BN26 6AA Tel: 01323 482368

Eat & drink

Arlington Tea Garden
BN26 6RU Tel: 01323 484549

Yew Tree Inn
BN26 6RX Tel: 01323 870590

The Six Bells Inn
BN8 6HT Tel: 01825 872227

The Railway Tavern
BN27 2BH Tel: 01323 842442

The Junction Tavern
BN26 6EB Tel: 01323 482010

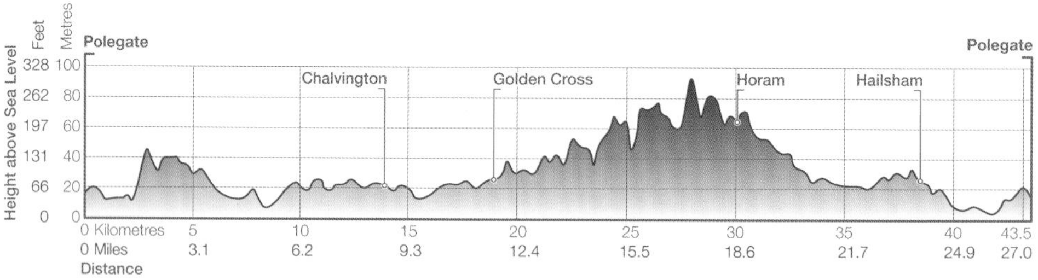

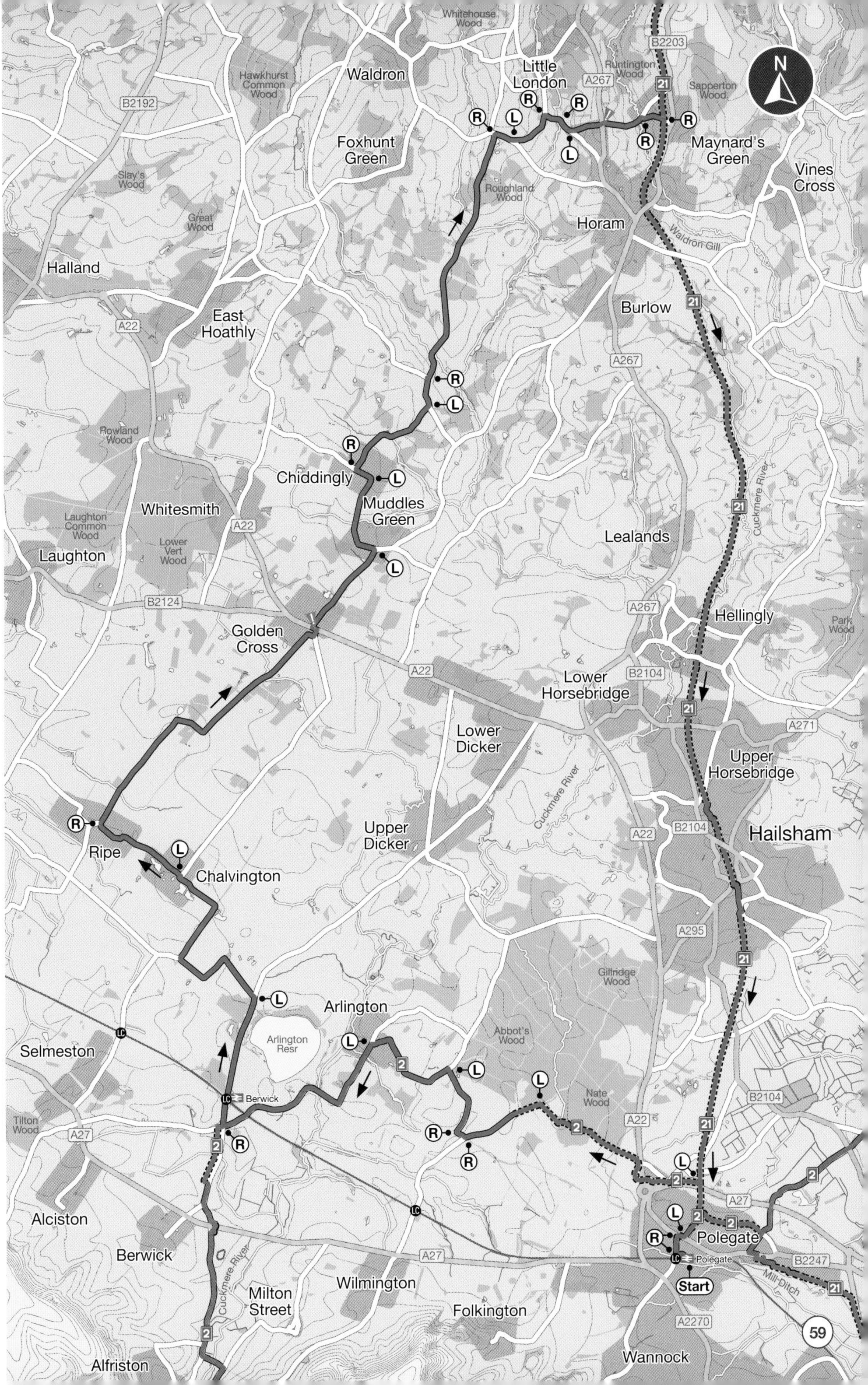

Whitehouse Wood
B2203
Waldron
Hawkhurst Common Wood
Little London
Runtington Wood
A267
Sapperton Wood
B2192
Foxhunt Green
Maynard's Green
Vines Cross
Slay's Wood
Roughland Wood
Great Wood
Horam
Waldron Gill
Halland
Burlow
East Hoathly
A22
A267
Rowland Wood
Chiddingly
Muddles Green
Whitesmith
Laughton Common Wood
Lower Vert Wood
Lealands
Cuckmere River
Laughton
B2124
A267
Hellingly
Park Wood
Golden Cross
A22
Lower Horsebridge
B2104
Lower Dicker
A271
Upper Horsebridge
Cuckmere River
Upper Dicker
A22
B2104
Hailsham
Ripe
Chalvington
A295
Gillridge Wood
Arlington
Arlington Resr
Abbot's Wood
Selmeston
Berwick
Nate Wood
Tilton Wood
A27
A22
B2104
Alciston
A27
Polegate
Berwick
A27
Polegate
B2247
Start
Mill Ditch
Cuckmere River
Milton Street
Wilmington
Folkington
A2270
Alfriston
Wannock
N

From either train station, make your way to the Canterbury War Memorial outside the Canterbury Cathedral gate. Head down Mercery Ln, turn **right** on High St and **left** on Stour St. Pass the church and turn **right**. Go under the A road, cross the river and turn **left** on Route 18. Follow the route south west along the Great Stour until it ends at Station Rd in Chartham. Turn **right** onto the road and then **left** on Church Ln. Continue **straight** on until the road ends, then turn **left** on Thruxted Ln. Turn **left** on Mystole Ln and then **right** on Penny Pot Ln. Continue **straight** on until you reach Waltam. Turn **right** following the sign for Bodsham and Wye, then turn **left** onto Whiteacre Ln. At the end of the road turn **right** towards Elmsted and then **left** on Clapper Hill. At the B2068 **jink left right** onto Curtis Ln to continue on. In Stelling Minnis turn **right** at the T-junction and follow Bossingham Rd straight on until it ends. Turn **left** following the sign for Regional Route 17. Continue following Route 17 towards Bridge. In Bridge turn **right** at the Plough and Harrow and then turn **left** at the Red Lion. Continue straight passing under the A2, then turn **left** onto Regional Route 16 towards Canterbury. Keep following the Route 16 signs. After crossing the rail tracks turn **left** on Spring Ln, **left** on the A257, then **right** on North Holmes Rd. Turn **left** on Military Rd, then **right** on the shared-use path signed Northgate. **Jink left right** on the narrow lane. Turn **left** on Northgate, then **left** on Palace St. Stay **left** and the Canterbury Cathedral gate will be on your left.

Bike shops

Canterbury Cycle Centre
CT1 2NZ Tel: 01227 787880

Cycles UK Canterbury
CT1 2SY Tel: 01227 457956

Biketart
CT1 2DR Tel: 01227 479353

Canterbury Cycle Hire
CT2 8BN Tel: 01227 388058

Eat & drink

The Artichoke
CT4 7JQ Tel: 01227 738316

Compasses Inn
CT4 7ES Tel: 01227 700300

The Rose & Crown
CT4 6AT Tel: 01227 709265

The Duck Inn
CT4 5PB Tel: 01227 830354

Red Lion Inn
CT4 5LB Tel: 01227 832213

Plough & Harrow
CT4 5LA Tel: 01227 830455

Various in Canterbury

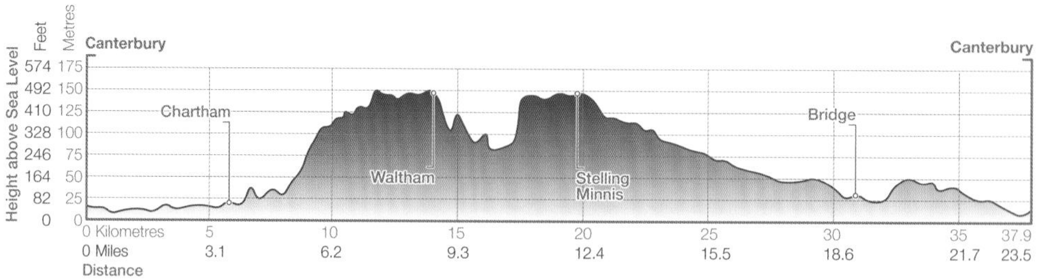

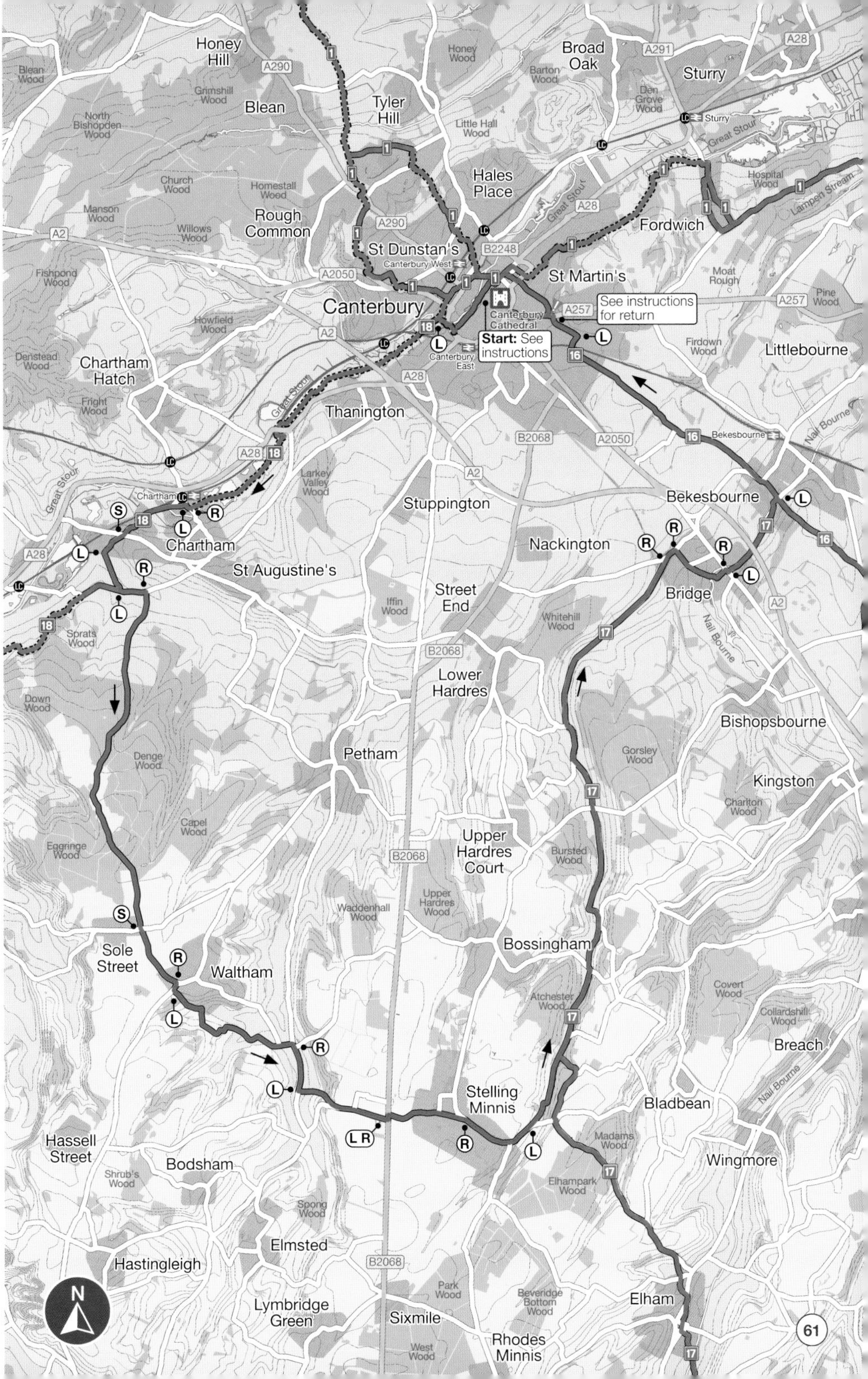
Honey Hill
Blean Wood
A290
Grimshill Wood
Blean
North Bishopden Wood
Honey Wood
Tyler Hill
Little Hall Wood
Broad Oak
Barton Wood
Den Grove Wood
A291
A28
Sturry
Great Stour
Hospital Wood
Lampen Stream
Hales Place
Fordwich
Church Wood
Homestall Wood
Rough Common
Manson Wood
Willows Wood
A290
A2
A28
St Dunstan's
Canterbury West
B2248
St Martin's
Moat Rough
Fishpond Wood
A2050
Canterbury
Canterbury Cathedral
See instructions for return
A257
Pine Wood
Howfield Wood
A2
Start: See instructions
Canterbury East
Firdown Wood
Littlebourne
Denstead Wood
Chartham Hatch
Fright Wood
A28
Thanington
B2068
A2050
Bekesbourne
Nail Bourne
A28
Great Stour
Larkey Valley Wood
A2
Chartham
Stuppington
Bekesbourne
A28
Chartham
St Augustine's
Nackington
Bridge
Street End
Iffin Wood
Whitehill Wood
A2
Sprats Wood
B2068
Lower Hardres
Down Wood
Bishopsbourne
Denge Wood
Petham
Gorsley Wood
Kingston
Charlton Wood
Capel Wood
Eggringe Wood
Upper Hardres Court
Bursted Wood
B2068
Upper Hardres Wood
Waddenhall Wood
Bossingham
Sole Street
Waltham
Atchester Wood
Covert Wood
Collardshill Wood
Breach
Stelling Minnis
Bladbean
Hassell Street
Bodsham
Madams Wood
Elhampark Wood
Wingmore
Shrub's Wood
Spong Wood
Elmsted
Hastingleigh
B2068
Park Wood
Beveridge Bottom Wood
Elham
Lymbridge Green
Sixmile
Rhodes Minnis
West Wood
N

07 Rye & Romney Marsh

26.8 miles / 42.3 km

Head straight out of the station and turn **left** at Cinque Ports. Follow the road straight, then turn **right** under the old stone gate signed Route 2. On your left after Tower Forge you will see the entrance to a path marked Route 2. At the end of the short path turn **left** onto the road, then **right** at the roundabout. Just after you cross the bridge over the River Rother, join the path on your **right** signed Route 2. Follow Route 2 through Camber and Lydd, turning **left** out of Lydd. When you reach a National Cycle Network signpost and sign for Route 11 towards Brookland and Rye, turn **left**. Follow the route on Clubb's Ln to Brookland. When the road ends **jink left right left** onto Straight Ln, turn **left** on King St, then **right** when the road ends. Follow the road to Appledore, there turn **left** to cross the stream and immediately turn **left** onto Military Rd. Follow this road **straight** all the way back to Rye. Stay **left** onto the A268 / Rye Rd. At the roundabout go **right** and then go back on the little path you took at the start (on your right). At the end of the path turn **left** on High St away from the old gate. Turn **right** on Market Rd, **left** on Cinque Ports St, **right** on Ferry Rd then **right** to the train station.

Bike shops

No bike shops

Eat & drink

The Owl
TN31 7RH Tel: 01797 225284

The George Hotel
TN29 9AJ Tel: 01797 321710

Dolphin Inn
TN29 9DQ Tel: 01797 320259

The Royal Oak
TN29 9QR Tel: 01797 344444

The Black Lion
TN26 2BU Tel: 01233 758206

The Globe Inn Marsh Rye
TN31 7NX Tel: 01797 225220

Various in Rye

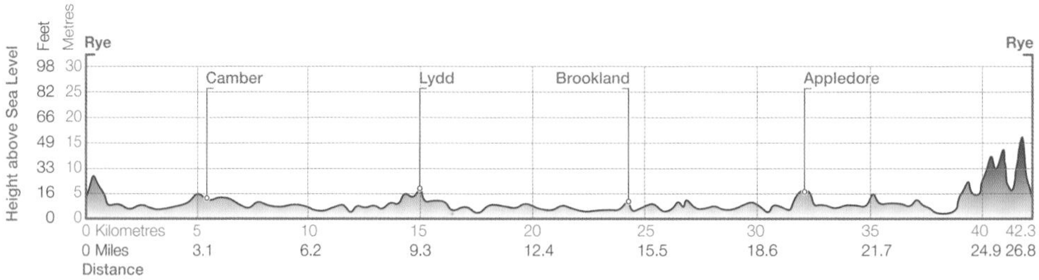

Small Hythe
Reading Street
Appledore
Snave
Snargate
Brenzett
Ivychurch
St Mary in the Marsh
St Mary's Bay
The Stocks
Stone in Oxney
Wittersham
Brookland
Old Romney
New Romney
Littlestone-on-Sea
Greatstone-on-Sea
Peasmarsh
Iden
Rye Foreign
Playden
East Guldeford
Start: See instructions
See instructions for return
Rye
Lydd
Ketchley Copse
Camber
Rye Harbour
Winchelsea
Winchelsea Beach
Lydd-on-Sea
River Rother
River Brede
River Tillingham
Reading Sewer
Newknock Channel
Otter Channel
Woodside Stream
New Sewer
Comb Wood
Cock Wood
Iden Wood
Morebread Wood
B2082
B2080
A2070
A259
A268
B2089
B2075
B2071
N

From Sandwich Station follow Route 1. Turn **left** on St George's Rd, **right** onto New St, **right** onto Harnet St, **left** on Strand St, **right** on Richborough Rd. Follow the route through Westmarsh, Elmstone, Preston and Grove. Between Grove and Stodmarsh Route 1 will be signed right through fields towards Stodmarsh. Don't turn, stay **straight** (leaving Route 1) on Green Ln with the wood fence on your left side. When Green Ln ends turn **right** on Grove Rd which will become Wickham Rd. Turn **left** on Wickham Ln towards Ickham. When you reach the A257 go **right** for Bramling and immediately **left** on Mill Rd. Turn **left** on Watercress Ln, when it ends turn **left** on Wingham Well Ln. Stay **right** to join Adisham Rd, then turn **left** on Crockshard Ln towards Goodnestone. Stay **left** at the fork in the road onto Cave Ln. Stay **straight** on this road until you pass The Griffin's Head pub, cross over Sandwich Rd, then turn **left** on Thornton Rd towards Northbourne. Turn **left** on Thornton Ln towards Eastry and Sandwich. Turn **right** on Heronden Rd which turns into Mill Ln, then **left** on High St. Stay right as it becomes Sandwich Rd. When you reach the A256, use the shared-use path to **jink left right** to cross the road onto Felderland Ln. Approaching the A258 / Deal Rd, join the shared-use path and go **left** along the road. Stay on the shared-use path to avoid the roundabout and turn **right** onto Deal Rd towards Sandwich. Immediately after crossing over the tracks there is a walking path on your **right** to the train station (please dismount), or you can turn **right** on St George's Rd and **right** on Delfside.

Bike shops

Locks of Sandwich Cycles
CT13 9BT Tel: 01304 617161

Eat & drink

The Half Moon & Seven Stars
CT3 1EB Tel: 01227 722296

The Red Lion
CT3 4BA Tel: 01227 721339

The Rose Inn
CT3 1RQ Tel: 01227 721763

Duke William
CT3 1QP Tel: 01227 721308

The Griffin's Head
CT3 1PR Tel: 01304 840325

The Five Bells
CT13 0HX Tel: 01304 611188

Hop & Huffkin
CT13 9AB Tel: 01304 448560

Various in Sandwich

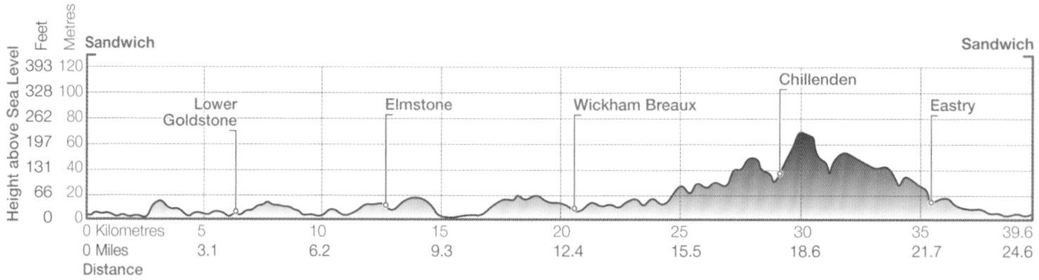

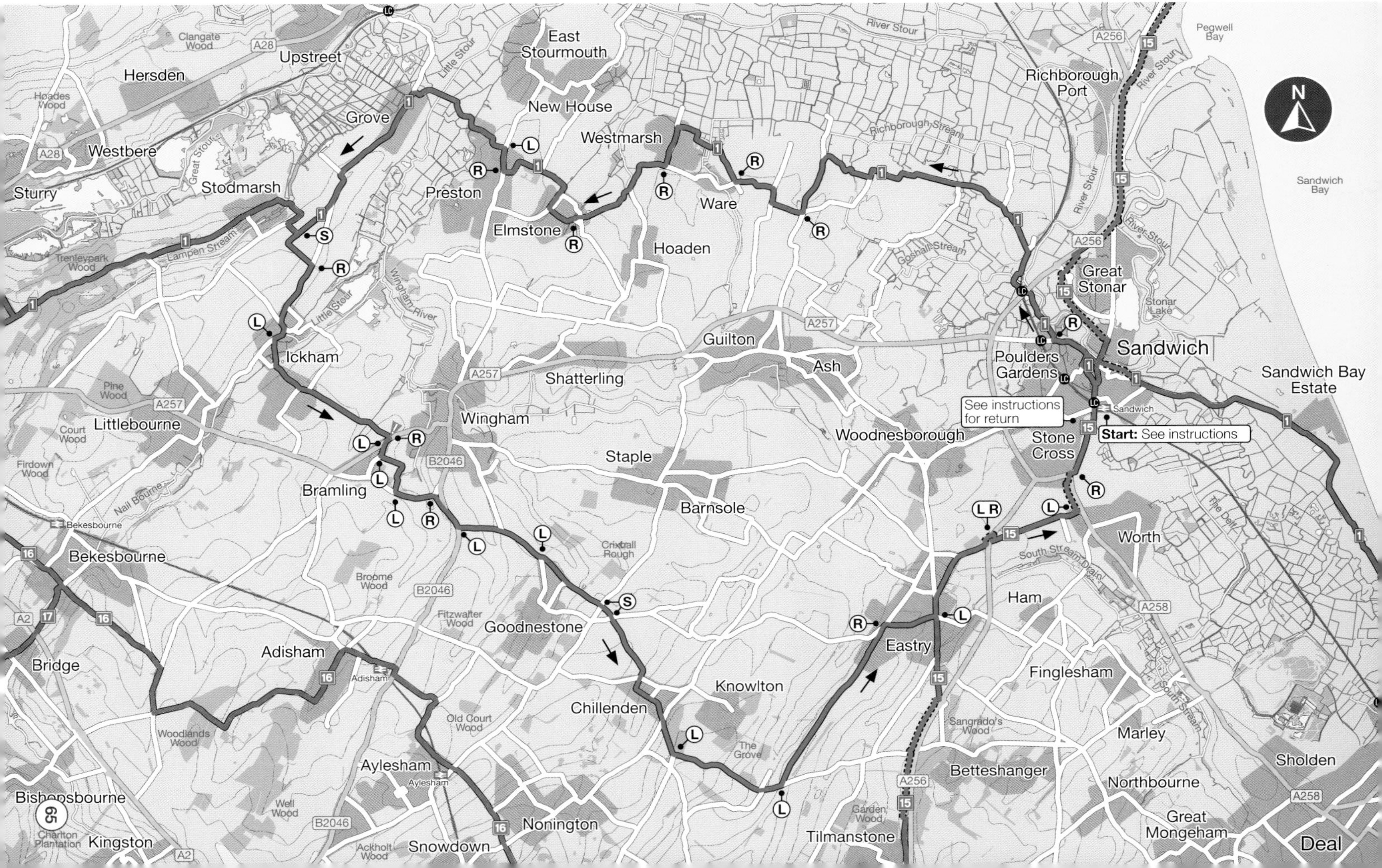
N
Pegwell Bay
Sandwich Bay
Sandwich Bay Estate
Sandwich
Great Stonar
Stonar Lake
Richborough Port
River Stour
Richborough Stream
Gosshall Stream
Poulders Gardens
See instructions for return
Start: See instructions
Stone Cross
Woodnesborough
Worth
The Delf
South Stream Drain
South Stream
Ham
Finglesham
Eastry
Sangrado's Wood
Betteshanger
Marley
Northbourne
Sholden
Great Mongeham
Deal
Tilmanstone
Garden Wood
Knowlton
The Grove
Chillenden
Goodnestone
Crixhall Rough
Barnsole
Staple
Ash
Guilton
Shatterling
Hoaden
Ware
Westmarsh
New House
East Stourmouth
Elmstone
Preston
Little Stour
Wingham River
Wingham
Ickham
Bramling
Grove
Upstreet
Hersden
Clangate Wood
Hoades Wood
Westbere
Sturry
Stodmarsh
Great Stour
Lampen Stream
Trenleypark Wood
Pine Wood
Littlebourne
Court Wood
Firdown Wood
Nail Bourne
Bekesbourne
Broome Wood
Fitzwalter Wood
Adisham
Bridge
Woodlands Wood
Aylesham
Old Court Wood
Nonington
Snowdown
Ackholt Wood
Well Wood
Bishopsbourne
Charlton Plantation
Kingston
A256
A257
A258
A28
A2
B2046
1
15
16
17
L
R
S
LC

From Headcorn Station head **right** on the main road, then stay **left** onto Smarden Rd. When the road ends turn **left** on Bell Ln, then **right** on Water Ln. In Smarden turn **left** on The Street (which becomes Smarden Rd again) and follow through Pluckley. Continue **straight** over the M20 and the road becomes Pluckley Rd, follow into Charing. Keep **straight** on over the A20 continuing on The High Street, which becomes The Hill. When the road ends in a T-junction you will see a path that begins in front of you. Take the path and turn **left** – this is Route 17 / Pilgrims Way. Follow the route **straight** all the way to Hollingbourne. At The Dirty Habit turn **left** on Upper St / B2163, leaving Route 17.

Optional visit to Leeds Castle: Continue on B2163 / Eyhorne St, pass under the M20. Follow the signs for Leeds Castle. At the first roundabout go left, at the second roundabout take the 3rd exit right. The entrance will be on your left. To re-join the route, exit right from the castle, go left at the roundabout onto the A20, just before the M20 turn right on Chegworth Road.

Turn **left** on Greenway Court Rd. When the road ends turn **right** onto the A20, pass under the M20 and turn **left** on Chegworth Road. Follow this road **straight** through Ulcombe all the way to Headcorn. At Kings Rd **jink left right** onto Forge Ln, follow the road and turn **left** on Station Rd. Headcorn Station will be on your right.

Bike shops

Wood's Cycles
TN27 9NN Tel: 01622 890664

Eat & drink

The Bell
TN27 8PW
Tel: 01233 770283

Chequers Inn
TN27 8QA
Tel: 01233 770217

Flying Horse
TN27 8QD
Tel: 01233 770432

Black Horse
TN27 0QS
Tel: 01233 841948

Dog & Bear Lenham
ME17 2PG
Tel: 01622 858219

The Dirty Habit
ME17 1UW
Tel: 01622 880880

The Sugar Loaves
ME17 1TS
Tel: 01622 880220

The Windmill
ME17 1TR
Tel: 01622 889000

The Park Gate Inn
ME17 1PG
Tel: 01622 880985

Harrow Inn
ME17 1DP
Tel: 01622 844422

The White Horse
TN27 9NN
Tel: 01622 890625

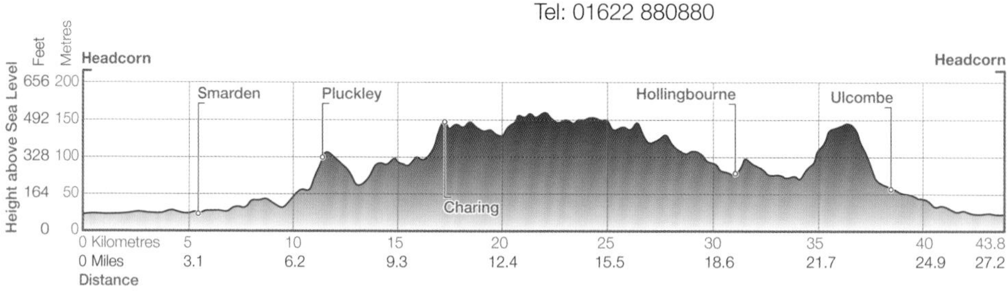

Bredgar
M2
Longton Wood
Hucking
Bicknor
Trundle Wood
Milstead
Kingsdown Wood
Sharsted Wood
Smokes Wood
Hogshaw Wood
Newnham
Wormshill
Doddington
Frinsted
Eastling
17
Broad Street
Wichling
Wichling Wood
Hollingbourne
Snarkhurst Wood
Hollingbourne
Stedehill Wood
West Street
Oakenpole Wood
Divan Wood
M20
Eyhorne Street
River Len
B2163
A20
Warren Street
Stalisfield Green
Leeds
Leeds Castle
Harrietsham
Lenham
Harrietsham
Broomfield
River Len
Lenham
Kite Hill Wood
Kingswood
King's Wood
Sandway
Great Stour
Liverton Street
Charing Heath
Charing
A252
Dencher Wood
Boughton Malherbe
Grafty Green
Ulcombe
Westwell Leacon
Great Stour
Egerton
Southpark Wood
Potter's Forstal
Pluckley
Little Chart
Frith Wood
Headcorn
Hothfield
River Sherway
Pluckley Thorne
Dering Wood
Headcorn
Start
A274
River Beult
Pluckley
The Forest
March Wood
Maltman's Hill
Hoad's Wood
Smarden
Hammer Stream
River Beult
Haffenden Quarter
Bethersden
Curteis Corner
Birch Wood
Twenty Acre Wood
A28
Three Chimneys
Honeyfield Wood
A262
Biddenden
N
Plurenden Wood
Hook Wood
High Halden
Harlakenden Wood
Roger's Wood
18
S
L
R

From Audley End Station turn **left** onto the B1039. Follow the road under the M11, it becomes Route 11. Follow the route through Arkesden, Clavering and Rickling. At Quendon leave Route 11 and stay **straight** on Belcham's Ln to the B1383. Turn **right** and then **left** towards Ugley – this is Regional Route 50. Follow the road passing under the M11 and keeping right, then turn **left** towards Henham. Continue **straight** through Henham, leaving Route 50, and continue on to Debden Green. Here turn **left** on Bolford St (becomes Debden Rd) and continue straight through Debden all the way to Saffron Walden. At the T-junction turn **left** on London Rd / Route 11. To visit Audley End House, follow the signs to the property and then return to the route. Follow Route 11 as it turns south towards Wendens Ambo. Using the shared-use paths, turn **left** along the B1383 then **right** along the B1039. At the roundabout turn **left** to return to the train station.

Bike shops

Newdales
CB10 1JZ Tel: 01799 513980

Bicicletta – Coffee con Velo
CB10 1JZ Tel: 01799 522814

Eat & drink

Axe & Compasses
CB11 4EX Tel: 01799 550272

The Cricketers
CB11 4QT Tel: 01799 550442

The Cricketer's Arms
CB11 3YG Tel: 01799 543210

The Chequers
CM22 6HZ Tel: 01799 540387

The Cock Inn
CM22 6AL Tel: 01279 850347

The Duke of York
CB10 1EA Tel: 01799 513113

The Fighting Cocks
CB11 4JN Tel: 01799 541279

The Bell Inn
CB11 4JY Tel: 01799 540382

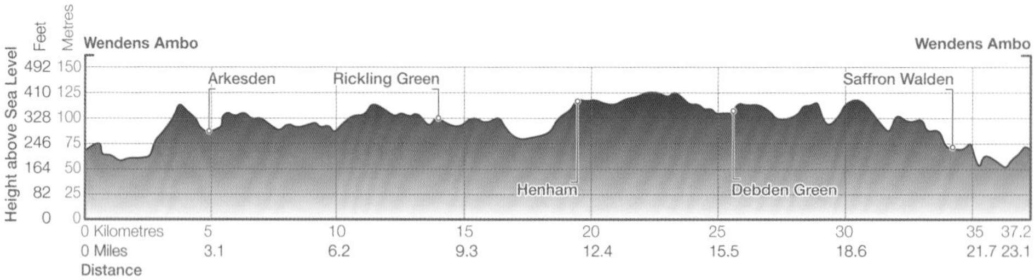

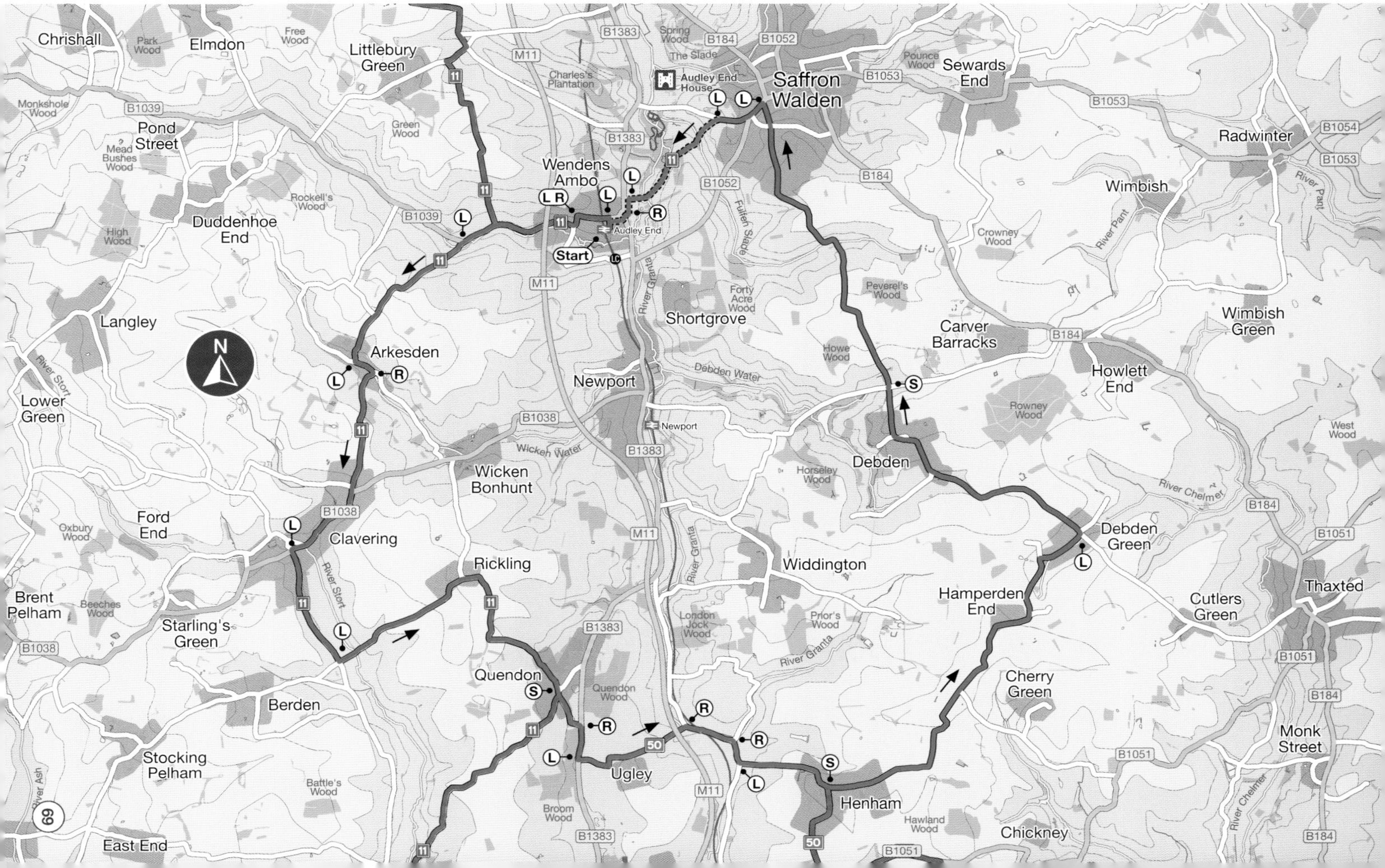
Chrishall
Elmdon
Littlebury Green
Saffron Walden
Sewards End
Radwinter
Wimbish
Wimbish Green
Pond Street
Duddenhoe End
Wendens Ambo
Audley End House
Start
Audley End
Shortgrove
Carver Barracks
Langley
Arkesden
Newport
Howlett End
Lower Green
Debden
Wicken Bonhunt
Ford End
Clavering
Debden Green
Rickling
Widdington
Hamperden End
Thaxted
Cutlers Green
Brent Pelham
Starling's Green
Quendon
Cherry Green
Berden
Ugley
Monk Street
Stocking Pelham
Henham
Chickney
East End
Park Wood
Free Wood
Monkshole Wood
Mead Bushes Wood
Green Wood
Rockell's Wood
High Wood
Charles's Plantation
Spring Wood
The Slade
Pounce Wood
Crowney Wood
Fulfen Slade
Forty Acre Wood
Peverel's Wood
Howe Wood
Rowney Wood
West Wood
Horseley Wood
London Jock Wood
Prior's Wood
Quendon Wood
Broom Wood
Hawland Wood
Battle's Wood
Oxbury Wood
Beeches Wood
River Stort
River Granta
River Pant
River Chelmer
River Ash
Debden Water
Wicken Water
B1039
B1383
B1184
B1052
B1053
B1054
B184
B1038
B1051
M11
11
50
L
R
S
N

11 Woolwich Ferry & Dartford Crossing

35.4 miles / 57.0 km

From Dartford Station turn **left** out and at the roundabout turn **left**. As the road bends left you will see a path entrance to your **right**, take this down to the river and head south away from the rail tracks – you are now on Route 1. When the path ends turn **left** onto the A226 briefly, then turn **right** on Darenth Rd. At the Ivy Leaf turn **left** on Brent Ln, **left** on Downs Ave, then **right** on Park Rd following Route 1. Turn **left** on Pilgrims Way leaving Route 1, when the road ends **jink right left** onto the shared-use path. The path follows the A282 all the way to Dartford Crossing. Cycling is not allowed over the bridge, please use the free transportation service via Dartford Tunnel. On the other side of the Thames take London Rd west towards Purfleet Station. At the Royal Hotel you will see a shared-use path to your **left**, get on and turn **right** along the river – this is Route 13. Follow Route 13 all the way to Rainham where you can visit National Trust property Rainham Hall. To continue turn **left** onto the A1306 shared-use path towards Dagenham. East of Beckton, the shared-use path will have a little roundabout (stay **left**) and then cross over rail tracks. At the fork stay **left** heading south along a residential road. The path will end at a roundabout, take the exit across from you onto Ferndale St. Follow the road as it bends to the right, then when you reach the roundabout turn **left** onto the path towards Cyprus Station / Docklands Campus. Turn **left** so that the marina is to your right and the rail tracks to your left. You will see Sir Steve Redgrave Bridge on your **right**, you can cross the bridge on the road or segregated path. Stay on Albert Rd as it curves to the right, then turn **left** on Pier Rd. This road also curves to the right and takes you to Woolwich Ferry. As an alternative to the ferry, take the Woolwich foot tunnel (cyclists must walk) entered via the round brick building. In Woolwich you have the option to visit the Greenwich Heritage Centre and Charlton House. Once you've crossed the Thames you can follow Route 1 along the river by going **left** from the ferry port / tunnel exit. The route takes you all the way back to Dartford Station.

Bike shops

Cycle King Dartford
DA1 2DT Tel: 01322 280050

Evans Cycles
RM20 3HH Tel: 01708 804988

Halfords
RM9 6SJ Tel: 02085 922163

Sports Direct
DA1 4LD Tel: 03443 325249

Eat & drink

Ivy Leaf
DA1 1LS
Tel: 01322 220993

The Fleet
RM19 1RJ
Tel: 01708 890999

The Phoenix
RM13 9YW
Tel: 01708 553700

Dial Arch
SE18 6GH
Tel: 02031 300700

Various in Woolwich

The Rose
DA1 1UP
Tel: 01322 225899

The Malt Shovel
DA1 1LP
Tel: 01322 224381

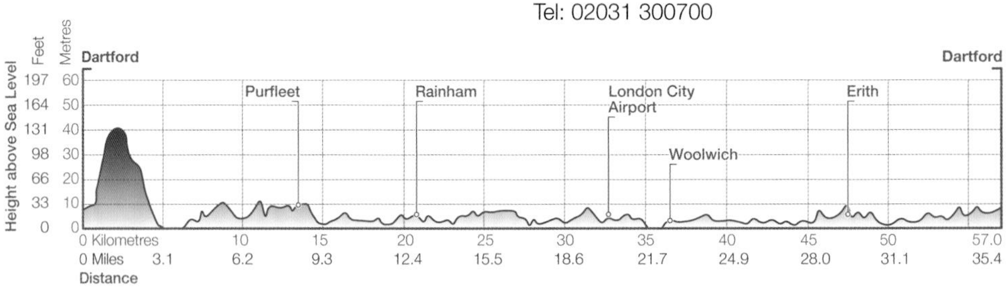

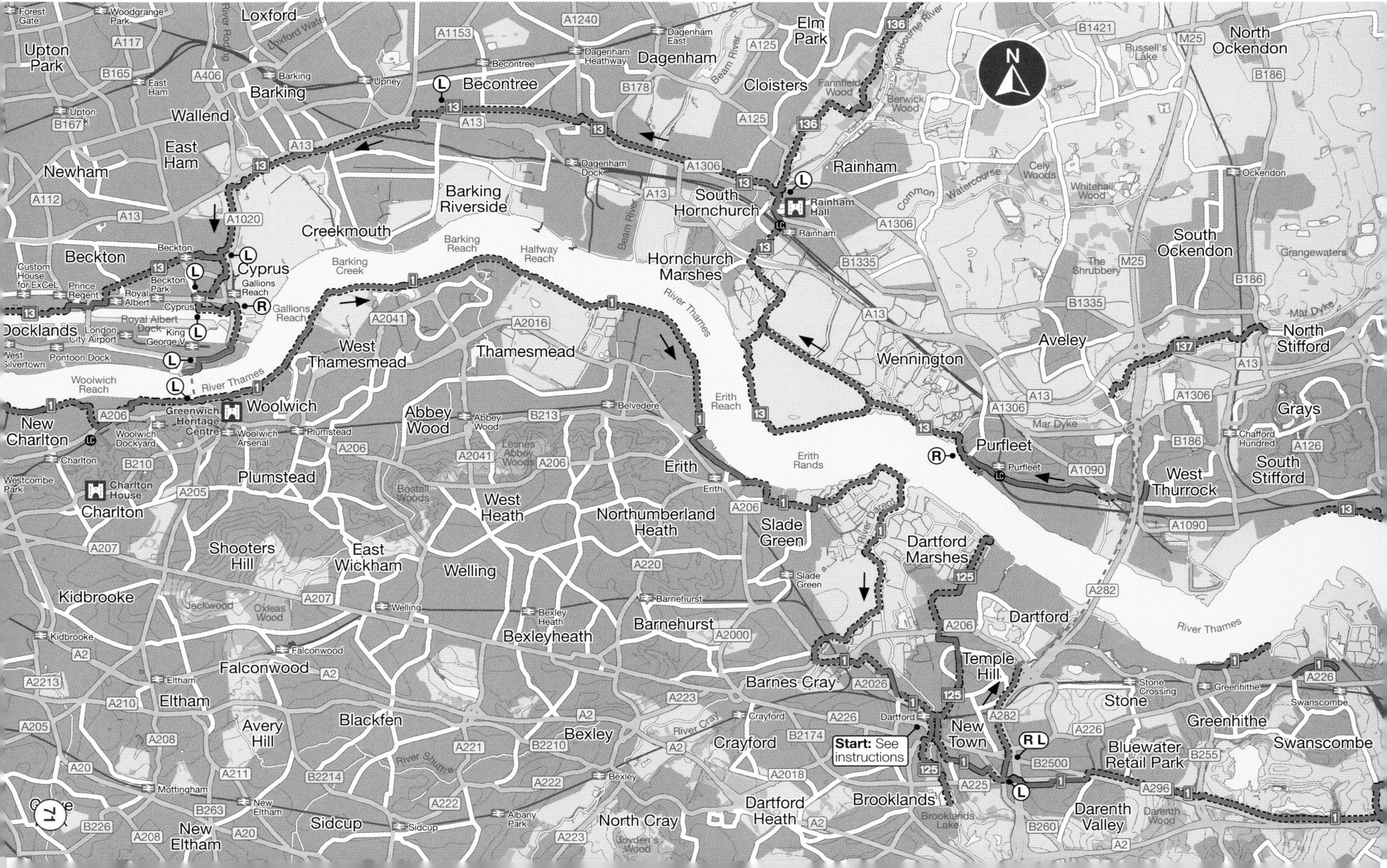
Upton Park
Loxford
Barking
Becontree
Dagenham
Elm Park
Cloisters
Rainham
North Ockendon
South Ockendon
Wallend
East Ham
Newham
Beckton
Cyprus
Creekmouth
Barking Riverside
South Hornchurch
Hornchurch Marshes
Rainham Hall
Docklands
Royal Albert Dock
London City Airport
Pontoon Dock
Woolwich Reach
Barking Reach
Barking Creek
Halfway Reach
Gallions Reach
River Thames
West Thamesmead
Thamesmead
Wennington
Aveley
North Stifford
Grays
Purfleet
West Thurrock
South Stifford
New Charlton
Woolwich
Greenwich Heritage Centre
Charlton House
Charlton
Plumstead
Abbey Wood
Erith Reach
Erith Rands
Erith
Slade Green
Dartford Marshes
Dartford
Shooters Hill
East Wickham
West Heath
Welling
Northumberland Heath
Kidbrooke
Falconwood
Bexleyheath
Barnehurst
Barnes Cray
Temple Hill
Stone
Greenhithe
Swanscombe
Eltham
Avery Hill
Blackfen
Bexley
Crayford
New Town
Bluewater Retail Park
Sidcup
New Eltham
North Cray
Dartford Heath
Brooklands
Darenth Valley
Start: See instructions

From Colchester Station go **right** onto the traffic-free path and **right** under the rail tracks. Turn **left** at Station Car Sales just after the tracks and follow the path as it curves right and ends at Mason Rd. Go slight **left** on Mason Rd and then **left** again at the car park. The road curves to the right and at the A133 you will see signs for the shared-use path. Use the crossing to cross the A133 and go **right** on the shared-use path. You are now on Route 1. Follow the path straight to cross the River Colne. Turn **left** along the river on Route 51 and follow all the way to Wivenhoe. Here the traffic-free section ends. Head straight on West St, then **right** at the church and **left** on East St. Keep following the route as it zig zags through residential streets, then turn **right** on Rectory Hill and **left** on Keelars Ln towards Elmstead Market. At the B1027 turn **right**, then turn **left** on School Rd. At Colchester Rd turn **right** and then **left** on Bromley Rd (becomes Harwich Rd). Follow Route 51 on this road towards Little Bentley. Do not take the right turn on Rectory Rd, but leave Route 51 and continue **straight** on Harwich Rd. When the road ends turn **left** on Little Bromley Rd. Carefully turn **right** onto the A120 and then go immediate **left** onto Bentley Rd. Continue on to Little Bromley, then turn **left** on Ardleigh Rd. Keep **right** towards Lawford. At the fork in the road, go **left** towards Dedham. Follow the road until it ends at a T-junction and turn **right** on Crown St. Optionally, you can turn left and visit the Munnings Art Museum. Crown St will take you into Dedham and curve left turning into High St. Turn **right** on Stratford Rd, cross over the A12 and then turn **left** on Gun Hill. You are now back on Route 1. Follow the route towards Colchester, and after crossing over the A12, get on the shared-use path. This will take you all the way back to where you joined Route 1 at the A133. Turn **left** on Mason Rd to return to the path that takes you back to the station, or continue on Route 1 to go into Colchester centre.

Bike shops

Colchester Cycle Stores
CO2 7AD Tel: 01206 563890

Globe G Sports
CO1 2AN Tel: 01206 502502

Cycle King Colchester
CO1 2TG Tel: 01206 867756

Eat & drink

Rose & Crown
CO7 9BX
Tel: 01206 826371

The Black Buoy
CO7 9BS
Tel: 01206 822425

The Court House
CO7 7JG
Tel: 01206 250322

Bricklayer's Arms
CO7 8SL
Tel: 01206 250405

The Haywain Pub
CO11 2PL
Tel: 01206 390004

Marlborough Head Inn
CO7 6DH
Tel: 01206 323250

The Sun Inn
CO7 6DF
Tel: 01206 323351

The Shepherd
CO4 5NR
Tel: 01206 272711

Various in Colchester

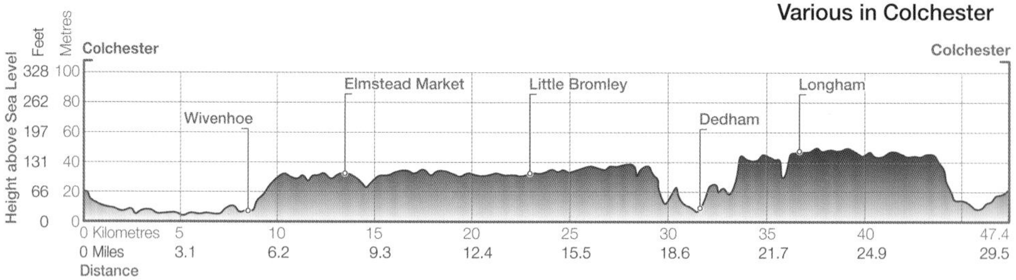

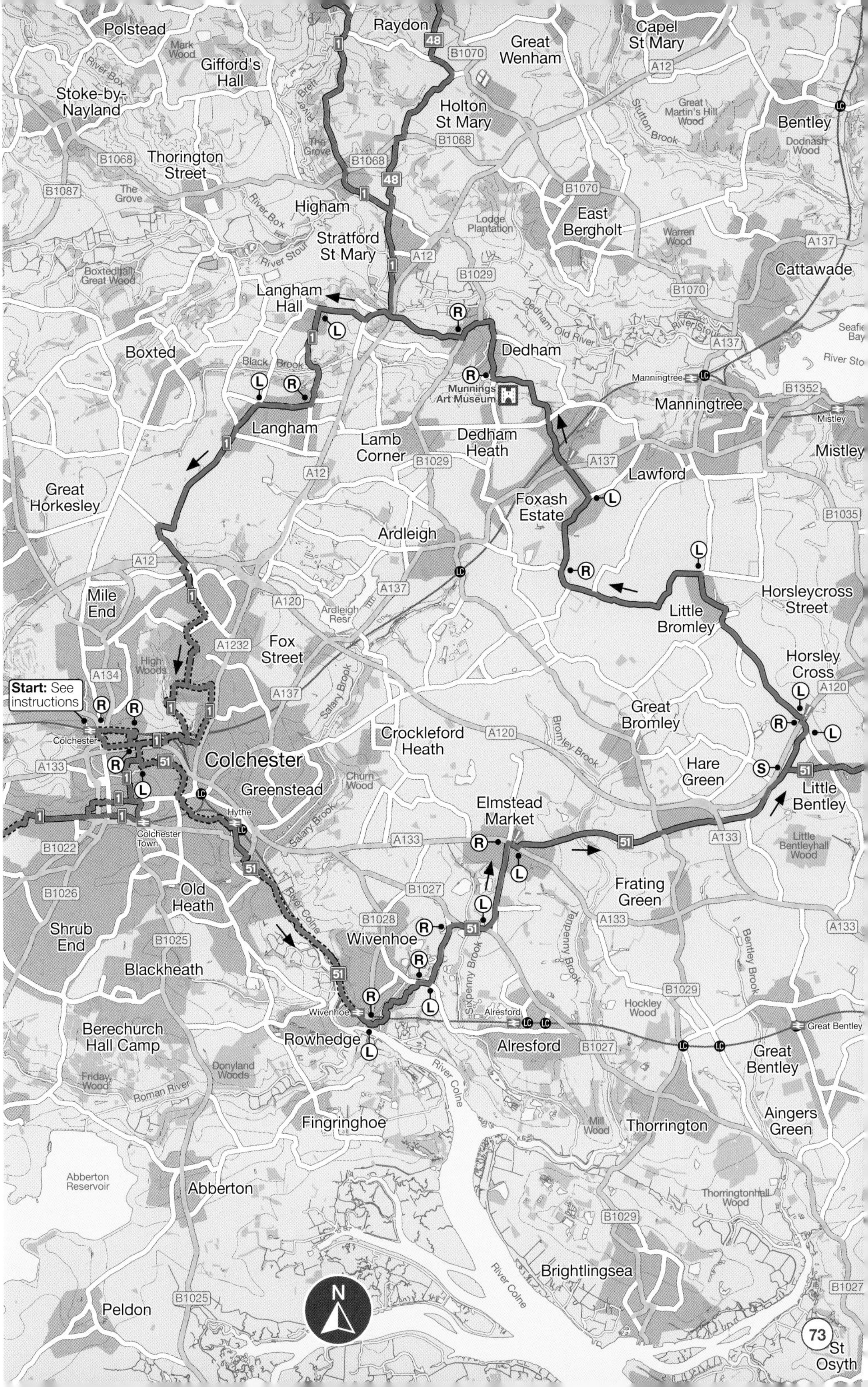

Polstead
Mark Wood
Raydon
Capel St Mary
Great Wenham
B1070
A12
Gifford's Hall
River Box
Stoke-by-Nayland
River Brett
The Grove
Holton St Mary
Great Martin's Hill Wood
Stutton Brook
Bentley
Dodnash Wood
B1068
Thorington Street
B1087
The Grove
River Box
Higham
Stratford St Mary
B1070
East Bergholt
Lodge Plantation
Warren Wood
A137
River Stour
Boxtedhall Great Wood
A12
B1029
Cattawade
B1070
Langham Hall
Dedham Old River
River Stour
Seafield Bay
A137
River Stour
Dedham
Boxted
Black Brook
Munnings Art Museum
Manningtree
B1352
Manningtree
Mistley
Langham
Lamb Corner
Dedham Heath
A137
Mistley
B1029
A12
Lawford
Great Horkesley
Foxash Estate
B1035
Ardleigh
A12
A137
Mile End
A120
Ardleigh Resr
Little Bromley
Horsleycross Street
A1232
Fox Street
High Woods
Horsley Cross
A134
Start: See instructions
A137
Salary Brook
A120
Colchester
Crockleford Heath
A120
Great Bromley
Bromley Brook
A133
Colchester
Greenstead
Churn Wood
Hare Green
Little Bentley
Hythe
Salary Brook
Elmstead Market
Colchester Town
A133
A133
Little Bentleyhall Wood
B1022
River Colne
B1027
Frating Green
B1026
Old Heath
B1028
A133
A133
Shrub End
Wivenhoe
Sixpenny Brook
Tenpenny Brook
Bentley Brook
B1025
Blackheath
B1029
Hockley Wood
Wivenhoe
Alresford
Great Bentley
Berechurch Hall Camp
Rowhedge
Alresford
B1027
Great Bentley
River Colne
Friday Wood
Donyland Woods
Roman River
Fingringhoe
Mill Wood
Thorrington
Aingers Green
Abberton Reservoir
Abberton
Thorringtonhall Wood
B1029
River Colne
Brightlingsea
B1025
B1027
Peldon
N
St Osyth

From Braintree Station go **left** following the signs for Route 16. Follow the traffic-free path until you come to Station Rd, turn **left** leaving Route 16. Turn **right** on Mill Rd towards North End. When the road splits go **right** on Bennett's Ln. **Jink right left** at the B1008 to continue and stay **left** at both forks in the road towards Pleshey. When you reach Pleshey turn **left** towards the Walthams and then turn **left** on The Street. You are now on Regional Route 50. Follow the route to Howe Street (town) then turn **left** on Hyde Hall Ln and **left** on Littley Green Rd. Follow the road through Littley Green and then turn **right** on Felstead Road towards Great Leighs. There turn **left** on Main Rd – this becomes Route 16. At the A131 roundabout take the shared-use path to go **right** along London Rd, then after the small roundabout turn **left** onto the signed shared-use path towards Braintree. Take Route 16 all the way back to the station.

Bike shops

Cycles UK Braintree
CM7 1TX Tel: 01376 345858

Sports Direct
CM77 8YH Tel: 03443 325120

Halfords
CM77 8YH Tel: 01376 550993

Eat & drink

The Swan Inn Felstead
CM6 3DG Tel: 01371 820245

The Leather Bottle
CM3 1HG Tel: 01245 237291

The Compasses
CM3 1BU Tel: 01245 362308

The Castle
CM3 1NE Tel: 01245 362630

The Dog & Partridge
CM3 1NR Tel: 01245 361331

Green Dragon
CM77 8QN Tel: 01245 361030

Various in Braintree

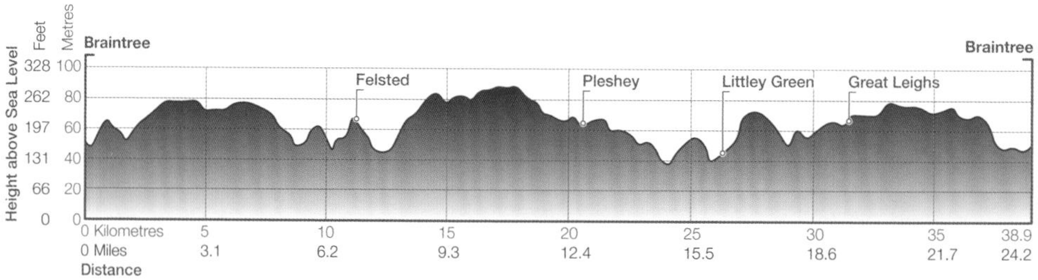

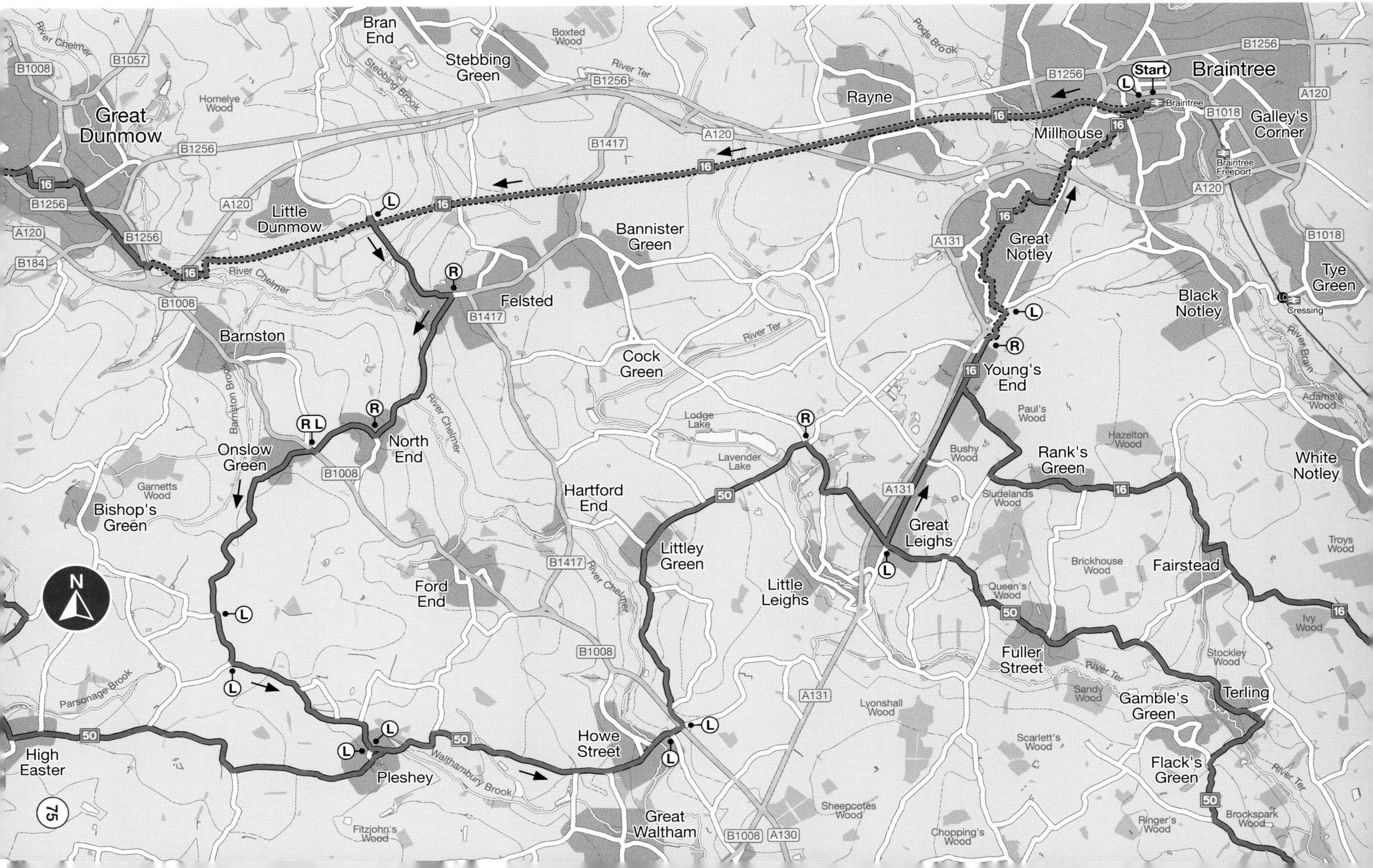
Start
Braintree
Galley's Corner
Braintree Freeport
Tye Green
Cressing
Black Notley
White Notley
Millhouse
Great Notley
Young's End
Rayne
Bran End
Stebbing Green
Stebbing Brook
Boxted Wood
River Ter
Pods Brook
Great Dunmow
Homelye Wood
River Chelmer
Little Dunmow
Bannister Green
Felsted
Barnston
Barnston Brook
Cock Green
Lodge Lake
Lavender Lake
Onslow Green
North End
Hartford End
Bishop's Green
Garnetts Wood
Ford End
Littley Green
Little Leighs
Great Leighs
Bushy Wood
Paul's Wood
Rank's Green
Hazelton Wood
Sludelands Wood
Brickhouse Wood
Fairstead
Troys Wood
Ivy Wood
Queen's Wood
Fuller Street
Stockley Wood
Terling
Sandy Wood
Gamble's Green
Flack's Green
Scarlett's Wood
Lyonshall Wood
Sheepcotes Wood
Chopping's Wood
Ringer's Wood
Brocksparks Wood
River Brain
Adams's Wood
Howe Street
Great Waltham
Pleshey
Walthambury Brook
Fitzjohn's Wood
High Easter
Parsonage Brook
N
16
50
A120
A131
A130
B1256
B1057
B1008
B1018
B1417
B184
L
R

14 Chelmsford & Maldon

34.2 miles / 55.5 km

From Chelmsford Station go **right** under the tracks on Duke St. At the second mini roundabout go **right** on Victoria Rd South. At the next roundabout take the 1st exit **straight** towards County Cricket Ground and follow the sign for the path to your **left**. This is Route 1 – follow until the A1099 and turn **right** on Route 13. Take the path under the large roundabout and follow the sign for Route 13 / Tile Kiln to go south on Manor Rd. Follow Route 13 through residential streets, then take the shared-use path that goes under Princes Rd. Continue **straight** on Longstomps Ave and at the small roundabout get on the shared-use path to your left. Turn **left** to follow the shared-use path, then when it ends go **left** on Dove Ln. Keep following the signs for Route 13. After passing through Chelmer Park turn **left** on Skinner's Ln then **left** on Watchouse Rd, leaving Route 13. Turn **right** on Brook Ln, then when you reach West Hanningfield Rd turn **right** to cross the A12. Keep following this road as it turns south (keep left) and passes through West Hanningfield. The road becomes Church Rd, keep **straight** crossing over the A130, then **jink right left** onto Pan Ln towards East Hanningfield. Keep **left** to go through East Hanningfield and at the fork in the road go **right** on Bicknacre Rd. Follow this road to Bicknacre, then at The White Swan turn **right** on White Elm Rd. Turn **right** on Slough Rd, then **right** on Marlpits Rd towards Cock Clarks. Turn **left** on Birchwood Rd and follow to Purleigh, stay **right** towards Mundon, then when you come to a T-junction turn **left** on Simmonds Ln (no street sign). At the next T-junction go **right**, then **jink right left** across the B1010 towards Mundon. At the next junction turn **left** on Mundon Rd towards Maldon. When Mundon Rd ends at a roundabout, take the 3rd exit **right** onto Park Dr. When the road ends turn **right** on Mill Rd, then **right** on London Rd. You are now on Route 1. Cross over the A414 and then turn **right** on Abbey Turning. Keep following the signs for Route 1. Eventually the route will take a **left** turn through a black gate onto a traffic-free path. When the path ends turn **left** on Hammonds Rd, then turn **right** on the next dirt road. Follow the path under the A12 and continue on Route 1 all the way back to Chelmsford. Return to the station the same way by turning **right** on Victoria Rd South and **left** on Duke St.

Bike shops

Chelmer Cycles
CM2 0RR Tel: 01245 287600
The Cycle Company
CM1 1PP Tel: 01245 283929
Cycles UK Chelmsford
CM1 1AN Tel: 01245 264477
Riverside Cycle Centre
CM9 5ET Tel: 01621 858240

Eat & drink

White Bear
CM2 8NH
Tel: 01245 353034
The Folly Bistro
CM3 8AA
Tel: 01245 400315
The White Swan
CM3 4EX
Tel: 01245 222826
The Bell
CM3 6QJ
Tel: 01621 828348
The White Horse
CM9 6P
Tel: 01621 740276
Various in Maldon
The Cat's Pub
CM9 6LS
General's Arms
CM3 4SX
Tel: 01245 222069
Various in Chelmsford

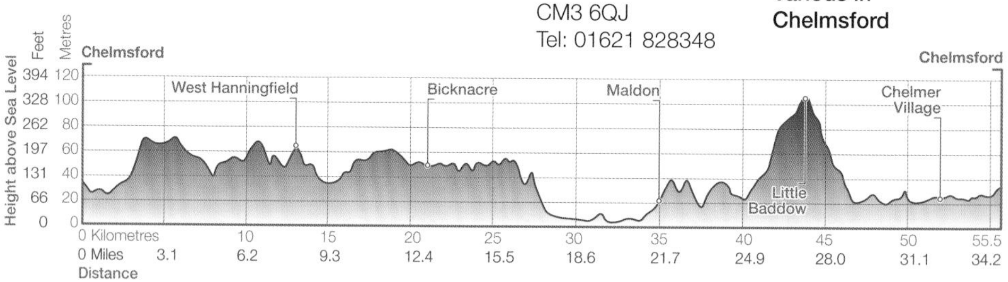

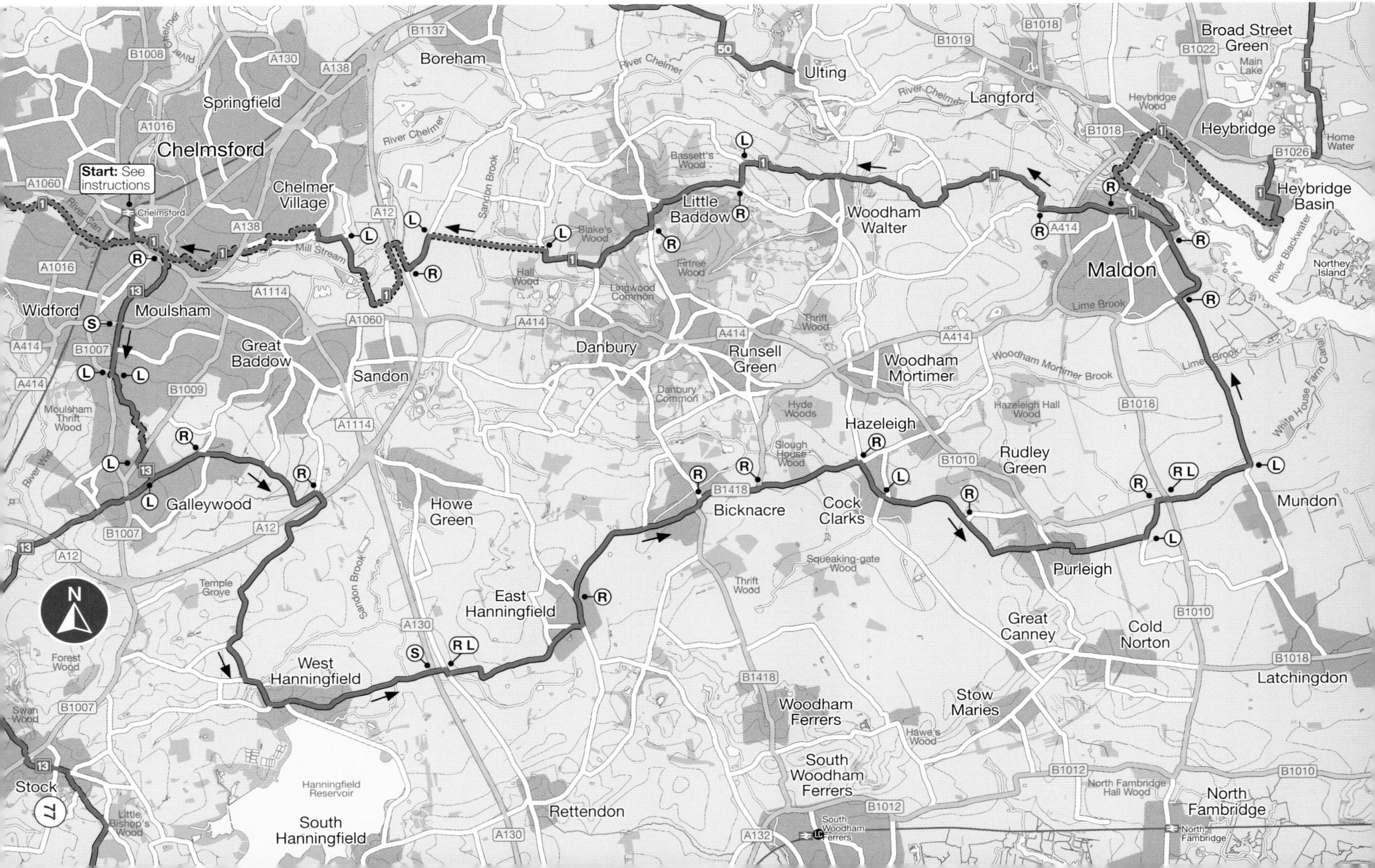

Start: See instructions
Chelmsford
Springfield
Chelmer Village
Boreham
Ulting
Langford
Broad Street Green
Heybridge
Heybridge Basin
Home Water
Heybridge Wood
Main Lake
River Blackwater
Northey Island
Maldon
Lime Brook
Little Baddow
Bassett's Wood
Blake's Wood
Woodham Walter
Widford
Moulsham
Great Baddow
Sandon
Danbury
Runsell Green
Woodham Mortimer
Woodham Mortimer Brook
White House Farm Canal
Hall Wood
Lingwood Common
Firtree Wood
Thrift Wood
Danbury Common
Hyde Woods
Slough House Wood
Hazeleigh
Hazeleigh Hall Wood
Rudley Green
Mundon
Moulsham Thrift Wood
River Wid
Galleywood
Howe Green
Bicknacre
Cock Clarks
Purleigh
Squeaking-gate Wood
East Hanningfield
West Hanningfield
Temple Grove
Forest Wood
Swan Wood
Great Canney
Cold Norton
Latchingdon
Stow Maries
Woodham Ferrers
Hawe's Wood
South Woodham Ferrers
North Fambridge Hall Wood
North Fambridge
Stock
Little Bishop's Wood
Hanningfield Reservoir
South Hanningfield
Rettendon
River Chelmer
River Can
Mill Stream
Sandon Brook
N

From the clock tower in the centre of Chesham, with your back to Chesham Museum, go **left** and cross towards the Red Lion. Continue along Germaine St and follow the road around **right** as it becomes Wey Ln. At The Queen's Head turn **right** then **left** on Pednormead. Soon after bear **left** and then bear **right** at the fork towards Pednor Bottom. Turn **right** on Westdean Ln, then **right** on Chartridge Ln. Turn **left** on Buslins Ln, then next **left** on Route 30. Follow Route 30 to Oak Ln and at the split go **right** towards Cholesbury, then take the next **left** towards Cholesbury. Turn **right** towards Wigginton, then the next **left**. Turn **left** towards Tring, and stay **left** at Marlin Hill. Cross under the A41 and turn **left** on Park Rd. When the road ends turn **left** and **left** onto Duckmoor Ln. Continue south on this road and after passing the Chiltern Boarding Kennels, turn **right** on Gilbert's Hill. At Jenkins Ln turn **right** then **left** towards The Lee. At Chesham Ln turn **right** on Route 3 towards Kings Ash and Wendover. Follow Route 3 south going **left** and **right**. At the crossroads turn **left** on Route 57 towards Ballinger. Follow the route **right** towards The Pednors. Stay **left** at Little Hundridge Ln, then **right** towards Lt. Pednor. Follow Route 57 back towards Chesham until you return to The Queen's Head. Follow Wey Ln / Germaine St back to the centre.

Bike shops

L.J. Stronnell Cycles
HP5 3DX Tel: 01494 784255

Mountain Mania Cycles Tring
HP23 4BX Tel: 01442 822458

The Bicycle Workshop Great Missenden
HP16 9AN Tel: 01494 867358

Eat & drink

The Bell at Chartridge
HP5 2TF Tel: 01494 782878

The Blue Ball
HP5 2UX Tel: 01494 758305

The Full Moon
HP5 2UH Tel: 01494 758959

Castle Inn
HP23 6BN Tel: 01442 823552

Various in Tring

The Old Swan
HP16 9NU Tel: 01494 837239

The Cock & Rabbit Inn
HP16 9LZ Tel: 01494 837540

The Queen's Head
HP5 1JD Tel: 01494 778690

Various in Chesham

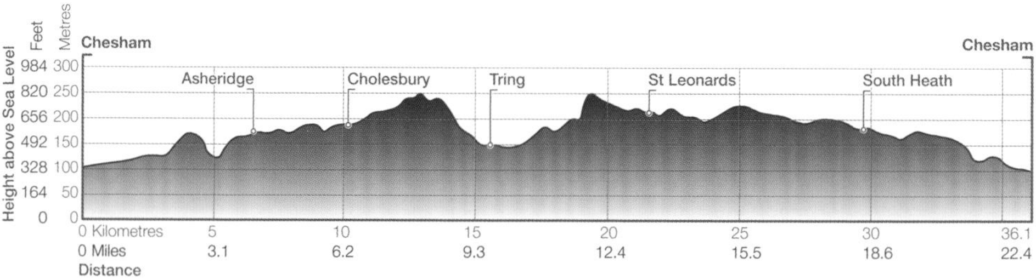

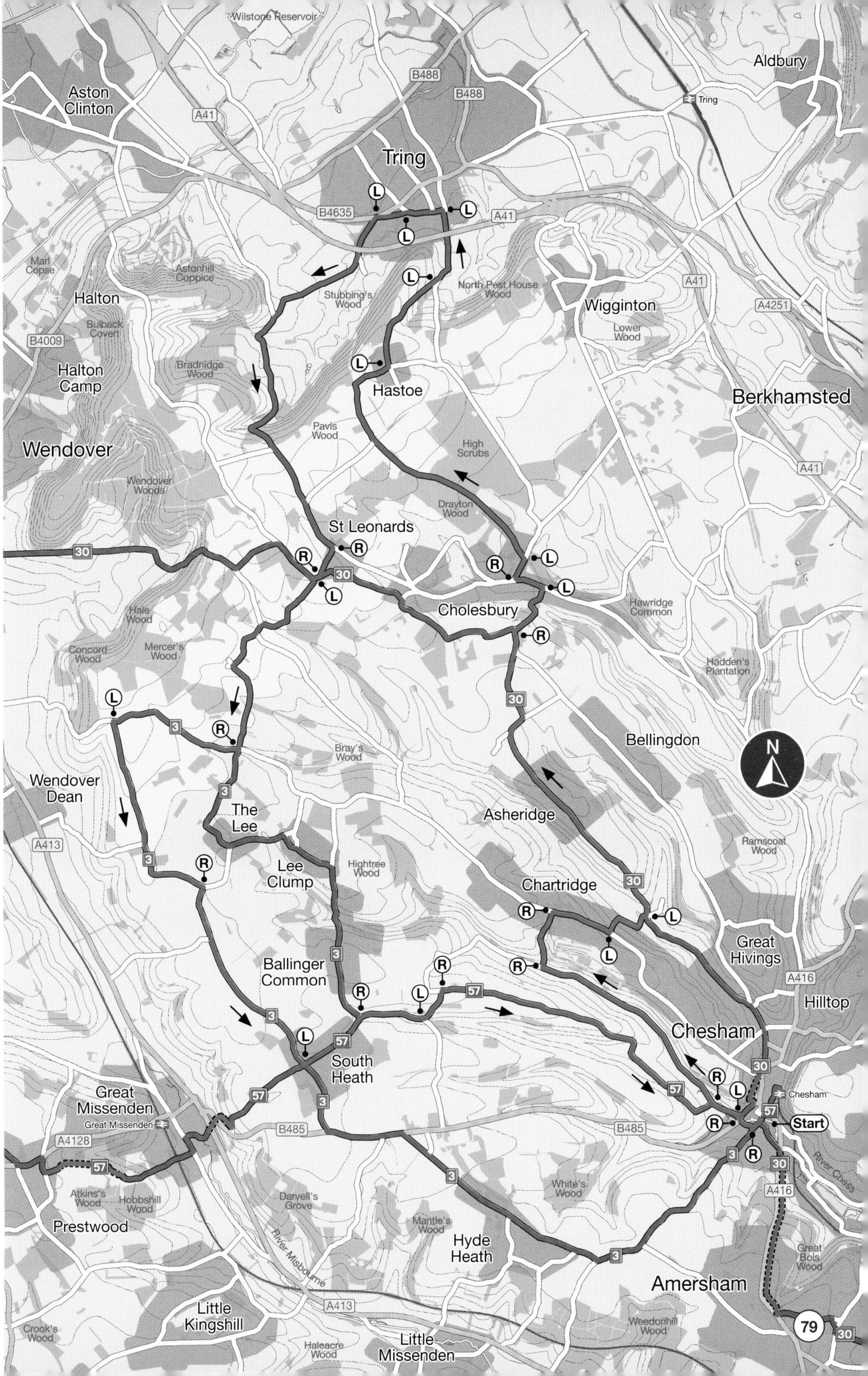
Wilstone Reservoir
Aldbury
Aston Clinton
Tring
Marl Copse
Astonhill Coppice
Stubbing's Wood
North Pest House Wood
Wigginton
Lower Wood
Halton
Bulback Covert
Halton Camp
Bradnidge Wood
Hastoe
Berkhamsted
Wendover
Pavis Wood
High Scrubs
Wendover Woods
Drayton Wood
St Leonards
Cholesbury
Hawridge Common
Hale Wood
Concord Wood
Mercer's Wood
Hadden's Plantation
Bellingdon
Bray's Wood
Wendover Dean
The Lee
Asheridge
Ramscoat Wood
Lee Clump
Hightree Wood
Chartridge
Great Hivings
Ballinger Common
Hilltop
Chesham
South Heath
Great Missenden
Great Missenden
Chesham
Start
River Chess
White's Wood
Atkins's Wood
Hobbshill Wood
Darvell's Grove
Prestwood
Mantle's Wood
Hyde Heath
River Misbourne
Great Bois Wood
Amersham
Little Kingshill
Crook's Wood
Weedonhill Wood
Haleacre Wood
Little Missenden
B488
A41
B4635
A4251
B4009
A413
A416
B485
A4128
30
3
57
L
R
N

Wales

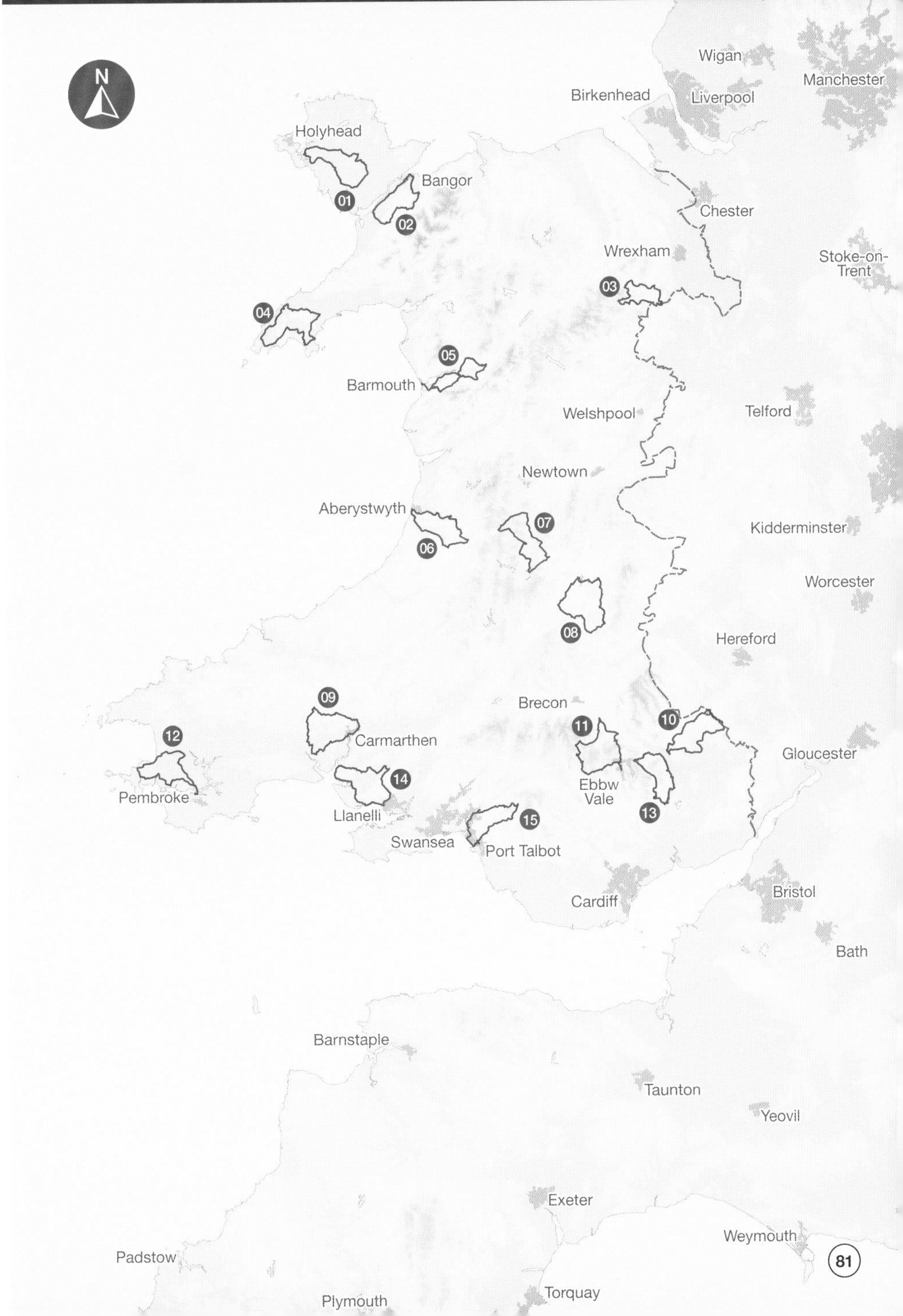
N
Wigan
Manchester
Birkenhead
Liverpool
Holyhead
Bangor
01
02
Chester
Wrexham
Stoke-on-Trent
03
04
05
Barmouth
Welshpool
Telford
Newtown
Aberystwyth
07
06
Kidderminster
Worcester
08
Hereford
09
Brecon
10
11
12
Carmarthen
Gloucester
14
Pembroke
Ebbw Vale
13
Llanelli
15
Swansea
Port Talbot
Cardiff
Bristol
Bath
Barnstaple
Taunton
Yeovil
Exeter
Weymouth
Padstow
Torquay
Plymouth

01 Anglesey: Valley, Malltraeth & Llangefni

34.2 miles / 55.5 km

From Valley Station go **right** on Station Rd. Cross over the A55 and turn **left** on Route 8. The route is well signed, follow through Dothan, Soar, Bethel and Trefdraeth. Cross the stone bridge over Afon Cefni and turn **left** onto the off-road path signed Lon Las Cefni / Route 566. Follow the path until it ends after passing Cefni Reservoir and turn **right**. Take the fourth **left** (unsigned). At the T-junction turn **left**, then turn **right** on the B5109 towards Trefor. At the A5025 turn **left** towards Y Fali / Valley. Go **right** at the fork. At the A5 **jink left right** to continue straight. Turn **left** on Station Rd (where you crossed the A55) to return to the station.

Bike shops

Summit to Sea
LL65 3DP Tel: 01407 740963

Eat & drink

Hotel Cymyran Restaurant
LL65 3LD Tel: 01407 742858

Joiner's Arms
LL62 5AS Tel: 01407 840692

Bull Hotel
LL77 7LR Tel: 01248 722119

The Foundry Vaults
LL77 7LT Tel: 01248 724512

The Crown Hotel
LL65 3TU Tel: 01407 238577

Bull Hotel
LL65 3DP Tel: 01407 740351

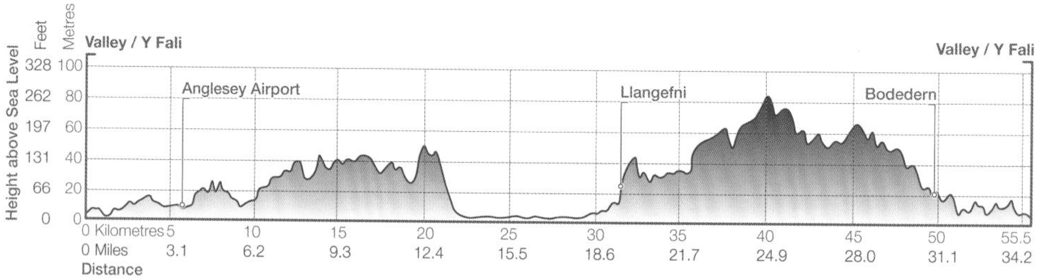

Llanynghenedl
Bodedern
Llechcynfarwy
Trefor
Tregaian
Beddmanarch Bay
Y Fali / Valley
Valley
Start
Caergeiliog
Bryngwran
Llynfaes
Llangwyllog
Rhosmeirch
Pont-rhydbont / Four Mile Bridge
Llanfairyneubwll
Bodior
Llanfihangel yn Nhowyn
Llyn Dinam
Coed Gareg-wen
Coed Fadog
Coed Tan-y-Bryn
Silver Bay
HOLY ISLAND
Traeth Cymyran / Cymyran Bay
Rhosneigr
Llanfaelog
Llyn Maelog
Penseri
Ty Croes
Capel Gwyn
Dothan
Gwalchmai
Llyn Hendref
Afon Caradog
Afon Crigyll
Bodffordd
Llyn Frogwy
Cefni Reservoir
Llangefni
Rhostrehwfa
Mona
Coed Trer-gof
Cerrigceinwen
Llangristiolus
Pentre Berw
Gaerwen
Llyn Padrig
Soar
Bethel
Coed y Green
Trefdraeth
Coed Henblas
Llynnau Gwaith-glo
Porth y Tywod
Porth Trecastell
Afon Ffraw
Llyn Coron
Bodorgan
Llangadwaladr
Hermon
Aberffraw
Malltraeth
Afon Cefni
Llangaffo
Coed Ffynnon
Coed Gorsedd
Coed Twr
Coed Llyn
Coed Singrug
Plevna Covert
Bonc-gch Covert
Bridge Covert
Vaynol Covert
Minffordd Covert
Ty'n-y-coed Covert
Coed Bath
Afon Erddreiniog
Coed Plas
A5025
A5
A55
B4545
B5112
B5111
B5109
B5110
B5420
B4422
A5114
A4080
B4419
5
8
566
L
R
LC
N

From Bangor Station cross the road and turn **left**, then turn **left** on Convent Ln (signed as a dead-end). When you emerge in front of the sports hall turn **left** on Ffriddoedd Rd / Route 5. Turn **left** on Belmont Rd. Turn **right** at the mini roundabout. Turn **right** at the roundabout in front of the car showroom. Carefully turn **right** signed Route 5 and turn **left** on the Route 8 path under the dual carriageway. Follow Route 8 to Caernarfon. Turn **left** in front of the medieval city wall and follow around. If you have time to visit Caernarfon Castle go right to the entrance, otherwise turn **left** in front of the harbour car park. Join the off-road path on your **left** along the heritage railway. Fork **left** onto Regional Route 61 under the A487. Cross the bridge over the river and turn **left** on the path along Pwllheli Rd, keep **left** on Penybryn Rd. Follow Route 61 to the A4085. Turn **right** on the shared-use path, then first **left** leaving Route 61 (crossing the road with care). Turn **left** towards Ceunant. Cross the A4086 and the river and follow the road **right**. Carefully cross the A4244, then turn **right** at the T-junction. Take the first **left** up the hill. Turn **left** towards Mynydd Llandegai. At the B4409 **jink right left** to cross, then join the Route 82 shared-use path to your **left**. Follow the route to Garth - it becomes Route 5 along the way. Follow the road around the coast back towards Bangor. At the A5 T-junction turn **right** and then **left** on Menai Ave. Turn **left** on Victoria Dr, **right** on Ffriddoedd Rd and **left** at the sports hall onto Convent Ln where you started. Turn **right** and **right** again to return to the station.

Bike shops

Evolution Bikes
LL57 4DA Tel: 01248 355770

Siop Y Modur
LL55 1AT Tel: 01286 673943

Beics Menai Bikes (hire & repair)
LL55 4BJ Tel: 01286 650721

Eat & drink

Garddfon Inn
LL56 4RQ
Tel: 01248 670359

Black Boy Inn
LL55 1RW
Tel: 01286 673604

Anglesey Arms
LL55 1SG
Tel: 01286 672158

Various in Caernarfon

Y Glyntwrog Inn
LL55 4AN
Tel: 01286 671191

The Wellington
LL55 3HR
Tel: 01286 870227

Pant Yr Ardd
LL57 4PL
Tel: 01248 605546

The Boatyard Inn
LL57 2SF
Tel: 01248 362462

The Waverley Hotel Bangor
LL57 1LZ
Tel: 01248 370819

Various in Bangor

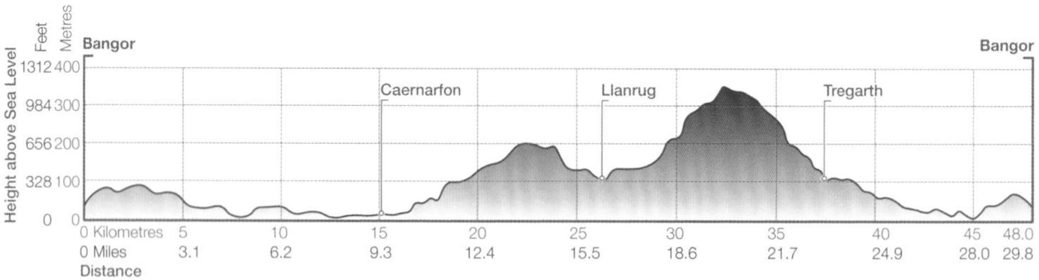

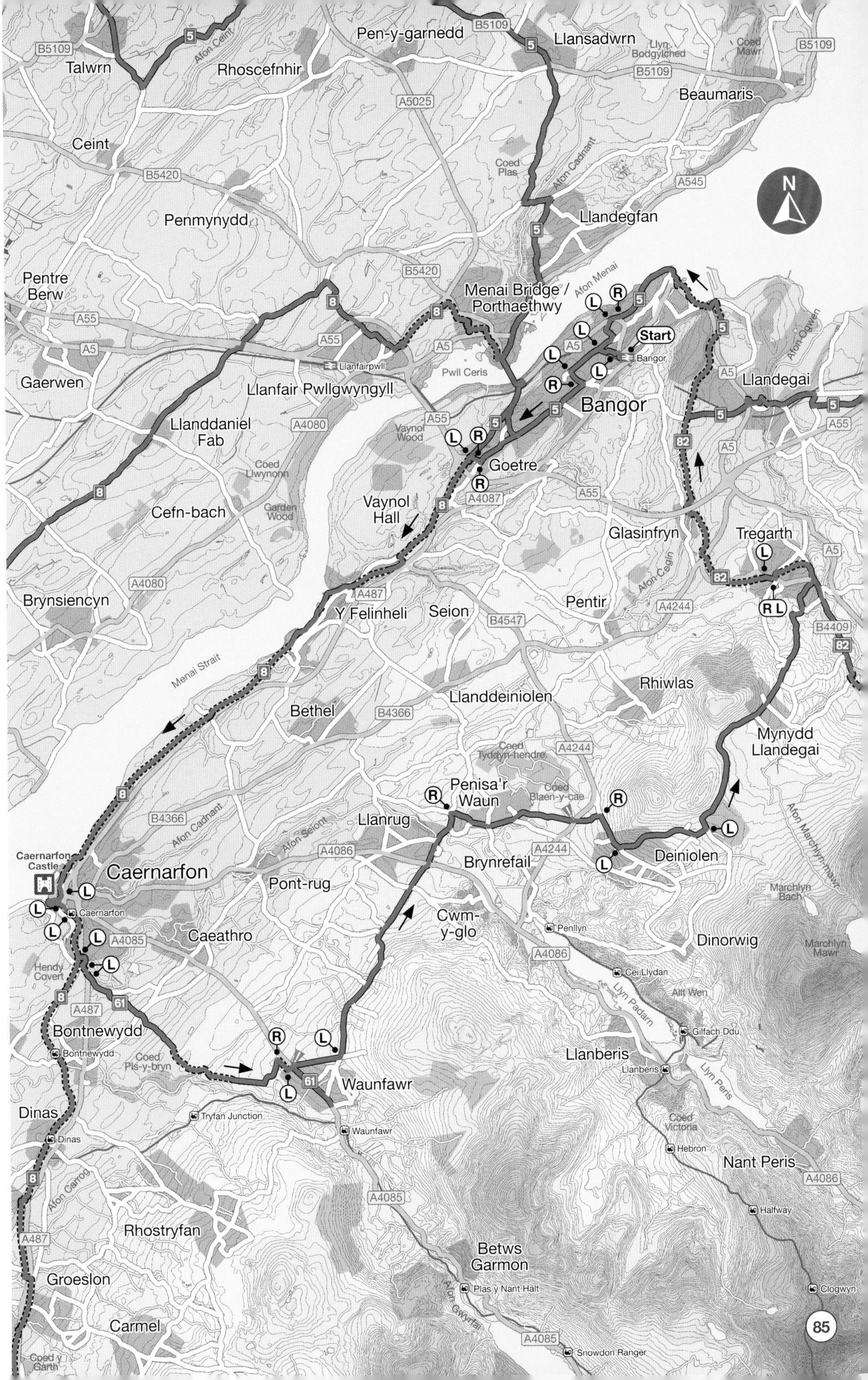

Talwrn
Rhoscefnhir
Pen-y-garnedd
Llansadwrn
Llyn Bodgylched
Coed Mawr
Beaumaris
B5109
A5025
Ceint
B5420
Coed Plas
Afon Cadnant
A545
Penmynydd
Llandegfan
Pentre Berw
Menai Bridge / Porthaethwy
Afon Menai
Start
Bangor
A55
A5
Llanfairpwll
Pwll Ceris
Gaerwen
Llanfair Pwllgwyngyll
Llandegai
Afon Ogwen
Llanddaniel Fab
A4080
Vaynol Wood
Goetre
Coed Llwynonn
Garden Wood
Vaynol Hall
A4087
Cefn-bach
Glasinfryn
Tregarth
Brynsiencyn
A487
Y Felinheli
Seion
Pentir
Afon Cegin
A4244
B4547
B4409
Menai Strait
Rhiwlas
Bethel
B4366
Llanddeiniolen
Mynydd Llandegai
Coed Tyddyn-hendre
Coed Blaen-y-cae
Penisa'r Waun
Llanrug
Afon Cadnant
Afon Seiont
A4086
Brynrefail
Deiniolen
Afon Marchlyn-mawr
Caernarfon Castle
Caernarfon
Pont-rug
Marchlyn Bach
Cwm-y-glo
Penllyn
Dinorwig
A4085
Caeathro
Marchlyn Mawr
Hendy Covert
Cei Llydan
Llyn Padarn
Allt Wen
Gilfach Ddu
Bontnewydd
Coed Pls-y-bryn
Llanberis
Llyn Peris
Waunfawr
Dinas
Tryfan Junction
Coed Victoria
Hebron
Nant Peris
Afon Carrog
Halfway
Rhostryfan
Betws Garmon
Groeslon
Plas y Nant Halt
Afon Gwyrfai
Clogwyn
Carmel
Snowdon Ranger
Coed y Garth

Go **right** out of Chirk Station, straight at the roundabout and over the tracks, and turn **right** down the canal path / Route 84. After crossing Pontcysyllte Aqueduct, turn **left** off the path and go around underneath, then up to the B5434. Turn **right**, cross the bridge and then turn **left** on the towpath / Route 85. At the Chainbridge Hotel go **right** over the little bridge from the towpath to the B5103 and turn **left**. Stay **left** towards Corwen, cross the River Dee and go under the tracks. Turn **right** on the A5 and then bear **left** up the single-track road. At the T-junction turn **left**. Continue towards Glyn Ceiriog. At the T-junction turn **right** towards Glyndyfrdwy. At the fork stay **right** – start following brown Ceiriog Cycle Route signs. At the T-junction turn **left** and continue towards Glyn Ceiriog. Go **straight** at the roundabout up High St. Take the third **right** (unsigned), then turn **left** (brown CCR sign). Stay **right** at the fork, then turn **right** over the bridge and first **left**. At the crossroads in front of The Golden Pheasant turn **left**. Stay **left** towards Pontfadog. Turn **right** on the B4500, then bear **right** at the fork and cross the bridge. Follow the road through Bronygarth, then follow the route **left**. Turn **right** away from the bridge and then **left**. Take two more **lefts** and then turn **left** on the B5070. At the war memorial turn **left** on Station Ave to return to the station.

If you have time to visit National Trust property Chirk Castle, continue straight over the tracks and go right at the ornate white gates, following the signs for the entrance.

Bike shops

Cycles 2 Go Bike Hire
LL20 7TU Tel: 07889 855908

Derek's Cycles
LL14 3AE Tel: 01978 821841

Llan Velo Ltd
LL20 8NF Tel: 01978 806226

RM Trail Riding
LL20 8NS Tel: 07759 009019

Eat & drink

Aqueduct Inn
LL20 7PY
Tel: 01691 777118

The Telford Inn
LL20 7TT
Tel: 01978 820469

Chainbridge Hotel
LL20 8BS
Tel: 01978 860215

Glyn Valley Hotel
LL20 7EU
Tel: 01691 718896

The Oak Y Dderwen
LL20 7EH
Tel: 01691 718810

The Golden Pheasant
LL20 7BB
Tel: 01691 718281

The Swan Inn
LL20 7AR
Tel: 01691 718273

The Bridge Inn
LL14 6RG
Tel: 01691 773213

Castle Bistro & Tea Room
LL14 5EZ
Tel: 01691 239133

The Hand Hotel
LL14 5EY
Tel: 01691 773472

Chirk Castle Tea Room
LL14 5AF
Tel: 01691 777701

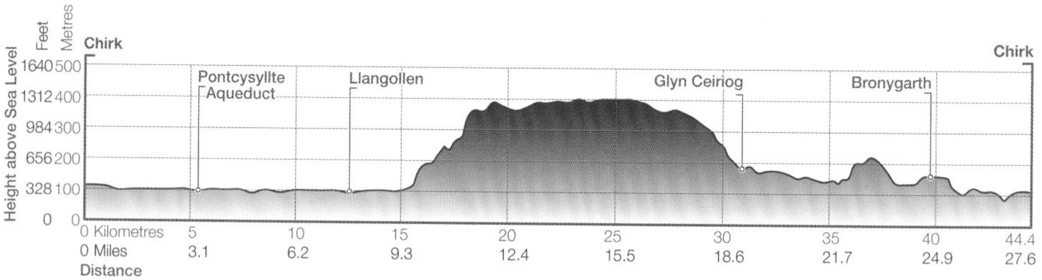

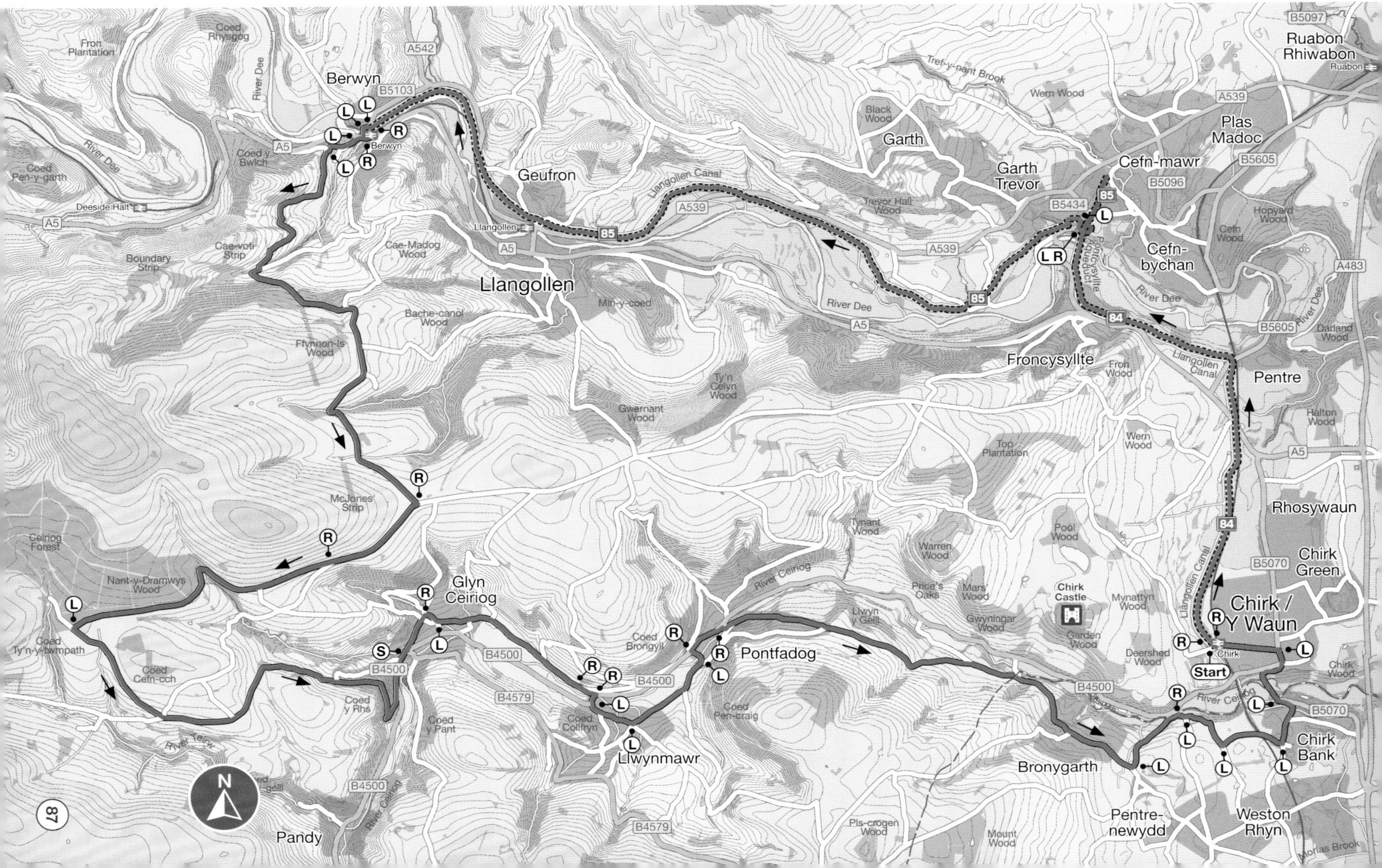
Ruabon
Rhiwabon
Plas
Madoc
Cefn-mawr
Cefn-
bychan
Garth
Garth
Trevor
Geufron
Berwyn
Llangollen
Froncysyllte
Pentre
Rhosywaun
Chirk
Green
Chirk /
Y Waun
Chirk
Bank
Weston
Rhyn
Pentre-
newydd
Bronygarth
Pontfadog
Llwynmawr
Glyn
Ceiriog
Pandy
Chirk
Castle
Pontcysyllte
Aqueduct
Llangollen Canal
River Dee
River Ceiriog
Ceiriog
Forest
Nant-y-Dramwys
Wood
McJones'
Strip
Ffynnon-Is
Wood
Boundary
Strip
Cae-voti
Strip
Coed y
Bwlch
Coed
Rhysgog
Fron
Plantation
Coed
Pen-y-garth
Deeside Halt
Cae-Madog
Wood
Bache-canol
Wood
Min-y-coed
Gwernant
Wood
Ty'n
Celyn
Wood
Top
Plantation
Wern
Wood
Fron
Wood
Halton
Wood
Darland
Wood
Hopyard
Wood
Cefn
Wood
Trevor Hall
Wood
Black
Wood
Wern Wood
Tref-y-nant Brook
Pool
Wood
Warren
Wood
Tynant
Wood
Price's
Oaks
Mars
Wood
Gwyningar
Wood
Garden
Wood
Mynattyn
Wood
Deershed
Wood
Chirk
Wood
Llwyn
y Gelli
Coed
Brongyll
Coed
Pen-craig
Coed
Collfryn
Coed
y Pant
Coed
y Rhs
Coed
Cefn-cch
Coed
Ty'n-y-twmpath
River Teirw
Pls-crogen
Wood
Mount
Wood
Morlas Brook
N

From Abersoch head north over the bridge. Turn **left** towards Llangian. At the fork go **right** towards Mynytho. At the next fork stay **left** on Regional Route 42. At the T-junction turn **right** towards Rhyd-y-clafdy. At the B4415 turn **left** towards Aberdaron on Route 41. Turn **right** towards Dinas. Turn **right** at the graveyard. At the crossroads keep **straight** on Route 42. At the B4417 turn **right**, then first **left**. Turn **right** on Route 43 and follow **straight** towards Llangwnnadl. Look out for the car park and trail on your right down to Traeth Penllech Beach. Turn **right** then **left** to continue. After Methlem there is a road down to Porth Oer Beach. At Capel Carmel turn **left** towards Aberdaron. At the coast T-junction turn **left** and then **right** and continue east. After the crossroads turn **left** on the unsigned road across from the stone farmhouse. Turn **right** towards Rhiw then immediate **left**. Turn **left** at the stone house. Take the second **right** on Route 42, then the next **left** downhill (no signs). Turn **right** at the T-junction on the bend, then **right** signed Plas yn Rhiw. Turn **left** towards Mynytho, or if you would like to visit National Trust property Plas yn Rhiw, turn right and follow the road for 2.5 miles. Turn **right** towards Abersoch then first **right** (unsigned). Turn **right** at Towyn and follow the route all the way back to Abersoch.

Bike shops

Llyn Cycle Centre
LL53 5BU Tel: 01758 612414

Eat & drink

Tu Hwnt I'r Afon
LL53 7YH Tel: 01758 741031

Lion Hotel
LL53 8ND Tel: 01758 770244

Caffi Porthor
LL53 8LH

The Ship Hotel
LL53 8BE Tel: 01758 760204

Plas yn Rhiw Tea Room
LL53 8AB Tel: 01758 780219

The Sun Inn
LL53 7LG Tel: 01758 712660

The Vaynol
LL53 7AP Tel: 01758 712776

St Tudwals Inn
LL53 7DS Tel: 01758 712539

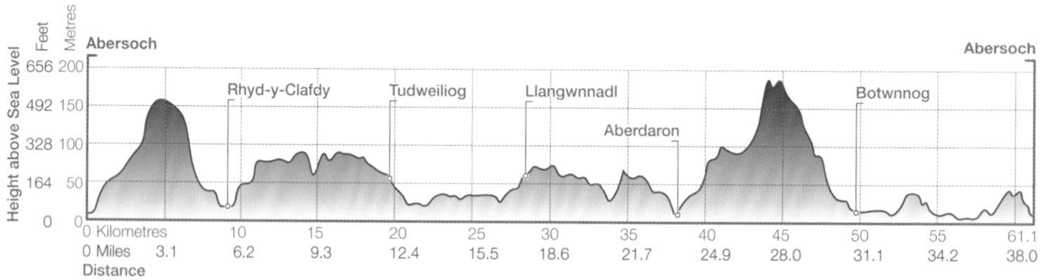

Rhos-y-llan
Porth Ysglaig
Tudweiliog
Llandudwen
Boduan
Coed Bodfel
Coed Mynydd-Meilian
Coed Nant-ffrancon
Coed Bryn Hendre
Coed Tal Hirion
Coed y Gledrydd
Efailnewydd
Dinas
Coed Garn Fadryn
Rhyd-y-clafdy
Coed Bodgadle
Drive Plantation
Porth Colmon
Traeth Penllech Beach
Penllech
Garnfadryn
Coed Tyddyn
Penrhos
Morfa
Coed Cefnamwlch
Llaniestyn
Coed Bodlas
Coed Cefn Llanfair
Llangwnnadl
Sarn Meyllteyrn
Rhedyn
Coed Cae-rhs
Y Gamlas
Gwinllan Cefn-y-gaer
Llanbedrog
Botwnnog
Bryncroes
Ty-hen
Nanhoron
Mynytho
Methlem
Porth Oer Beach
Rhydlios
Llandegwning
Llangian
St Tudwal's Roads
Rhoshirwaun
Llawr Dref
Capel Carmel
Rhiw
Plas yn Rhiw
Start
Abersoch
Porth Neigwl / Hell's Mouth
Towyn
Llanengan
Borth Fawr
Aberdaron
Uwchmynydd
Llanfaelrhys
Sarn Bach
Bodermid
Aberdaron Bay
Bwlchtocyn
B4417
B4415
B4413
A497
A499
41
42
43
N

Turn **right** out of Barmouth Station, **right** over the level crossing and **left** onto the beachfront path / Route 8. At the double gates turn **right** off the trail and then **left** on the A493. Take a hairpin **right** turn uphill towards Llynnau Cregennen. Turn **left** towards Dolgellau on Route 82. Turn **right** on Route 8 and follow the one-way roads through the town onto Arran Rd. Fork **right** on Fron Serth towards Tabor and keep **straight**, leaving Route 8. Continue on the A470 / Regional Route 21 towards Dinas Mawddwy. Turn **left** on Gwanas. Turn **right** on the B4416, then stay **straight** at the bend. At the A494 turn **left**, then turn **right** up the single track road signed Llanfachreth. Bear **left** towards Tyn y Groes, then turn **left** on Route 82 / 8. At the T-junction follow route **left**. At the A470 join the shared-use path **left** – it will become a road. At the T-junction turn **left** and then turn **right** on the public footpath (please dismount). Follow the path **right** (not over the bridge) and follow Route 8 back to Barmouth.

Bike shops

Dolgellau Cycles
LL40 1DE Tel: 01341 423332

Eat & drink

Gwesty'r Gwernan Hotel
LL40 1TL Tel: 01341 422488

Royal Ship Hotel
LL40 1AR Tel: 01341 422209

The Stag Inn
LL40 1AU Tel: 01341 421788

Various in Dolgellau

Cross Foxes
LL40 2SG Tel: 01341 421001

George III Hotel
LL40 1YD Tel: 01341 422525

The Last Inn
LL42 1BN Tel: 01341 280530

Barmouth Hotel
LL42 1EG Tel: 01341 280400

Tal Y Don Hotel
LL42 1DL Tel: 01341 280508

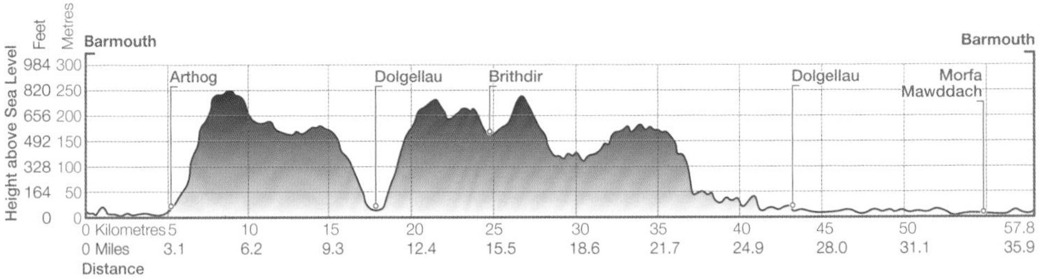

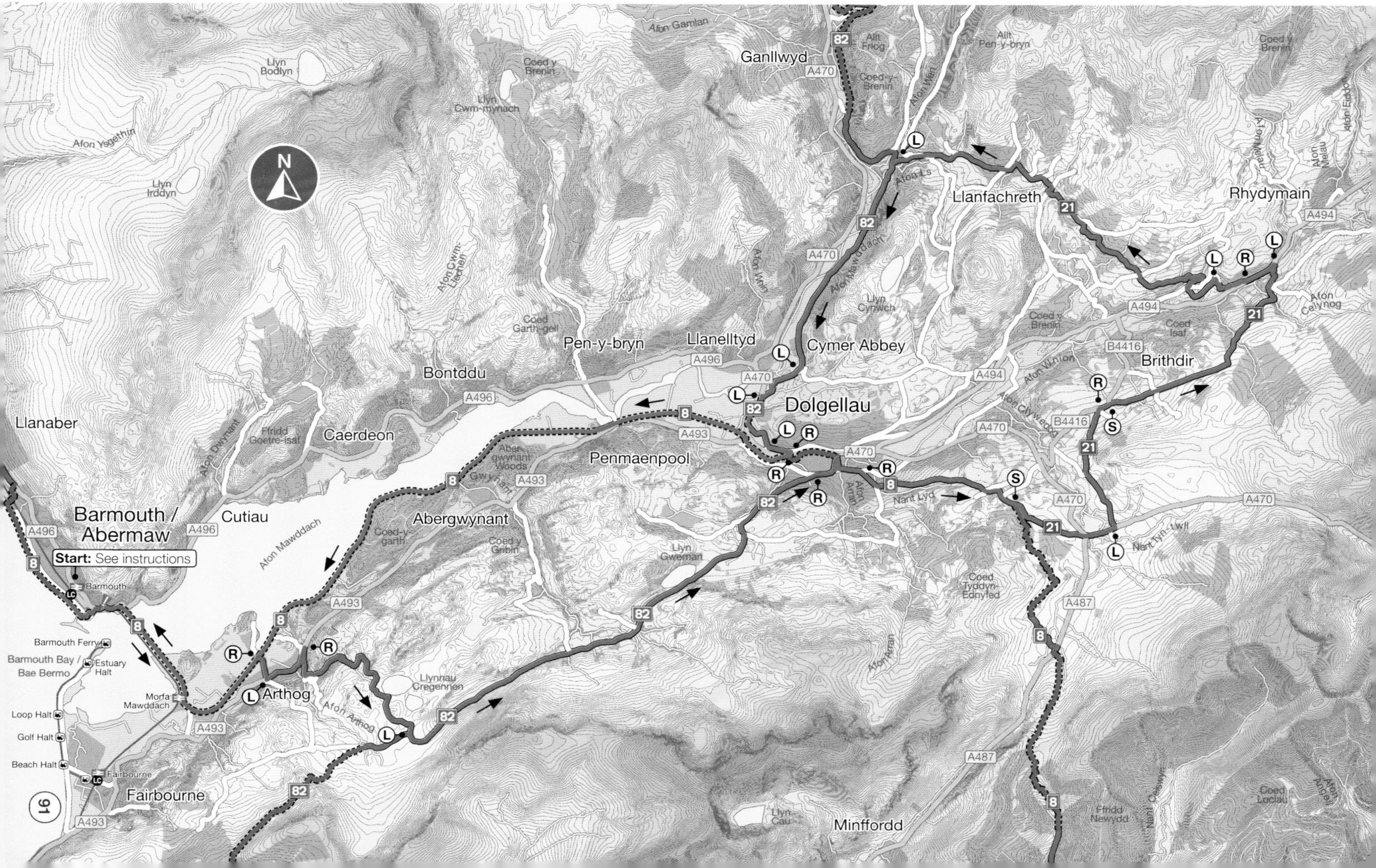
Barmouth / Abermaw
Start: See instructions
Barmouth
Llanaber
Cutiau
Caerdeon
Bontddu
Pen-y-bryn
Llanelltyd
Cymer Abbey
Dolgellau
Penmaenpool
Abergwynant
Arthog
Fairbourne
Minffordd
Llanfachreth
Rhydymain
Brithdir
Ganllwyd
Afon Mawddach
Barmouth Ferry
Barmouth Bay / Bae Bermo
Estuary Halt
Morfa Mawddach
Loop Halt
Golf Halt
Beach Halt
Fairbourne
Llynnau Cregennen
Llyn Gwernan
Llyn Cau
Llyn Bodlyn
Llyn Irddyn
Llyn Cwm-mynach
Llyn Cynwch
Afon Ysgethin
Afon Dwynant
Afon Cwm-Llechen
Afon Gamlan
Afon Wnin
Afon Arthog
Afon Arran
Nant Lyd
Afon Clywedog
Afon Wnion
Afon Melau
Afon Eiddon
Afon Celynog
Afon Angell
Nant Oeswyn
Nant Tyn-Lwll
Ffridd Goetre-isaf
Ffridd Newydd
Coed y Brenin
Coed Garth-gell
Coed-y-garth
Coed y Gribin
Coed Isaf
Coed Tyddyn-Ednyfed
Coed Lociau
Allt Ffrog
Allt Pen-y-bryn
Aber-gwynant Woods
A496
A470
A493
A494
A487
B4416
8
21
82
N
91

Turn **left** out of Aberystwyth Station and go **straight** at the roundabout. Turn **left** on Riverside Terrace before the bridge. Join the Route 81/ 82 shared-use path to the **right** and cross the river. Follow the Ystwyth Trail to the B4340 and turn **left** to follow Route 81. At the bridge fork **right** and follow the river. Join the B4343 and turn **left** immediately after crossing the river, leaving Route 81. At the crossroads turn **right** towards Trisant. Go **left** at the lake. At the fork go **right** up the hill. Turn **left** on the A4120, then take a sharp **right** down into the valley. Turn **right** towards Capel Bangor. After crossing the weir turn **left**. Turn **left** on the A44, then **left** at the crossroads. Keep **right** after crossing the tracks. Turn **right** at Depot Glanyrafon, then **left** towards the recycling centre. At the end of the trading estate join the traffic-free path. Follow the path until it ends at a roundabout and go **left** to return to the station.

Bike shops

Summit Cycles
SY23 2JN Tel: 01970 626061

Sports Direct
SY23 2LJ Tel: 03443 325352

Halfords
SY23 3TL Tel: 01970 627187

Eat & drink

The Falcon Inn
SY23 4PA Tel: 01974 241189

Cwtch Café
SY25 6DF Tel: 01974 282563

The Miner's Arms
SY25 6DN Tel: 01974 282238

Y Maes
SY23 3LT Tel: 01970 880621

Tynllidiart Arms
SY23 3LR Tel: 01970 880248

The Starling Cloud
SY23 3TL Tel: 01970 623743

Yr Hen Orsaf
SY23 1LN Tel: 01970 636080

Lord Beechings
SY23 1LE Tel: 01970 625069

Various in Aberystwyth

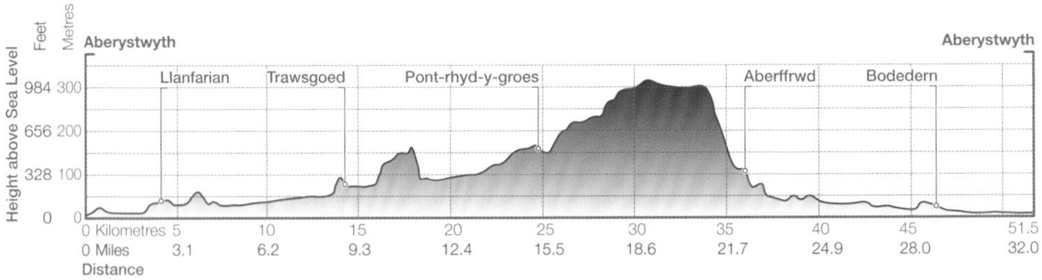

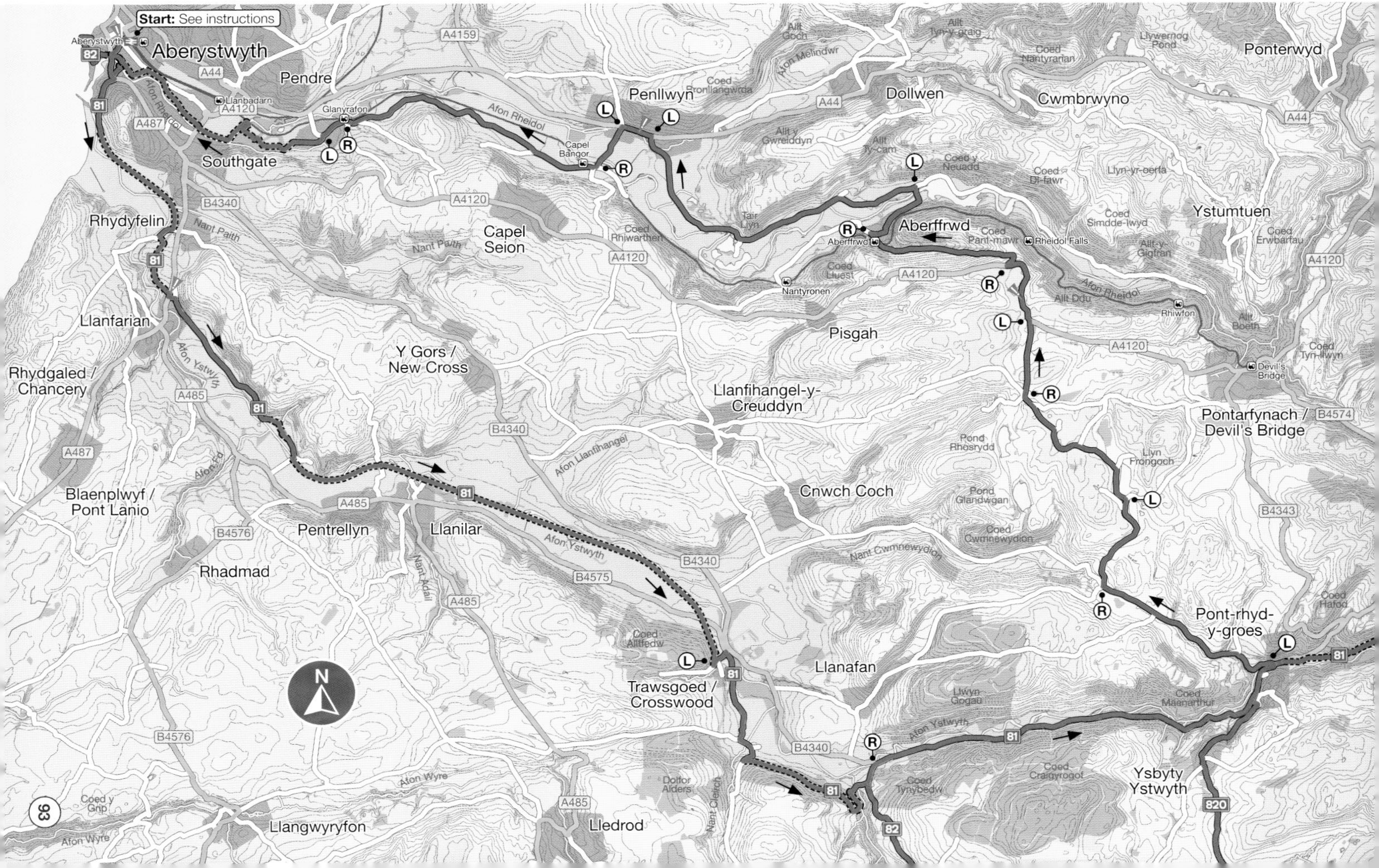
Start: See instructions
Aberystwyth
Pendre
Southgate
Glanyrafon
Llanbadarn
Capel Bangor
Penllwyn
Dollwen
Cwmbrwyno
Ponterwyd
Rhydyfelin
Capel Seion
Llanfarian
Y Gors / New Cross
Rhydgaled / Chancery
Blaenplwyf / Pont Lanio
Pentrellyn
Llanilar
Rhadmad
Llangwyryfon
Lledrod
Trawsgoed / Crosswood
Llanafan
Cnwch Coch
Llanfihangel-y-Creuddyn
Pisgah
Aberffrwd
Nantyronen
Rheidol Falls
Rhiwfon
Ystumtuen
Devil's Bridge
Pontarfynach / Devil's Bridge
Pont-rhyd-y-groes
Ysbyty Ystwyth
Afon Rheidol
Afon Ystwyth
Afon Wyre
Nant Paith
Nant Adail
Afon Llanfihangel
Nant Cwmnewydion
Nant Clerch
Llyn Frongoch
Pond Rhosrydd
Pond Glandwgan
Coed Cwmnewydion
Llwyn Gogau
Coed Maenarthur
Coed Craigyrogof
Coed Tynybedw
Dolfor Alders
Coed Alltfedw
Coed Lluest
Coed Rhiwarthen
Coed Pant-mawr
Allt Ddu
Coed Hafod
Coed Tyn-llwyn
Allt Boeth
Coed Erwbarfau
Allt-y-Gigfran
Coed Simdde-lwyd
Llyn-yr-oerfa
Coed Dl-fawr
Coed y Neuadd
Allt Ty-cam
Allt y Gwreiddyn
Coed Bronllangwrda
Allt Goch
Afon Melindwr
Allt Tyn-y-graig
Coed Nantyrarian
Llywernog Pond
Tair Llyn
Coed y Gnip
A44
A4120
A4159
A487
A485
B4340
B4575
B4576
B4343
B4574
81
82
820
N

From the war memorial in Rhayader centre head straight down West St towards Elan Valley. Turn **right** on Route 8 / 81 towards Llangurig after the car park. At the A44 turn **left** on Route 818. Turn **left** down the single track road. Go through the gate, cross the stream and bend left. At the T-junction with the road turn sharp **left** to follow Route 81. Turn **right** signed Cym Elan / Elan Valley. Turn **left** over the dam, then go **right** to join the off-road path. When the path ends at the B4518, turn **right** and continue straight back to Rhayader centre.

Bike shops

Elan Cyclery
LD6 5AB Tel: 01597 811343

Eat & drink

The Bluebell Inn
SY18 6SG Tel: 01686 440254

Black Lion Hotel
SY18 6SG Tel: 01686 440223

Elan Valley Visitor Centre Café
LD6 5HP Tel: 01597 810899

The Triangle Inn
LD6 5AR Tel: 01597 810537

Cornhill Inn
LD6 5AB Tel: 01597 810853

The Elan Hotel
LD6 5AF Tel: 01597 811208

The Old Swan Tea Rooms
LD6 5AB Tel: 01597 811060

The Castle Carvery & Bars
LD6 5DL Tel: 01597 811896

The Crown Inn
LD6 5BU Tel: 01597 811099

The Lamb & Flag Inn
LD6 5BT Tel: 01597 810819

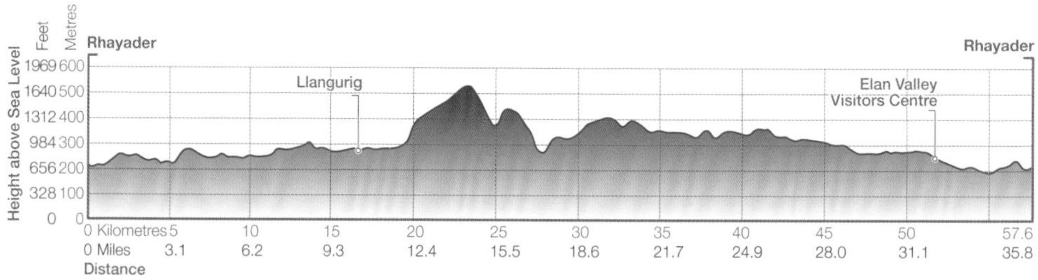

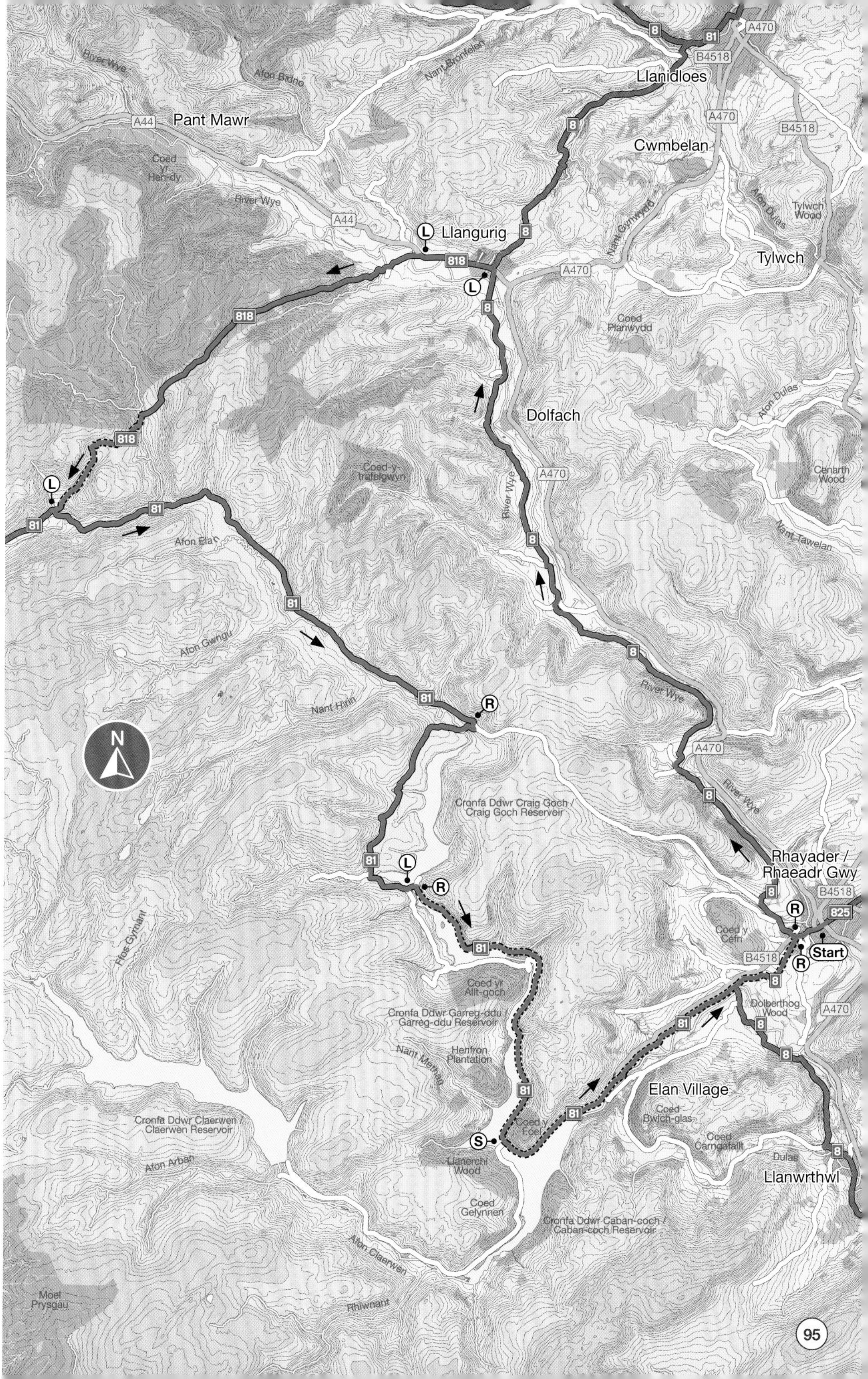
A470
B4518
Llanidloes
River Wye
Afon Biddno
Nant Bronfelen
A44
Pant Mawr
A470
B4518
Cwmbelan
Coed
yr
Hen-dy
River Wye
Nant Gwyddyd
Afon Dulas
Tylwch
Wood
A44
Llangurig
818
A470
Tylwch
818
Coed
Planwydd
Afon Dulas
Dolfach
818
Coed-y-
trafelgwyn
A470
Cenarth
Wood
River Wye
81
81
Afon Elan
Nant Tawelan
81
Afon Gwngu
81
Nant Hirin
River Wye
A470
N
Cronfa Ddwr Craig Goch /
Craig Goch Reservoir
River Wye
Rhayader /
Rhaeadr Gwy
81
B4518
825
Coed y
Cefn
Start
B4518
Rhos Gyrnant
81
Coed yr
Allt-goch
Cronfa Ddwr Garreg-ddu /
Garreg-ddu Reservoir
Dolberthog
Wood
A470
81
Henfron
Plantation
Nant Methan
81
Elan Village
Cronfa Ddwr Claerwen /
Claerwen Reservoir
81
Coed y
Foel
Coed
Bwlch-glas
Llanerchi
Wood
Coed
Carngafallt
Dulas
Afon Arban
Llanwrthwl
Coed
Gelynnen
Cronfa Ddwr Caban-coch /
Caban-coch Reservoir
Afon Claerwen
Moel
Prysgau
Rhiwnant

08 Llandrindod Wells & Builth Wells

34.8 miles / 56.1 km

Leave the station via the west exit and turn **left** on Waterloo Rd. Fork **right** and then turn **right** at the A4081 roundabout towards Rhayader. At the crossroads turn **left** following Route 25. Turn **left** on the B4358. At the New Inn Hotel turn **left** on the A470. Turn **right** towards Brynwern on Route 8. At the T-junction turn **left** towards Builth Wells. Turn **left** onto the off-road path along the river. When the path ends turn **left** and **left** to cross the bridge, then turn **right** on the off-road path. When the path ends join the road and bend to the left. Turn **right** at the roundabout, then **right** towards Aberedw. Turn **left** towards Aberedw, leaving Route 8. Stay **right** at the first fork and **left** at the second fork. Take the first **left** over the small stone bridge. Go **right** at the T-junction bend. Turn **left** at the next T-junction. Turn **left** towards Hundred House joining Route 25. At the crossroads turn **right**. Turn **left** towards Franksbridge. Stay **left** signed 'Bettws'. Turn **left** towards Pen-y-bont. Turn **left** and **left** again. When you reach the A483 in Llandrindod, you can visit the National Cycle Collection on your left. To continue turn **right** at the roundabout, then **left** on Station Crescent to return to the station.

Bike shops

Heart of Wales Bikes
LD1 6AG Tel: 01597 825533

Cycle-tec
LD2 3BB Tel: 01982 554682

Eat & drink

The Bell Country Inn
LD1 6DY Tel: 01597 823959

The New Inn Hotel
LD1 6HY Tel: 01597 860211

The Fountain Inn
LD2 3DT Tel: 01982 553888

The Lamb
LD2 3DT Tel: 01982 551119

The Llanelwedd Arms
LD2 3SR Tel: 01982 553282

Hundred House Inn
LD1 5RY Tel: 01982 570231

The Lakeside Restaurant
LD1 5HU Tel: 01597 825679

The Temple Bar
LD1 5HG Tel: 01597 825405

Arvon Ale House Micropub
LD1 5DP Tel: 07477 627267

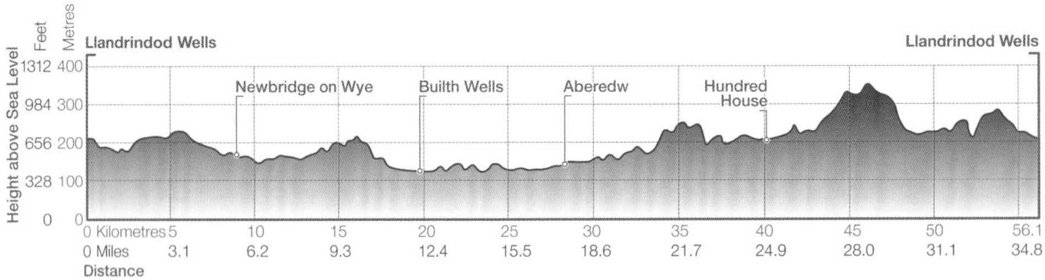

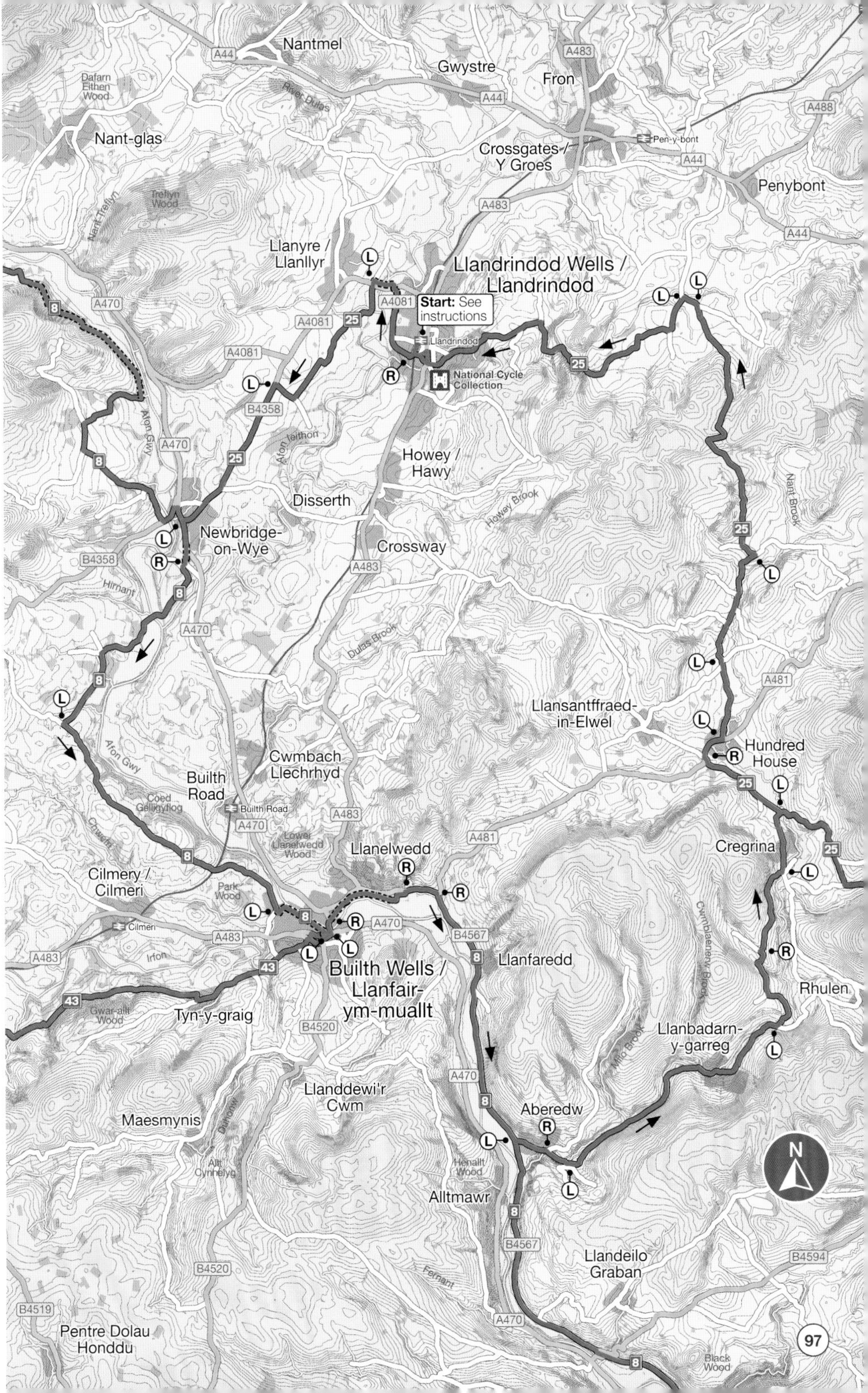

Nantmel
A44
A483
Gwystre
Fron
Dafarn Eithen Wood
River Dulas
A44
A488
Nant-glas
Pen-y-bont
Crossgates / Y Groes
A44
Penybont
Treflyn Wood
Nant Treflyn
A483
A44
Llanyre / Llanllyr
Llandrindod Wells / Llandrindod
A470
A4081
Start: See instructions
A4081
Llandrindod
A4081
National Cycle Collection
B4358
Afon Ieithon
Afon Gwy
A470
Howey / Hawy
Nant Brook
Disserth
Howey Brook
Newbridge-on-Wye
Crossway
B4358
A483
Hirnant
A470
Dulas Brook
A481
Llansantffraed-in-Elwel
Hundred House
Cwmbach Llechrhyd
Builth Road
Afon Gwy
Coed Gelligyflog
Builth Road
A483
A470
Lower Llanelwedd Wood
A481
Cregrina
Llanelwedd
Cilmery / Cilmeri
Park Wood
Cwmblaenerw Brook
A470
Cilmeri
A483
B4567
A483
Irfon
Llanfaredd
Rhulen
Builth Wells / Llanfair-ym-muallt
Gwar-allt Wood
Tyn-y-graig
B4520
Llanbadarn-y-garreg
Milo Brook
Llanddewi'r Cwm
A470
Maesmynis
Aberedw
Duhonw
Allt Cynhelyg
Henallt Wood
Alltmawr
B4567
Llandeilo Graban
B4594
B4520
Fernant
B4519
A470
Pentre Dolau Honddu
Black Wood
N
8
25
43
L
R

Go **left** out of Carmarthen Station and cross the river via the traffic-free bridge. Go **right** along the river on Route 47. After the road curves up to the left, turn **right** on the shared-use path which joins The Parade. Keep **straight** and join the shared-use path. When the path ends turn **left**. Turn **right** at the first roundabout, then take the **2nd exit** at the next roundabout. Keep **straight** at the big roundabout and turn **left** after crossing the river. Turn **left** at the T-junction, then next **left**. At the A484 turn hard **right**, then bear **left** on the single track road. Turn **right** at the T-junction. Turn **left** towards Carmarthen, then **right** towards Abernant. Keep straight towards Pen-y-Bont. Turn **left** over the bridge and next sharp **left**, leaving Route 47. At the B4299 turn **left**. At the T-junction turn **right** towards St Clears (but not up the hill). Take a sharp **left** towards Glasfryn Ford. At the A40 carefully cross and go **left** on the shared-use path. At the church turn **right** on Route 4 and follow to Johnstown. At the B4312 turn **left** (you can cross and then get on the shared-use path). Curve **right** onto St Clears Rd. Turn **right** at the Welsh Assembly Government Office and follow Route 4 back to the station.

Bike shops

Beiciau Hobbs Bikes
SA31 2BD Tel: 01267 236785

Cranc Cyclesport
SA31 2BL Tel: 01267 231701

Halfords
SA31 2NF Tel: 01267 237087

Eat & drink

Tafarn y Tanerdy
SA31 2EY Tel: 01267 231891

The Fountain Inn
SA33 5QG Tel: 01994 232132

Various in St Clears

The Forge Lodge & Restaurant
SA33 4NA Tel: 01994 230300

The Poplars Inn
SA31 3HU Tel: 01267 232544

Friends' Arms
SA31 3HH Tel: 01267 234073

Various in Carmarthen

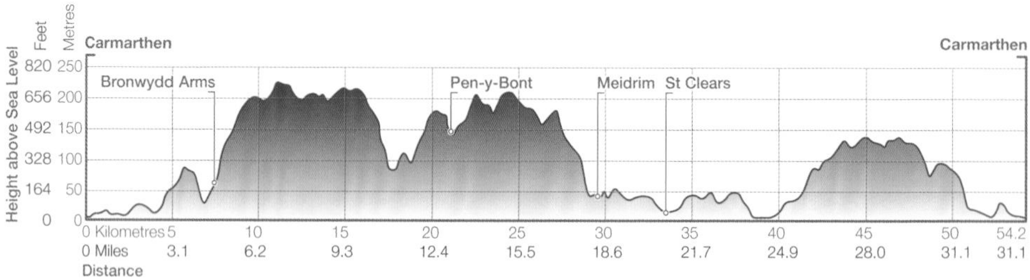

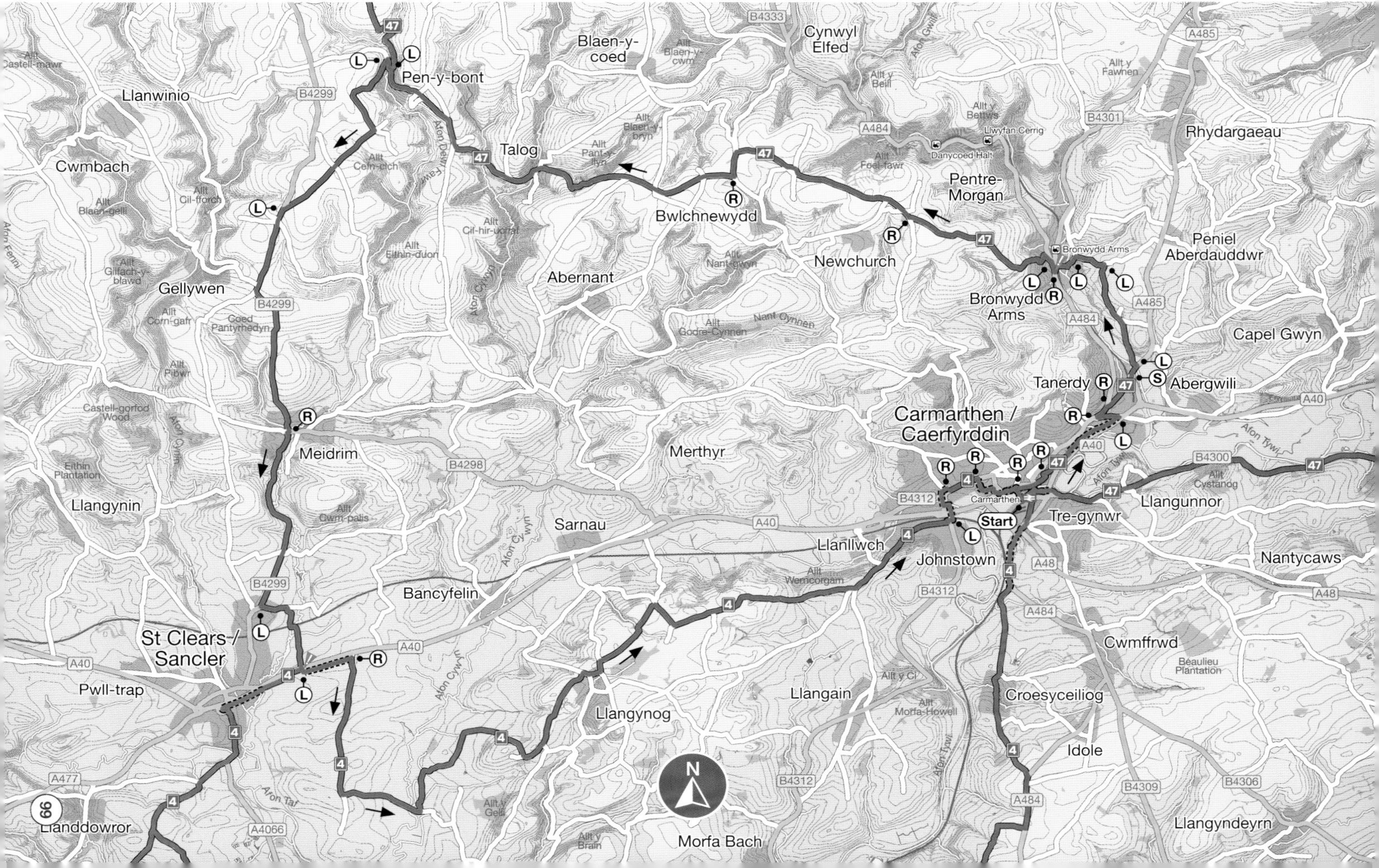
Pen-y-bont
Llanwinio
Cwmbach
Gellywen
Talog
Blaen-y-coed
Cynwyl Elfed
Bwlchnewydd
Newchurch
Abernant
Pentre-Morgan
Bronwydd Arms
Rhydargaeau
Peniel
Aberdauddwr
Capel Gwyn
Abergwili
Tanerdy
Carmarthen / Caerfyrddin
Start
Tre-gynwr
Llangunnor
Nantycaws
Merthyr
Meidrim
Llangynin
Sarnau
Llanllwch
Johnstown
Bancyfelin
St Clears / Sancler
Pwll-trap
Llangynog
Llangain
Croesyceiliog
Cwmffrwd
Idole
Llangyndeyrn
Morfa Bach
Llanddowror
Danycoed Halt
Llwyfan Cerrig
Beaulieu Plantation
Eithin Plantation
Castell-gorfod Wood
Coed Pantyrhedyn
Afon Tywi
Afon Taf
Afon Cywyn
Afon Cynin
Nant Cynnen
A40
A48
A484
A485
A477
A4066
B4299
B4298
B4312
B4300
B4301
B4306
B4309
B4333

From the station go **right** on Belmont Cres, **right** on Holywell Cres and **right** on Holywell Rd. Turn **left** at the mini roundabout, then **right** on Ross Rd / Route 42. Turn **right** on Tredilion Rd. Turn **left** on the B4233 and stay **straight**, leaving Route 42. Turn **left** towards White Castle, which is signed if you'd like to visit. Stay **right** twice, then turn **left** at the T-junction. At the B4521 turn **right** towards Skenfrith. Turn left towards Skenfrith Castle if you'd like to stop and visit. Continue on the B4521 and turn **left** after the bridge. At the T-junction turn **left** on Route 46. Turn **left** towards Grosmont where you can visit Grosmont Castle. Continue to follow Route 46 towards Abergavenny. At the T-junction turn **right**, leaving Route 46. Go **left** at the fork, then **left** at the T-junction on Route 42. Follow Route 42 back to Abergavenny. Use the crossing to cross the A40 and continue on King St. Turn **left** on Lion St, leaving Route 42. Stay **straight** on the B4233. Turn **right** at the mini roundabout on Holywell Rd, **left** on Holywell Cres and keep **left** on Belmont Cres back to the station.

Bike shops

Gateway Cycles
NP7 5UH Tel: 01873 858519

Eat & drink

The Hog's Head
NP7 8TA Tel: 01600 780410

Red Castle Tea Room
NP7 8PB Tel: 07914 234368

Apple County Cider Co
NP25 5NS Tel: 01600 750835

The Bell of Skenfrith
NP7 8UH Tel: 01600 750235

The Bridge Inn
HR2 0DB Tel: 01981 240228

The Angel Inn
NP7 8EP Tel: 01981 240646

The Crown Pantygelli
NP7 7HR Tel: 01873 853314

The Farmer's Arms
NP7 5NT Tel: 01873 855422

Various in Abergavenny

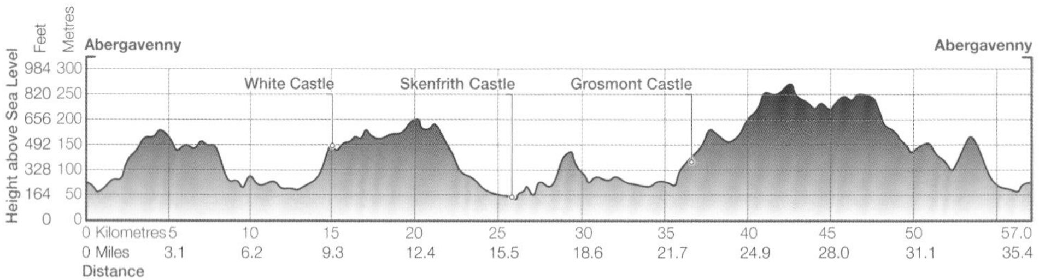

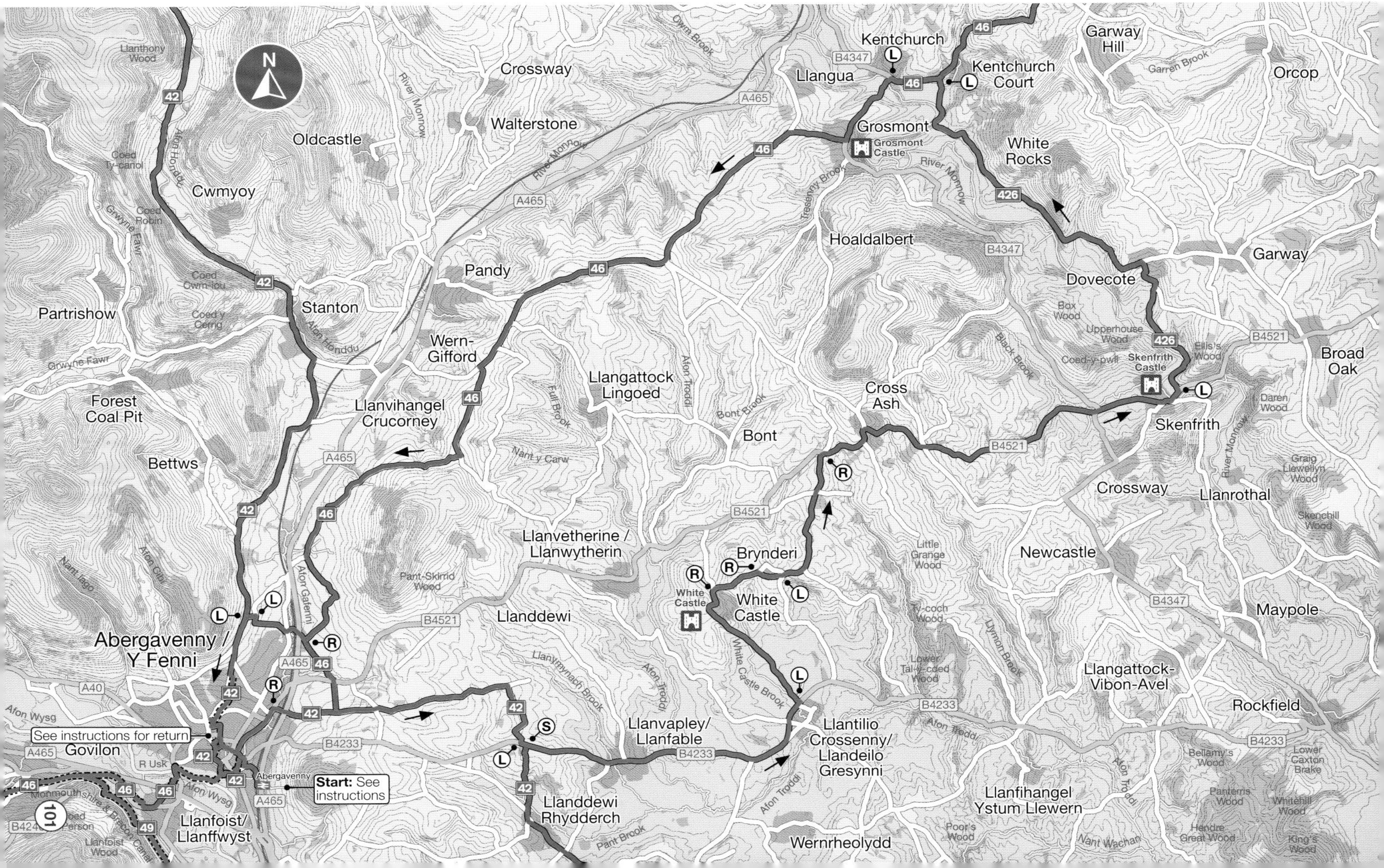
N
Kentchurch
Kentchurch Court
Garway Hill
Orcop
Llangua
Grosmont
Grosmont Castle
White Rocks
Crossway
Walterstone
Oldcastle
Cwmyoy
Hoaldalbert
Garway
Dovecote
Pandy
Stanton
Partrishow
Wern-Gifford
Llangattock Lingoed
Cross Ash
Skenfrith Castle
Skenfrith
Broad Oak
Forest Coal Pit
Llanvihangel Crucorney
Bont
Bettws
Llanrothal
Llanvetherine / Llanwytherin
Brynderi
Newcastle
White Castle
Llanddewi
Abergavenny / Y Fenni
Maypole
Llangattock-Vibon-Avel
Rockfield
Llanvapley/ Llanfable
Llantilio Crossenny/ Llandeilo Gresynni
See instructions for return
Govilon
Start: See instructions
Llanfoist/ Llanffwyst
Llanddewi Rhydderch
Llanfihangel Ystum Llewern
Wernrheolydd

From Ebbw Vale Town Station turn **right** on Lime Ave and follow Route 466 on the shared-use path. Pass under the bridge and go **right**. When the path ends turn **left** along the road and then **right** on Emlyn Ave. Go **straight** through the mini roundabout and then immediate **right**. **Jink right left** onto the A4047. Turn **left** on Llangynidr Rd / B4560 and follow towards Llangynidr. At the B4558 T-junction turn **left** into Llangynidr. Stay **left** along the canal. Turn **left** towards Talybont Reservoir. Turn **left** across the dam on Route 8, then turn **right** on the shared-use path. When the path ends turn **left** on the road, then **right** on the gravel track through the barrier. Continue **left** on Route 8. Turn **right** and **right** on the forest track. Turn **right** to rejoin the road. Take sharp **left** at the Red Cow Inn. Turn **right** at the T-junction and stay **straight** on the road / Route 46 (don't follow Route 8 off the road). Turn **left** off Pant Rd onto the off-road path. Briefly join the road **right** and then exit **right** onto the path and under the A road. Continue **straight** at the roundabout past the sculpture. After crossing over the A465 go **right** at the roundabout. Turn **right** off the path across the bridge back over the A465. Take the second **left**. Join the shared-use path **right** before the roundabout. Go **straight** at the roundabout on Badminton Grove / Route 466. Bear **right** on Emlyn Ave, then **left** at the end of the road. Join the shared-use path and follow back to the station.

Bike shops

Halfords
NP23 4PS Tel: 01495 314190

Bikes & Hikes
LD3 7YJ Tel: 07909 968135

Eat & drink

Coach & Horses Tavern
NP8 1LS
Tel: 01874 730245

Traveller's Rest Inn
LD3 7YP
Tel: 01874 676333

White Hart Inn
LD3 7JD
Tel: 01874 676227

The Star Inn
LD3 7YX
Tel: 01874 676635

Red Cow Inn
CF48 2UN
Tel: 01685 387775

Pant Cad Ivor Inn
CF48 2DD
Tel: 01685 377220

Prince of Wales Inn
NP22 3AE
Tel: 01865 844441

Nag's Head Inn
NP22 3AP
Tel: 01495 722867

Castle Inn
NP23 5DA
Tel: 01495 302087

The Bridge
NP23 5AZ
Tel: 01495 302171

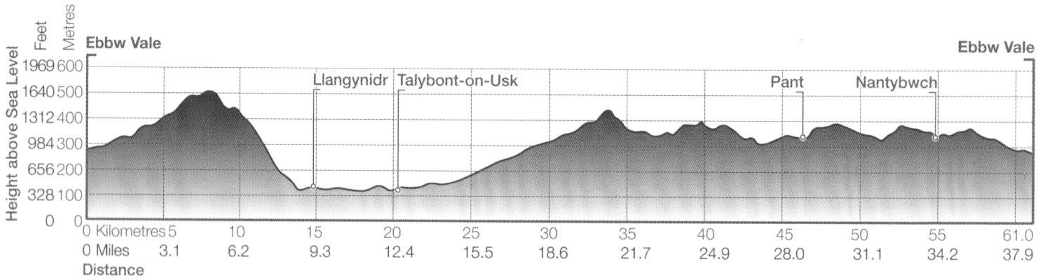

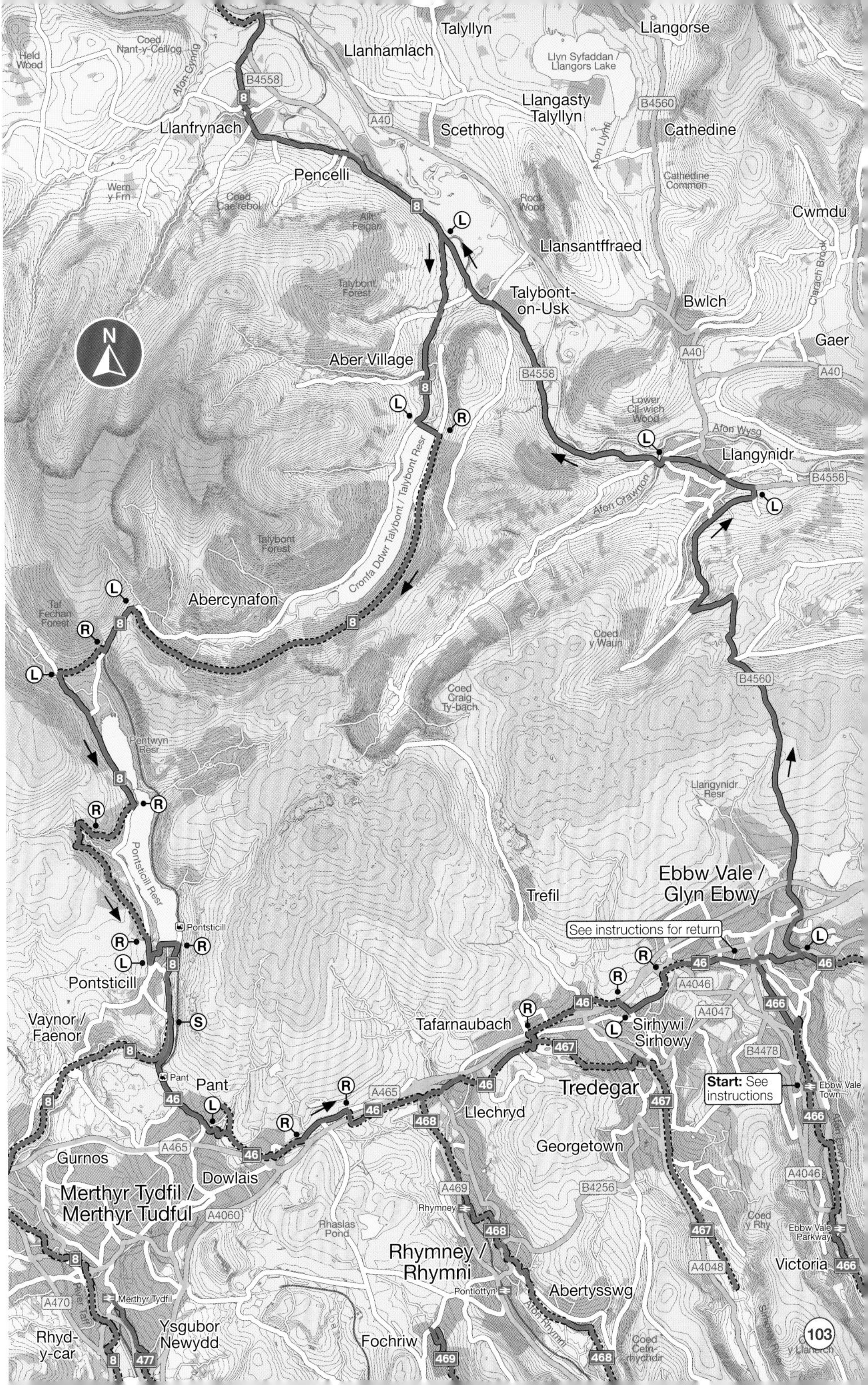
Talyllyn
Llangorse
Held Wood
Coed Nant-y-Ceiliog
Afon Cynrig
Llanhamlach
Llyn Syfaddan / Llangors Lake
B4558
8
Llangasty Talyllyn
B4560
A40
Llanfrynach
Scethrog
Cathedine
Afon Llynfi
Pencelli
Cathedine Common
Wern y Frn
Coed Cae'rebol
Rock Wood
Cwmdu
Allt Feigan
L
Llansantffraed
Talybont Forest
Talybont-on-Usk
Bwlch
Clarach Brook
N
Gaer
A40
Aber Village
B4558
A40
Lower Cil-wich Wood
R
Afon Wysg
Llangynidr
B4558
Cronfa Ddwr Talybont / Talybont Resr
Afon Crawnon
Talybont Forest
Abercynafon
Taf Fechan Forest
Coed y Waun
Coed Craig Ty-bach
B4560
Pentwyn Resr
Llangynidr Resr
Pontsticill Resr
Ebbw Vale / Glyn Ebwy
Trefil
Pontsticill
See instructions for return
46
Pontsticill
A4046
466
S
Tafarnaubach
A4047
Sirhywi / Sirhowy
Vaynor / Faenor
467
B4478
Pant
Pant
A465
Tredegar
Start: See instructions
Ebbw Vale Town
46
467
468
Llechryd
466
Gurnos
A465
Georgetown
Dowlais
Afon Ebwy
A4046
Merthyr Tydfil / Merthyr Tudful
A469
B4256
A4060
Rhymney
Coed y Rhy
Rhaslas Pond
Ebbw Vale Parkway
468
Rhymney / Rhymni
A4048
Victoria
A470
Merthyr Tydfil
Pontlottyn
Abertysswg
Afon Rhymni
Rhyd-y-car
Ysgubor Newydd
Fochriw
Coed Cefn-rhychdir
477
469
Sirhowy River

Turn **right** out of Pembroke Dock Station, **right** on Water St and **right** at the roundabout, using the Route 4 path. Turn **left** at the next roundabout and carry straight on across Cleddau Bridge. Cross the second bridge and then carefully cross the road **right** to follow the Route 4 traffic-free path. When the path ends turn **left**, follow the route to Broad Haven. At the coast follow the B4341 south towards Little Haven, leaving Route 4. At the T-junction turn **right** down the hill. If you have time definitely walk up the Pembrokeshire Coast Path for views over Rook's Bay. Continue south and stay **right** at the fork towards Talbenny. At the crossroads turn **right**. Turn **left** on the private road. Continue straight to visit St Brides, otherwise turn **left** towards Marloes to continue. Turn **right** at the T-junction and **left** towards St Ishmael's. Bear **left** and continue straight towards Herbrandston. Bear **left** towards Milford Haven. Turn **left** at the roundabout and then immediate **left** in front of Tesco following the road through the business park to the traffic-free path. Turn **right** when the path ends, then join the path **left** at the next T-junction. Follow the path along the A477 all the way back to Pembroke Dock (it becomes Route 4). Turn **left** on Water St and **left** on Dimond St to return to the station.

To visit Pembroke Castle, turn left at the second roundabout after Cleddau Bridge onto the A477 and then turn right on the A4139.

Bike shops

Bierspool Cycles
SA72 6DT Tel: 01646 681039

Mike's Bikes
SA61 2PE Tel: 01437 760068

Eat & drink

The Glen
SA61 1XA
Tel: 01437 760070

The Galleon Inn
SA62 3JW
Tel: 01437 781157

The Castle
SA62 3UG
Tel: 01437 781445

Swan Inn
SA62 3UL
Tel: 01437 781880

The Saint Brides Inn
SA62 3UN
Tel: 01437 781266

The Brook Inn
SA62 3TE
Tel: 01646 636277

Various in Milford Haven

Horse & Jockey
SA73 1AP
Tel: 01646 663778

The Ferry Inn
SA72 6UD
Tel: 01646 682947

Various in Pembroke Dock

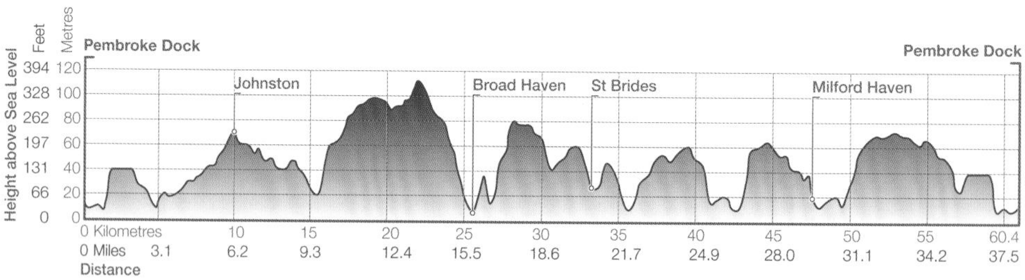

Haverfordwest / Hwlffordd
Milford Haven / Aberdaugleddau
Pembroke Dock / Doc Penfro
Start: See instructions
See instructions for return
St Brides Bay
Druidston
Lambston
Haroldston West
Broad Haven
Little Haven
Rook's Bay
Talbenny
St Brides
The Moors
Marloes
Dale
Dale Roads
Westdale Bay
Castlebeach Wood
Castlebeach Bay
Watwick Bay
Frenchman's Bay
Mill Bay
Hasguard
Rosepool
Walwyn's Castle
Sandy Haven
St Ishmael's
Lindsway Bay
Sleeping Bay
Herbrandston
Gelliswick Bay
Scotch Bay
Aberdaugleddyf / Milford Haven
Man of War Roads
West Angle Bay
Angle
Angle Bay
Oil Refinery
Pennar Mouth
Portfield Gate
Dreenhill
Tiers Cross
Johnston
Denant Wood
Boltonhill Wood
Merlin's Brook
Pope Hill
Lower Freystrop
Freystrop
Johnston Wood
Rosemarket
Waterston
Llanstadwell
Neyland
Houghton
Hill Mountain
Burton
Cosheston Pill
Llangwm
Badger Wood
Wright's Wood
Nash Wood
Hook
Nash Lake
Little Milford Wood
Northwell Green
Boulston
Ash Wood
East Wood
Shady Grove
Uzmaston
Black Backs Wood
Millin Brook
Bowen's Wood
Cartlett Brook
Cleddau Wen / Western Cleddau
Lambston Wood
King's Wood
Pembroke Dock
A487
B4330
B4329
A40
B4341
B4327
A4076
A477
B4325
B4320
B4322
A4139
4
L
R
N

Go **right** out of Pontypool and New Inn Station, then turn **right** on The Highway. After passing Panteg Cemetery turn **right** off the road and down the slope to the canal towpath / Route 49. Follow the Monmouthshire and Brecon Canal towards Abergavenny. Fork **right** away from the canal and turn **left** onto Route 46. There are two very sharp **left** and **right** zig zags before Route 46 meets Route 492. Turn **left** on Route 492 and follow towards Pontypool. (If you miss the zig zags and end up at the roundabout in Pontygof, turn left on the A467 and left on Darren-Felin Rd to re-join the route.) You can stop off to visit the Big Pit: National Coal Museum. After crossing over the A472, descend to the canal and take a sharp **left** onto Route 49. Pass under the A road and over the aqueduct, then turn **right** onto The Highway in front of the cemetery. Cross the tracks and turn **left** to return to the station.

Bike shops

Gateway Cycles
NP7 5UH Tel: 01873 858519

Hopyard Cycles (hire)
NP7 9SE Tel: 01873 830219

Eat & drink

The Star Inn
NP4 0JF Tel: 01495 785319

Hummingbird Café
NP7 9HA Tel: 01873 881044

Various in Abergavenny

Tafarn Y Bont
NP7 9RP Tel: 01873 830720

Jolly Colliers
NP7 0PW Tel: 01873 832496

The Racehorse Inn
NP7 0PU Tel: 01495 310282

Queen Victoria Inn
NP4 9BD Tel: 01495 524364

Little Crown Inn
NP4 6DR Tel: 01495 763148

The Unicorn
NP4 6LE Tel: 01495 751304

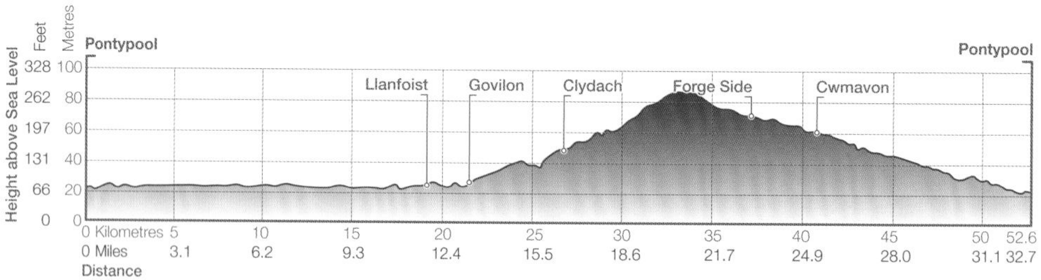

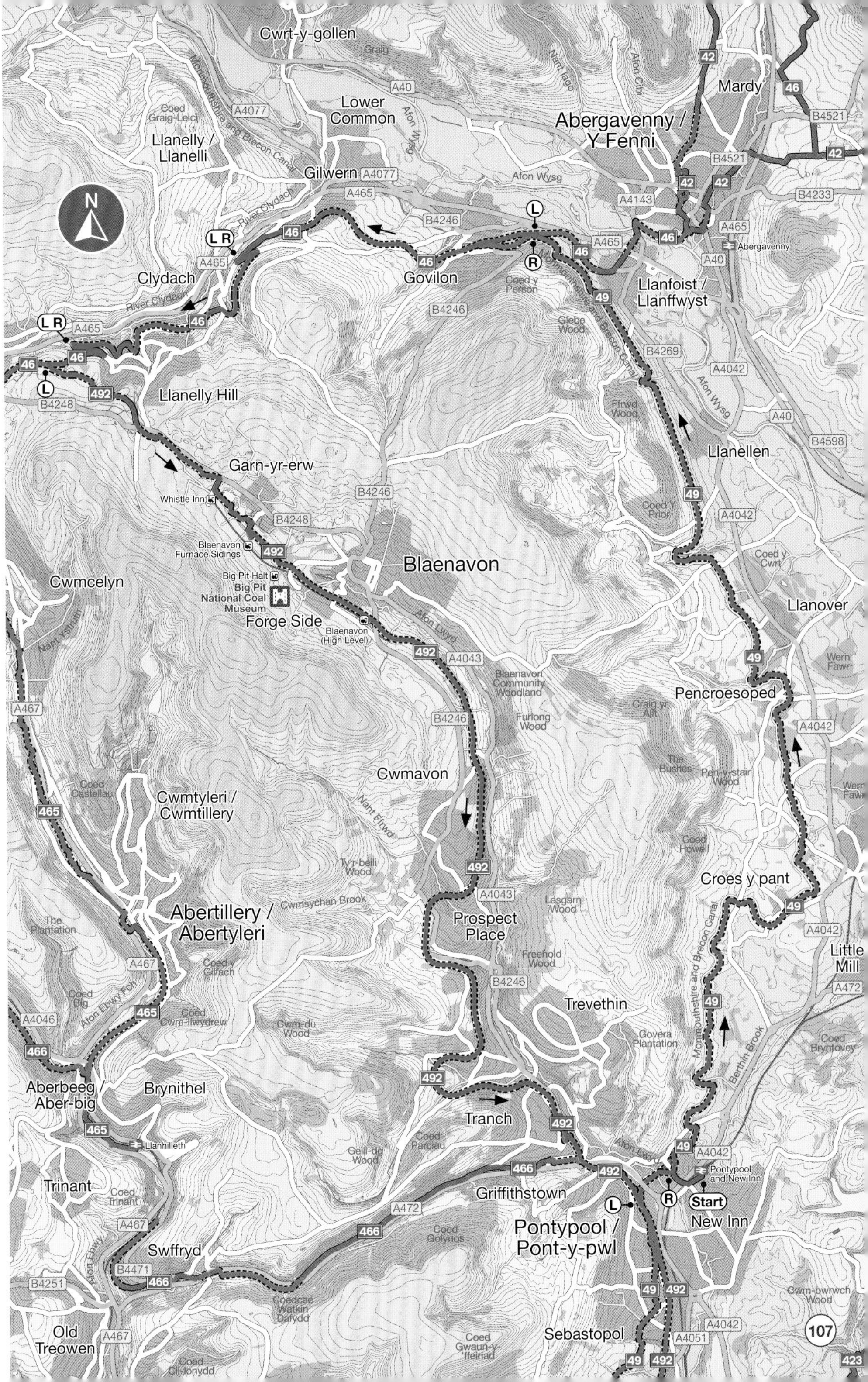
Cwrt-y-gollen
Graig
Lower Common
Coed Graig-Leici
Llanelly / Llanelli
Monmouthshire and Brecon Canal
Gilwern
River Clydach
Clydach
Govilon
Coed y Person
Abergavenny / Y Fenni
Mardy
Afon Wysg
Afon Cibi
Nant Iago
Afon Wysg
Abergavenny
Llanfoist / Llanffwyst
Glebe Wood
Ffrwd Wood
Llanellen
Coed Y Prior
Llanelly Hill
Garn-yr-erw
Whistle Inn
Blaenavon Furnace Sidings
Big Pit Halt
Big Pit National Coal Museum
Blaenavon
Forge Side
Blaenavon (High Level)
Afon Lwyd
Cwmcelyn
Nant Ystruth
Coed y Cwrt
Llanover
Wern Fawr
Pencroesoped
Blaenavon Community Woodland
Craig y Allt
Furlong Wood
The Bushes
Pen-y-stair Wood
Coed Howell
Cwmavon
Nant Ffrwd
Coed Castellau
Cwmtyleri / Cwmtillery
Ty'r-belli Wood
Cwmsychan Brook
Croes y pant
Abertillery / Abertyleri
The Plantation
Prospect Place
Lasgarn Wood
Freehold Wood
Coed y Gilfach
Coed Big
Afon Ebwy Fch
Coed Cwm-llwydrew
Cwm-du Wood
Trevethin
Govera Plantation
Berthin Brook
Little Mill
Coed Bryntovey
Aberbeeg / Aber-big
Brynithel
Tranch
Llanhilleth
Coed Parciau
Gelli-dg Wood
Afon Lwyd
Pontypool and New Inn
Start
Trinant
Coed Trinant
Griffithstown
Pontypool / Pont-y-pwl
New Inn
Coed Golynos
Swffryd
Afon Ebwy
Coedcae Watkin Dafydd
Cwm-bwrwch Wood
Old Treowen
Coed Gwaun-y-ffeiriad
Sebastopol
Coed Cil-lonydd
A40
A4077
A465
B4246
A4143
B4521
B4233
B4269
A4042
B4598
B4248
A4043
A467
A4046
A472
A4051
B4471
B4251
42
46
49
465
466
492
423
L
R
N

14 Ferryside, Coastal Path & Swiss Valley

35.2 miles / 56.6 km

From Ferryside Station turn **right**, with the tracks and water on your right. Follow Route 4 to Kidwelly, where you can visit the Kidwelly Castle ruins. Continue to follow Route 4 towards Burry Port. Use the path along the A484, then carefully cross **left**. Take the first **right**, then **left** to join the off-road path. At the stone circle stay **left** on Route 47 to go inland along the lake. Go **right** around the car park and over the bridge, looping north. You can stop and visit the free Parc Howard Musuem and Art Gallery. Follow Route 47 until it passes under the B4306. Turn sharp **left** up the slope to the road and turn **right**. Turn **left** on the B4317 towards Pontyates. Turn sharp **right** down the hill towards Baltic Inn. Turn **right** on the B4309, then **left** in front of the bus stop at the crossroads. Turn **left** at the stop sign. Turn **right** at the crossroads. Turn **right** and then fork **left**. **Jink right left** to carefully cross the A484. Turn **left** at the T-junction. Follow the road back to the station.

Bike shops

On Your Bike
SA15 3TW Tel: 01554 773200

Eat & drink

The Gatehouse
SA17 5AX Tel: 01554 891278

Fisherman's Arms
SA17 4UU Tel: 01554 891589

The Pembrey Inn
SA16 0UA Tel: 01554 834530

The Neptune
SA16 0EP Tel: 01554 834334

Pavilion Café
SA15 4AR Tel: 07767 818594

The York Palace
SA15 3YA Tel: 01554 758609

The Waun Wyllt Inn
SA15 5AQ Tel: 01269 862941

The New Inn
SA15 5EB Tel: 01269 871152

The Baltic Inn & Restaurant
SA15 5RE Tel: 01269 861409

White Lion Hotel
SA17 5RW Tel: 01267 267214

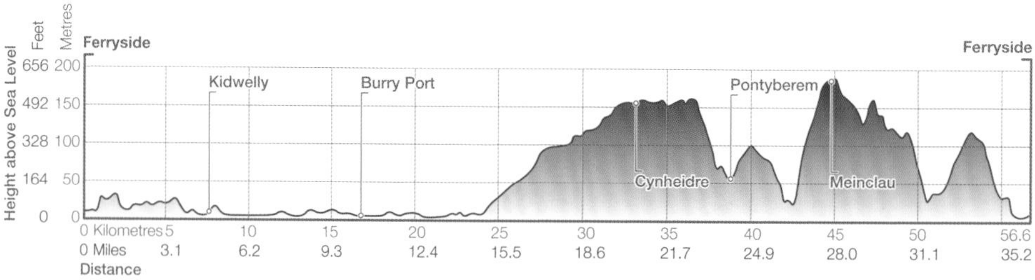

Start
Ferryside
Llansteffan
St Ishmael
Broadlay
Llansaint
Broadway
Llandefaelog
Kidwelly / Cydweli
Kidwelly Castle
Mynyddygarreg
Pontyates / Pont-iets
Meinciau
Pont Henri
Pontyberem
Tumble / Y Tymbl
Llannon
Sylen
Cynheidre
Carway / Carwe
Five Roads / Pum Heol
Trimsaran
Pen-y-mynydd
Burry Port / Porth Tywyn
Pembrey / Pen-bre
Pwll
Llanelli
Parc Howard Museum & Art Gallery
Swiss Valley
Cwmcarnhywel
Bigyn
Pembrey Forest
Afon Tywi / River Towy

Go **right** out of Port Talbot Parkway, turn **right** over the level crossing then **right** on Cramic Way. Bear **right** to cross the river and follow the shared-use path around the roundabout. Follow the path alongside the railway, around the car park and under the M4. Follow Route 887 along the Afan Valley. Take a sharp **left** up the forest track, then turn **left** on Route 47. Alternatively, follow Route 887 around to Route 47 and go left. At the cemetery turn **right**. Turn **left** down the shared-use path and then **left** along the Neath Canal. If you want to visit the Neath Castle ruins, come off the canal path and cross at the B4434. When Route 47 ends go **left** on Route 4 towards Port Talbot. Turn **right** towards Sandfields Young Business Centre, then cross the road to turn **left**. Curve left and follow the path along Aberavon Beach. Follow the route left along the River Afan. When the path ends turn **right** over the bridge and **left** along the river. At the roundabout join the shared-use path, go over the pedestrian bridge and around to continue along the river. Pass under the A road and then **right** on Cramic Way. Turn **left** and **left** to return to the station.

Bike shops

Welsh Coast Cycles
SA13 1NU Tel: 01639 894169

Halfords
SA12 7BZ Tel: 01639 816320

Skyline Cycles
SA13 3EA Tel: 01639 850011

Halfords
SA10 7AY Tel: 01639 635731

Eat & drink

The Brit Pub
SA12 9AH Tel: 01639 680247

Afan Tavern
SA12 9AS Tel: 01639 898283

Refreshment Rooms
SA13 3HY Tel: 01639 850901

The Whittington Arms
SA11 3JF Tel: 01639 632577

St Ives Inn
SA11 3NA Tel: 01639 638297

Castle Hotel & Restaurant
SA11 1RB Tel: 01639 641119

The Britannia Inn
SA11 2HQ Tel: 01639 812542

Café Remos
SA12 6QP Tel: 01639 882121

The Grand Hotel
SA13 1DE Tel: 01639 882830

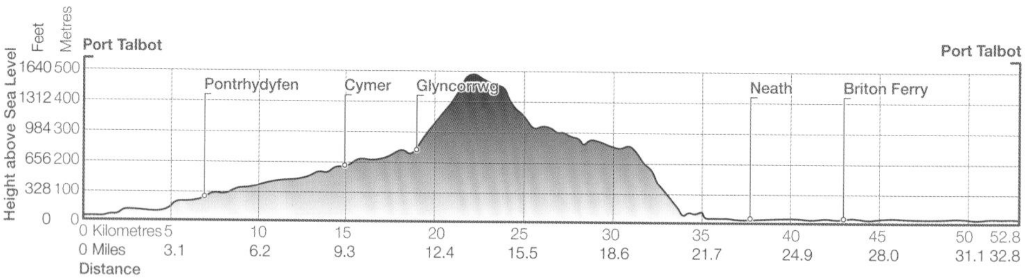

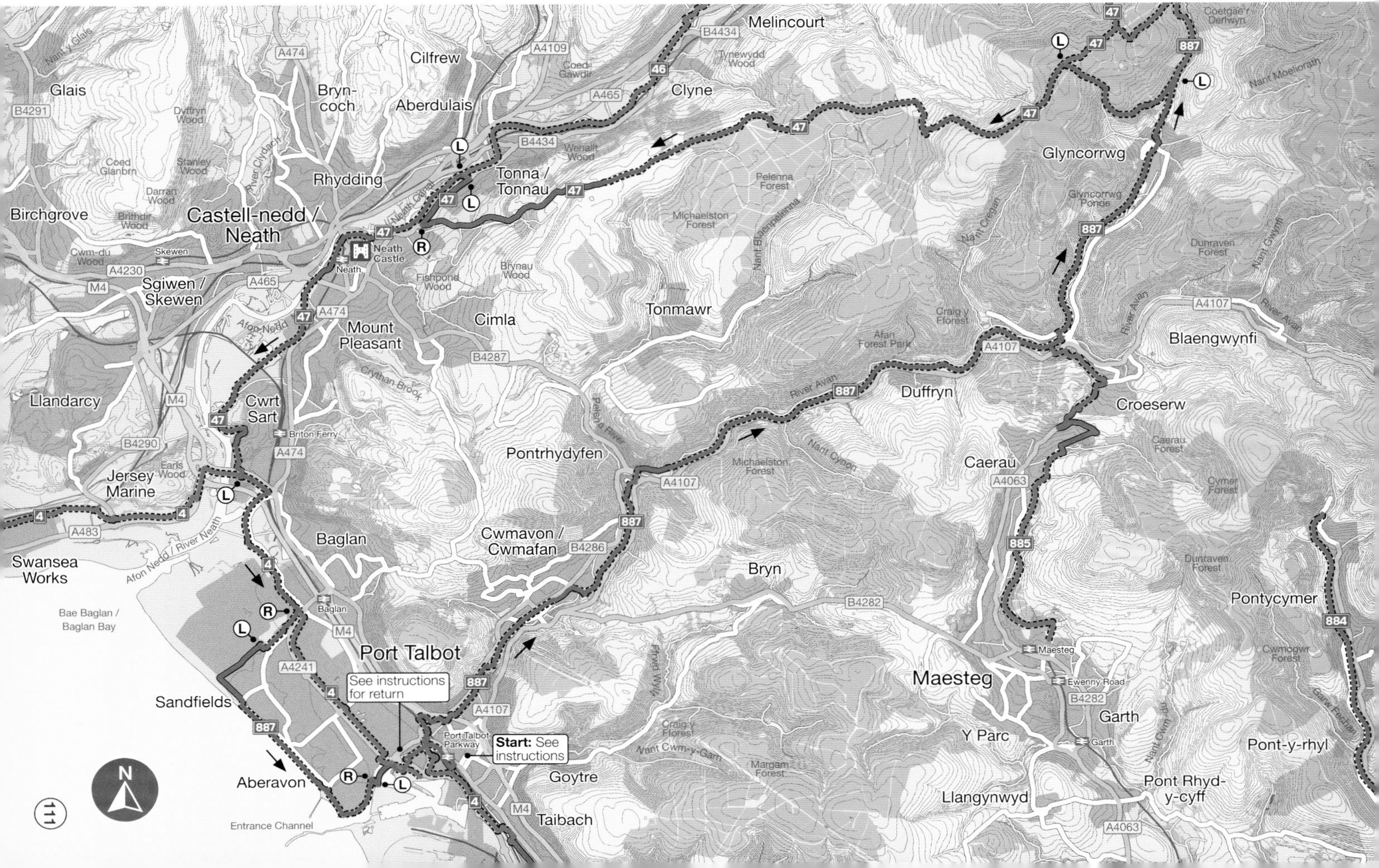

Start: See instructions
See instructions for return
Port Talbot
Port Talbot Parkway
Aberavon
Sandfields
Baglan
Bae Baglan / Baglan Bay
Entrance Channel
Afon Nedd / River Neath
Swansea Works
Jersey Marine
Llandarcy
Birchgrove
Glais
Sgiwen / Skewen
Castell-nedd / Neath
Neath Castle
Neath
Cwrt Sart
Briton Ferry
Bryn-coch
Rhydding
Cilfrew
Aberdulais
Tonna / Tonnau
Clyne
Melincourt
Tonmawr
Cimla
Mount Pleasant
Pontrhydyfen
Cwmavon / Cwmafan
Bryn
Duffryn
Afan Forest Park
Glyncorrwg
Glyncorrwg Ponds
Blaengwynfi
Croeserw
Caerau
Maesteg
Garth
Pontycymer
Pont-y-rhyl
Pont Rhyd-y-cyff
Y Parc
Llangynwyd
Goytre
Taibach
Michaelston Forest
Pelenna Forest
Margam Forest
Craig y Fforest
Dunraven Forest
Caerau Forest
Cymer Forest
River Avan
Pelenna River
River Clydach
887
47
46
4
884
885
M4
A474
A465
A4107
A4063
B4282
B4286
B4287
B4434
A4109
A4230
A4241
A483
B4290
B4291

Midlands

N
Birkenhead
Liverpool
Manchester
Sheffield
Lincoln
Chester
Wrexham
Stoke-on-Trent
Nottingham
Derby
07
13
12
11
10
Telford
Cannock
08
Leicester
Welshpool
Peterborough
Newtown
Birmingham
09
Corby
Kidderminster
Coventry
Northampton
Worcester
05
01
02
Hereford
Bedford
03
04
06
Brecon
Luton
Gloucester
Ebbw Vale
Oxford
Port Talbot
Swindon
London
Cardiff
Bristol
Reading
Bath
Aldershot
Crawley
Taunton
Yeovil
Southampton
Brighton
Portsmouth
Bournemouth
Exeter
Weymouth
Torquay

The Malvern Hills Circular

25.4 miles / 40.8 km

This route does not use the National Cycle Network, but follows quiet lanes around the Malvern Hills AONB. From Colwall Station head **straight** on Stone Dr. At the T-junction turn **right** on Old Church Rd, then **left** on Mathon Rd. Turn **left** twice towards Mathon. Stay **left** towards Mathon and Cradley. After Mathon stay **right** towards Cradley. At the A4103 turn **left** and then first **right**. Turn **right** towards Suckley. Turn **right** twice towards Alfrick and Worcester. Turn **left** at the single track road sign. At the T-junction turn **left**. If you would like to visit National Trust property Brockhampton Estate keep straight through Linley Green, turn right on the B4220, then right on the A44. At the crossroads turn **left** towards Cradley. Turn **right** towards Acton and Beauchamp. Turn **left** towards Greenhill and Cradley. Turn **right** towards Cradley and Bosbury. At the A4103 turn **right** and then **left** on the B4220. Follow the road south and then turn **left** towards Mathon. Stay **straight** towards Coddington. Turn **right** towards Bosbury. Turn **left** towards Wellington Heath, then **left** at the T-junction. Turn **right** towards Wellington Heath, then **left** at the post box. Turn **right** at the brick barn. Turn **left** then **left** again towards Coddington and Mathon. At St James the Great Colwall turn **right**, then turn **left** towards Upper Colwall. Turn **right** on Stone Dr and stay **straight** to return to the station.

Bike shops

Detour Cycles
WR14 1NY Tel: 01684 891555

Back on Track Bikes
WR14 4LT Tel: 01684 565777

The Malvern Bike Hire Company
WR14 3QP Tel: 01684 589414

Eat & drink

The Red Lion Inn
WR13 5NN Tel: 01886 880318

The Nelson Inn
WR6 5EF Tel: 01886 884530

The Cross Keys
WR6 5DJ Tel: 01886 884494

Brockhampton Estate Tea Room & Granary Shop
WR6 5TB Tel: 01885 482077

The Glasshouse Café at Holloways
WR6 5DE Tel: 01886 884665

Crown Inn
WR13 6QP Tel: 01684 541074

Colwall Park Restaurant
WR13 6QG Tel: 01684 540000

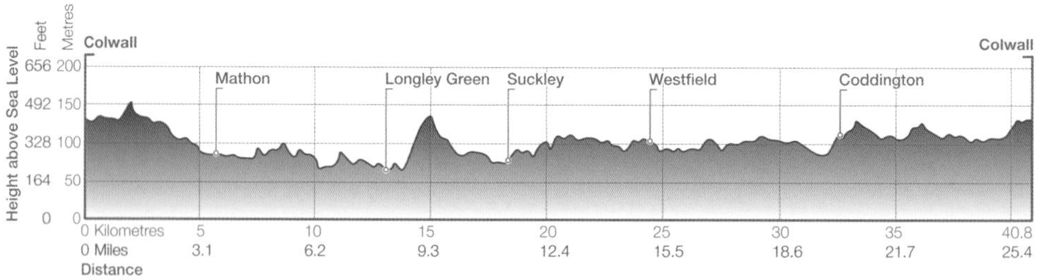

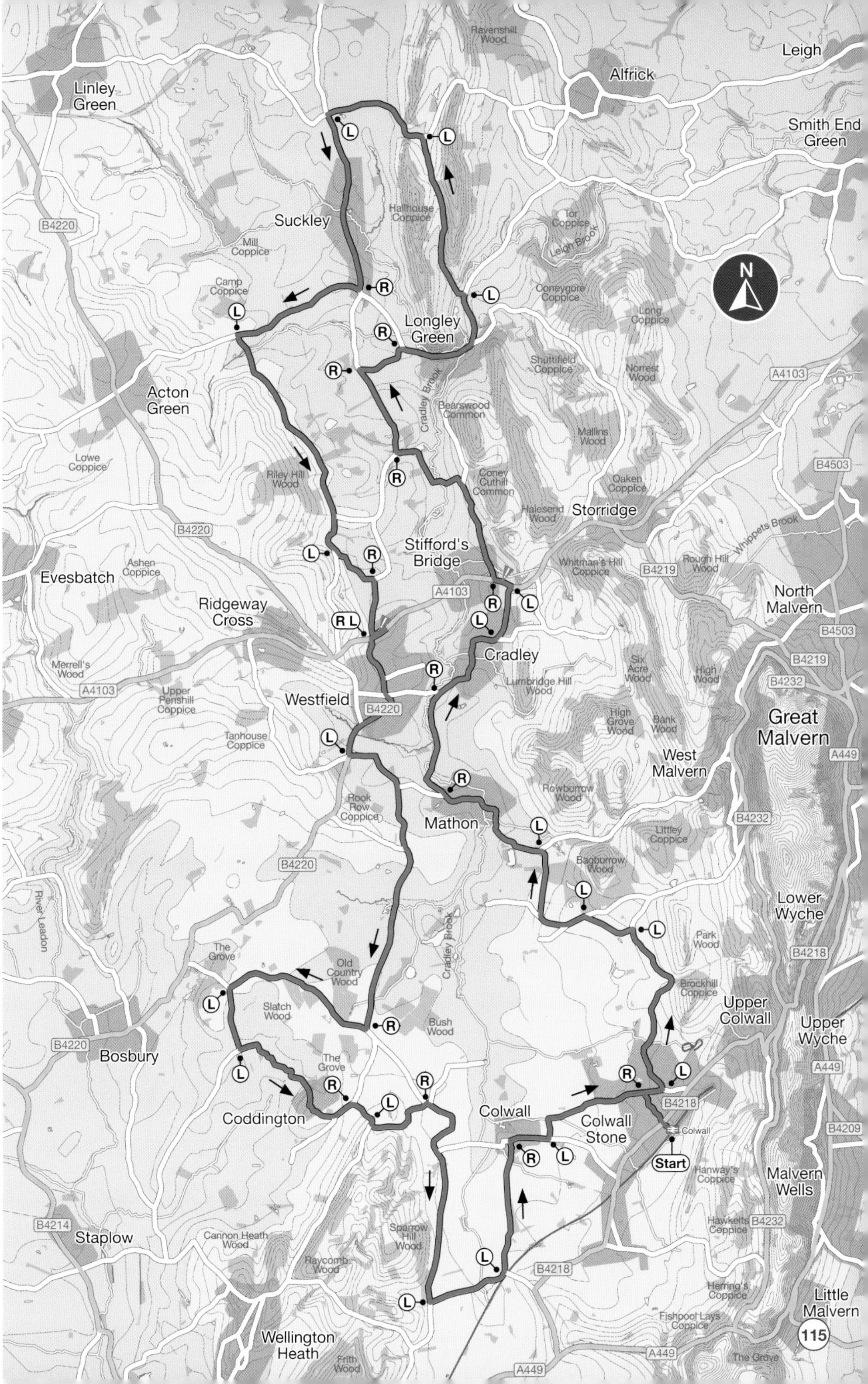
Ravenshill Wood
Leigh
Alfrick
Linley Green
Smith End Green
Suckley
Hallhouse Coppice
Tor Coppice
Leigh Brook
B4220
Mill Coppice
Camp Coppice
Coneygore Coppice
Long Coppice
Longley Green
Shuttifield Coppice
Norrest Wood
A4103
Acton Green
Cradley Brook
Bearswood Common
Mallins Wood
Lowe Coppice
Riley Hill Wood
Coney Cuthill Common
Oaken Coppice
B4503
Halesend Wood
Storridge
Whippets Brook
Stifford's Bridge
Whitman's Hill Coppice
Rough Hill Wood
B4219
Evesbatch
Ashen Coppice
Ridgeway Cross
North Malvern
Cradley
Merrell's Wood
Six Acre Wood
High Wood
Lumbridge Hill Wood
Upper Penshill Coppice
Westfield
High Grove Wood
Bank Wood
B4232
Great Malvern
Tanhouse Coppice
West Malvern
A449
Rook Row Coppice
Rowburrow Wood
Mathon
Littley Coppice
Bagburrow Wood
Lower Wyche
River Leadon
Park Wood
The Grove
Old Country Wood
Brockhill Coppice
B4218
Upper Colwall
Slatch Wood
Bush Wood
Upper Wyche
Bosbury
The Grove
Coddington
Colwall
Colwall Stone
Start
B4209
Hanway's Coppice
Malvern Wells
B4214
Staplow
Cannon Heath Wood
Sparrow Hill Wood
Hawkelts Coppice
Raycomb Wood
Herring's Coppice
Little Malvern
Fishpool Lays Coppice
Wellington Heath
Frith Wood
The Grove
N
L
R

From Evesham Station turn **left** and head north on Greenhill / A4184. Cross the A44 and pass through Norton. Near Harvington turn **left** on Leys Rd. At Church Lench turn **right** on Low Rd. Turn **left** towards Inkberrow and Flyford Flavell. Turn **left** towards Bishampton. Turn **left** towards Lenches and Fladbury. Turn **right** towards The Lenches. At the silos go **left** towards Evesham. At the church turn **right** towards Lenchwick and Evesham. If you fancy some trout fishing, stop off at the Lenches Lakes. Continue straight to Lenchwick. When Kings Ln ends turn **right** on Evesham Rd / A4184 which will take you back to the station.

Bike shops

Vale Cycles
WR11 3LF Tel: 01386 41204

Eat & drink

Norton Grange
WR11 4TL Tel: 01386 871477

The Golden Cross
WR11 8PQ Tel: 01386 871900

The Wheelbarrow Castle
WR7 4LR Tel: 01386 792207

The Boot Inn
WR7 4BS Tel: 01386 462658

The Dolphin Inn
WR10 2LX Tel: 01386 462343

The Railway Hotel
WR11 4EJ Tel: 01386 422582

Various in Evesham

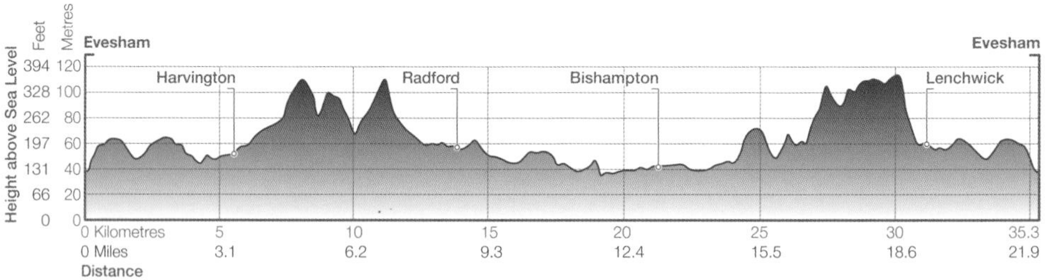

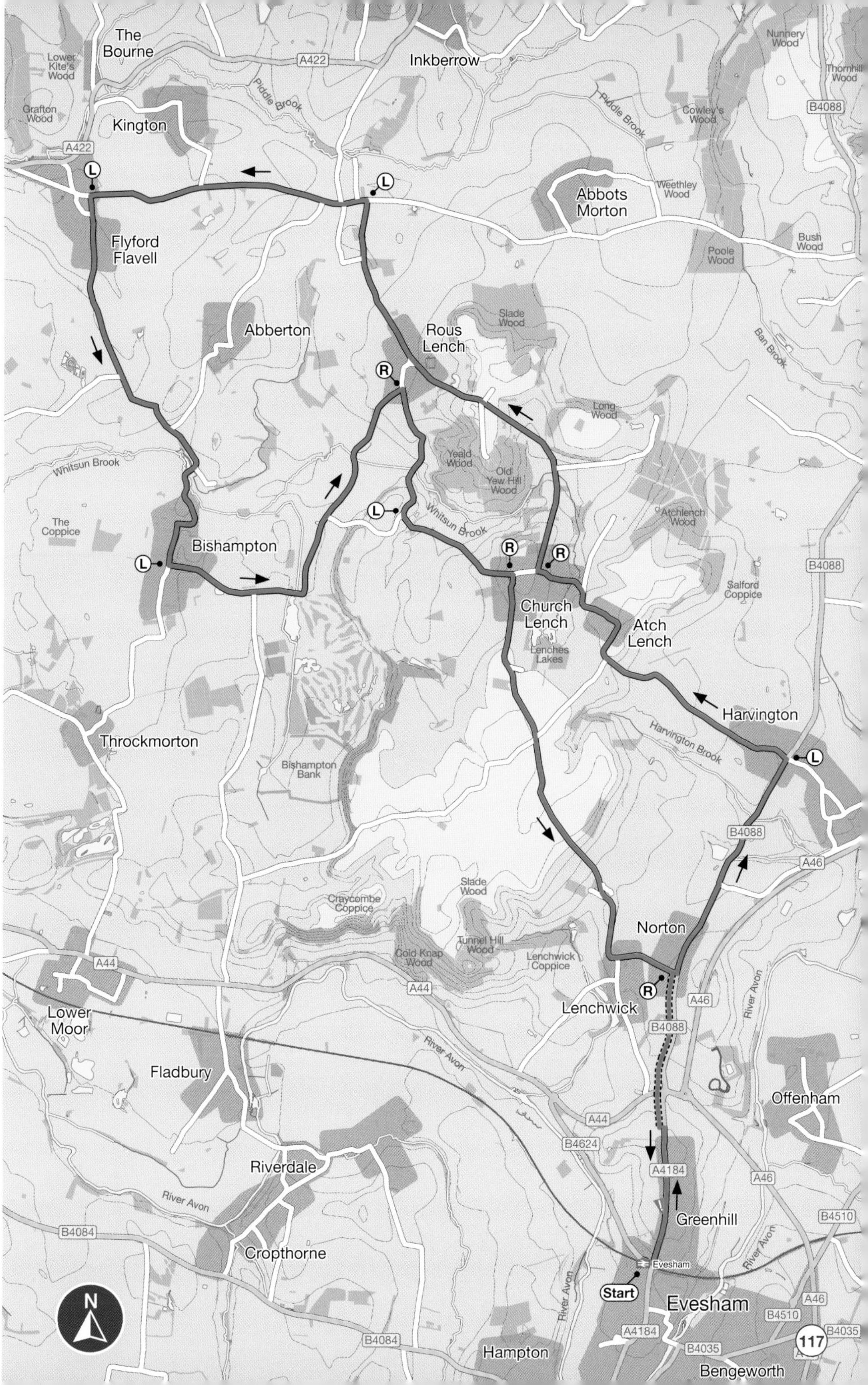
The Bourne
Lower Kite's Wood
Grafton Wood
A422
Inkberrow
Piddle Brook
Nunnery Wood
Thornhill Wood
Cowley's Wood
B4088
Kington
L
Weethley Wood
Abbots Morton
Flyford Flavell
Bush Wood
Poole Wood
Slade Wood
Abberton
Rous Lench
R
Ban Brook
Long Wood
Whitsun Brook
Yeald Wood
Old Yew Hill Wood
Atchlench Wood
The Coppice
Bishampton
Church Lench
Atch Lench
Salford Coppice
Lenches Lakes
Harvington
Harvington Brook
Throckmorton
Bishampton Bank
A46
Craycombe Coppice
Slade Wood
Norton
Tunnel Hill Wood
Cold Knap Wood
Lenchwick Coppice
A44
Lower Moor
Lenchwick
Fladbury
River Avon
Offenham
B4624
A4184
Riverdale
Greenhill
B4510
B4084
Cropthorne
Evesham
Start
A46
B4035
Hampton
Bengeworth
N

This route follows parts of the National Byway's Ledbury Loop. From Ledbury Station turn **right**, staying on the shared-use path, and then join the signed shared-use path to your **left**. Turn **right** on Little Marcle Rd, then **left** back onto the signed shared-use path. When the path comes to the roundabout go **right** to continue on the path. Turn **left** towards Leadington. Follow the route sign **left**. Turn **left** towards Brooms Green. Turn **right** towards Knights Green. Turn **left** towards Ryton, then **left** again. Follow the road over the M50 and turn **right** towards Ketford. Before passing through Poolhill you can take a detour to visit Three Choirs Vineyard. Turn **left** at Pool Hill Rd, then **left** towards Pauntley. Continue **straight** on Drury Ln (don't follow Newent Loop). **Jink right left** towards Lowbands. Turn **right** towards Lowbands then **left** towards Pendock. Stay **left** and then turn **right** into Pendock. Turn **left** on Wyndbrook Ln. Turn **left** towards Bromsberrow. At the T-junction turn **right** and then take first **left**. Turn **left** towards Bromsberrow. At the ford you can use the footbridge. If you have time to visit the stunning Eastnor Castle (limited open days), the entrance will be on your right. Stay **left** through Eastnor. Carefully join the A438. Stay **left** on the A449, then exit slight **right**. Turn **left** towards Hereford. At the T-junction turn **right**. Turn **right** on High St, then **left** at the clock tower. Join the shared-use path on your **right** and return to the station. You can also stay straight at the clock tower to return to the station if you would like to go through central Ledbury.

Bike shops

Cycles Clements
HR8 1AA Tel: 01531 632213

Ledbury Cycle Hire
HR8 1LG Tel: 01531 635024

Eat & drink

The Full Pitcher
HR8 2EN Tel: 01531 632352

Beauchamp Arms Inn
GL18 2AQ Tel: 01531 890266

Three Choirs Vineyard
GL18 1LS Tel: 01531 890223

Rose & Crown
GL19 3NB Tel: 01531 650234

Various in Ledbury

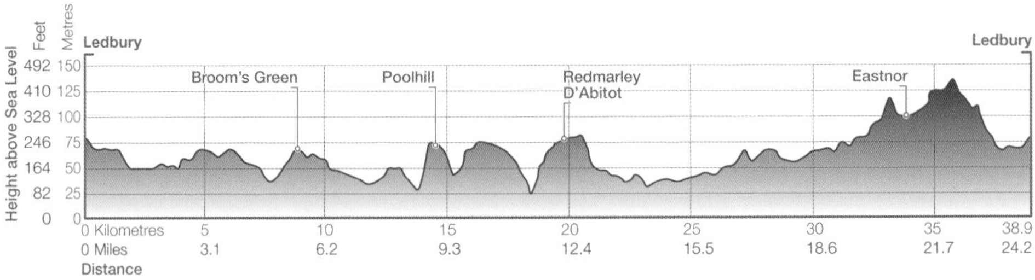

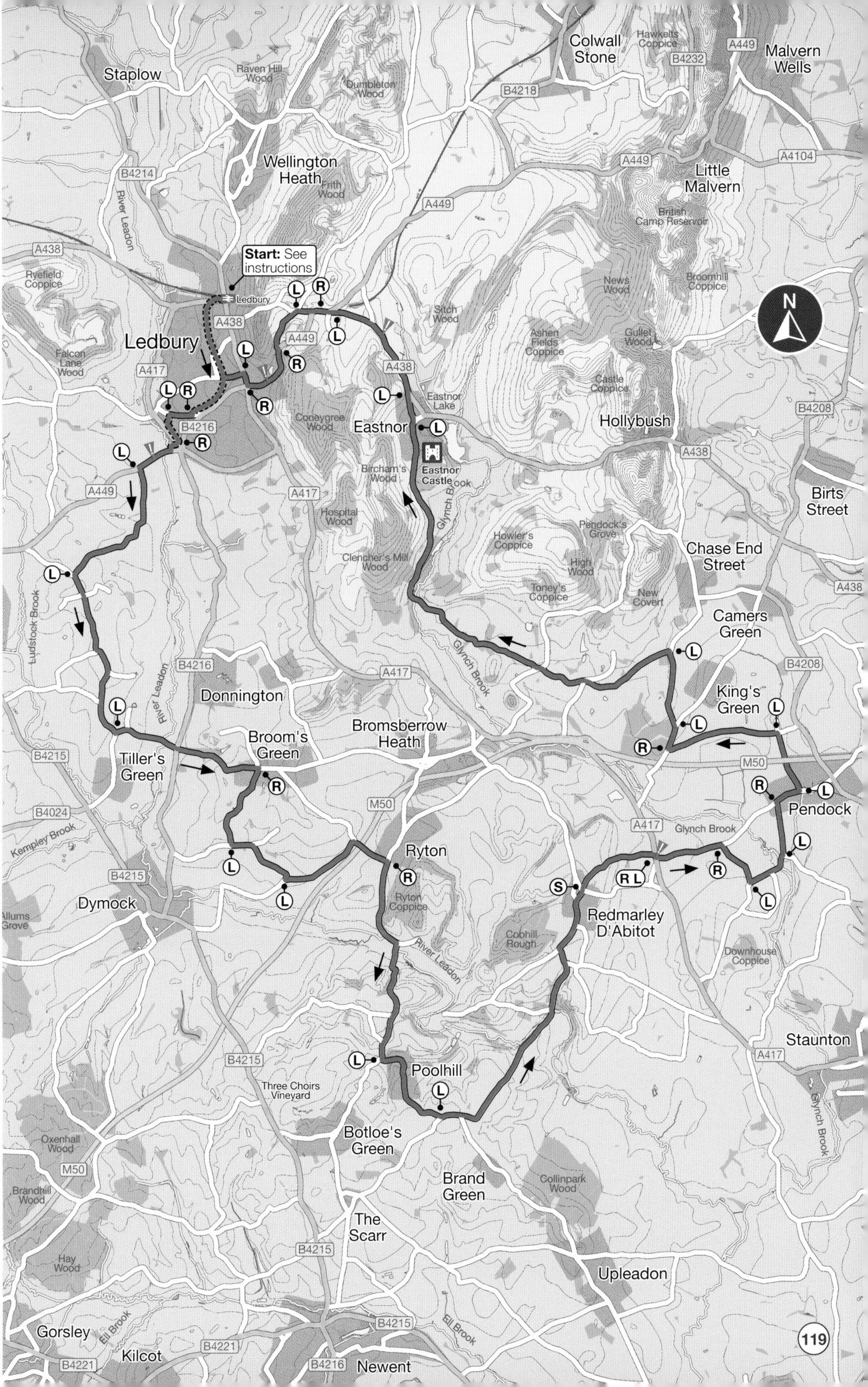
Staplow
Raven Hill Wood
Dumbleton Wood
Colwall Stone
Hawkelts Coppice
B4232
A449
Malvern Wells
B4218
Wellington Heath
Frith Wood
B4214
River Leadon
A449
Little Malvern
A4104
British Camp Reservoir
A438
Start: See instructions
Ryefield Coppice
Ledbury
A438
A449
Sitch Wood
News Wood
Broomhill Coppice
Ashen Fields Coppice
Gullet Wood
Falcon Lane Wood
Ledbury
A417
A438
Castle Coppice
Eastnor Lake
Coneygree Wood
Eastnor
Hollybush
B4216
Eastnor Castle
A438
B4208
A449
Bircham's Wood
A417
Glynch Brook
Hospital Wood
Birts Street
Howler's Coppice
Pendock's Grove
Chase End Street
Clencher's Mill Wood
High Wood
Toney's Coppice
New Covert
A438
Camers Green
Ludstock Brook
B4216
A417
Glynch Brook
B4208
Donnington
King's Green
River Leadon
Bromsberrow Heath
Broom's Green
Tiller's Green
B4215
M50
M50
Pendock
B4024
A417
Glynch Brook
Kempley Brook
Ryton
Ryton Coppice
B4215
Dymock
Redmarley D'Abitot
Allums Grove
Cobhill Rough
River Leadon
Downhouse Coppice
Staunton
B4215
A417
Poolhill
Three Choirs Vineyard
Glynch Brook
Oxenhall Wood
Botloe's Green
M50
Brand Green
Collinpark Wood
Brandhill Wood
The Scarr
B4215
Hay Wood
Upleadon
B4215
Gorsley
Ell Brook
Ell Brook
B4221
Kilcot
B4221
B4216
Newent

37.0 miles / 59.6 km

From Charlbury Station turn **left** on the B4437 heading west. Turn **left** on Catsham Ln towards Leafield, then **right** to continue towards Leafield. At Leafield turn **right** towards Minster Lovell, then **right** on Fairspear Rd towards Shipton-under-Wychwood. Turn **left** on Swinbrook Rd, then **right** on Fiddlers Hill. Continue **straight** ahead until the road ends in a T-junction and go **right** then **left** towards Westcote. After passing the church in Church Westcote turn **left**, then turn **right** on the A424 towards Stow. Turn **left** towards Little Rissington, then if you would like to visit Bourton-on-the-Water or Birdland continue straight. Otherwise turn **right** twice towards Little Rissington and Bourton-on-the-Water. Turn **left** towards Wyck Rissington and continue to the A429. Here turn **left** then **right** onto Copsehill Rd. Follow the road around turning **right** at the church, and continue to Lower Swell. At the B4068 turn **right** towards Stow. After crossing the A429, take the first **left** on Church St. At Market Square go **left** to join Route 48. Turn **right** on Parson's Corner, then **left** signed 'to the wells'. Follow the off-road path, then turn **right** when it ends. Go **right** twice for Evenlode, then **left** on Chapel St. Turn **right** towards Adlestrop, then before reaching it turn **right** towards Stow. Join the A436 **left** towards Chipping Norton, then turn **right** towards Daylesford – you are now on Route 442. Continue on to Kingham, then turn **left** towards Churchill and **right** towards Lyneham. Follow the route **left** towards Sarsden, then **right** towards Chadlington. **Jink left right** to cross the A361. Turn **right** at the T-junction, then **jink left right** towards Charlbury. At the B4437 turn **left**. The station will be on your right. If you'd like to stop in Charlbury, continue straight past the station and turn right on Market St.

Bike shops

No bike shops

Eat & drink

The Lamb Inn
OX7 6DQ
Tel: 01993 830465

The Feathered Nest Country Inn
OX7 6SD
Tel: 01993 833030

The Slaughters Country Inn
GL54 2HS
Tel: 01451 822143

The Golden Ball Inn
GL54 1LF
Tel: 01451 833886

The Talbot
GL54 1BQ
Tel: 01451 870934

Queen's Head Inn
GL54 1AB
Tel: 01451 830563

The Fox Inn
GL56 0UF
Tel: 01451 870909

The Kingham Plough
OX7 6YD
Tel: 01608 658327

The Chequers
OX7 6NJ
Tel: 01608 659393

The Tite Inn
OX7 3NY
Tel: 01608 676910

The Bull Inn
OX7 3RR
Tel: 01608 810689

Rose & Crown
OX7 3PL
Tel: 01608 810103

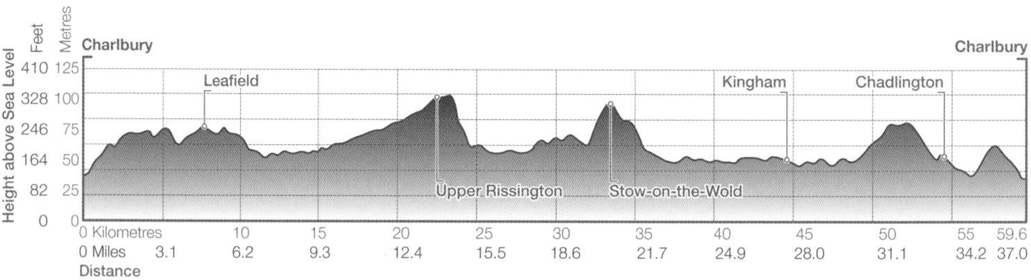

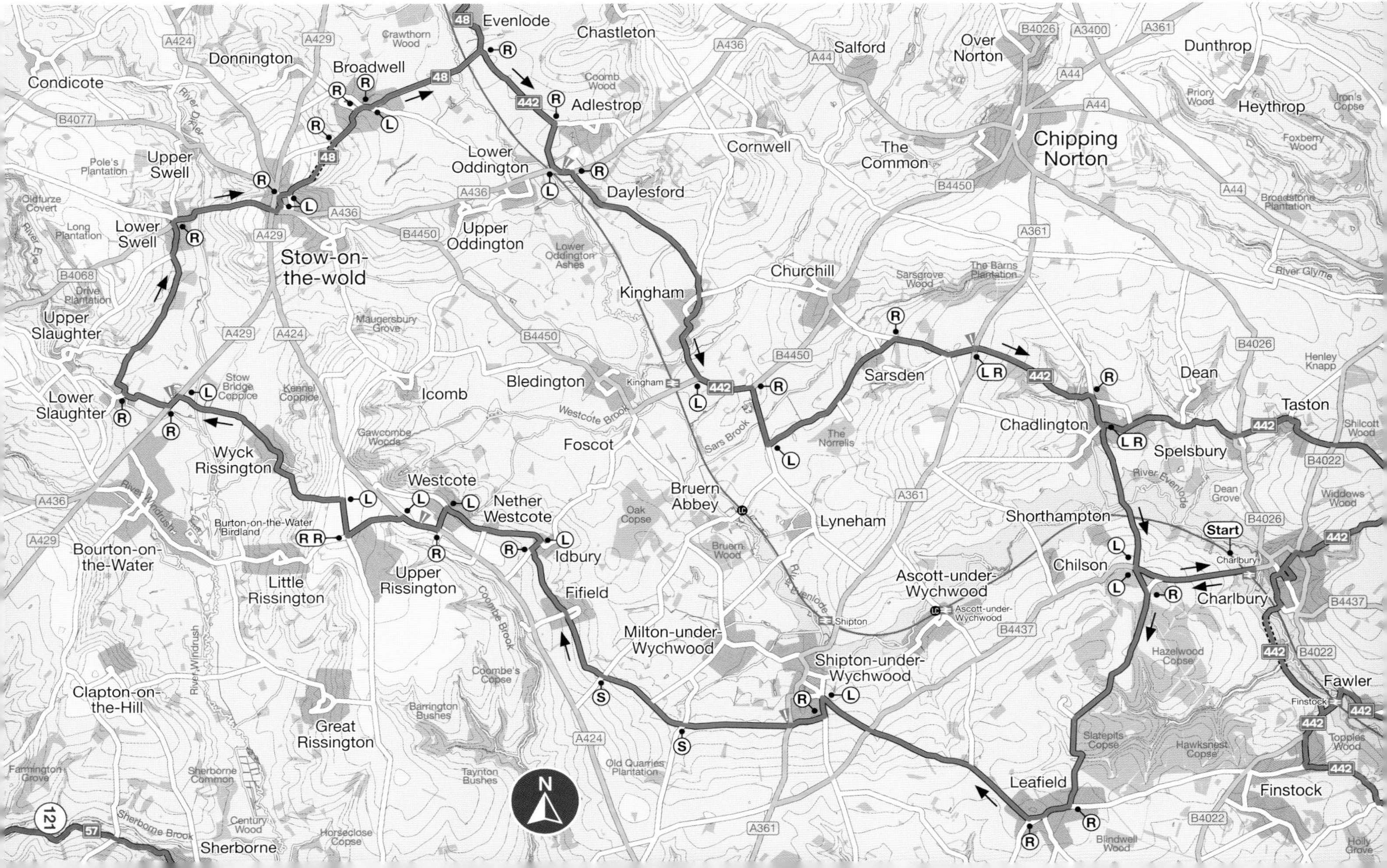

Start
Charlbury
Spelsbury
Taston
Dean
Chadlington
Shorthampton
Chilson
Ascott-under-Wychwood
Shipton-under-Wychwood
Leafield
Finstock
Fawler
Chipping Norton
Over Norton
Salford
The Common
Churchill
Sarsden
Lyneham
Kingham
Daylesford
Adlestrop
Chastleton
Evenlode
Cornwell
Lower Oddington
Upper Oddington
Broadwell
Donnington
Stow-on-the-wold
Upper Swell
Lower Swell
Condicote
Upper Slaughter
Lower Slaughter
Wyck Rissington
Little Rissington
Great Rissington
Bourton-on-the-Water
Clapton-on-the-Hill
Sherborne
Icomb
Westcote
Nether Westcote
Upper Rissington
Idbury
Fifield
Foscot
Bledington
Bruern Abbey
Milton-under-Wychwood
Dunthrop
Heythrop
River Evenlode
River Windrush
Westcote Brook
Coombe Brook
Sars Brook

From Leamington Spa Station follow Route 41 / Lias Line under the tracks and over the River Learn and east towards Long Itchington. When you reach the Blue Lias Inn, leave the towpath and go **right** on the road over the bridge, leaving Route 41. Continue **straight** on this road, then at the T-junction turn **right** for Napton. Stay **right** at the fork. Pass through Napton and then turn **right** towards Priors Marston. At the T-junction turn **right** for Southam. Continue **straight** and use the subway to cross under the A423, then continue on Pound Way. Turn **left** on Pendicke St and then **right** on Oxford St. Turn **left** on Welsh Rd West towards Offchurch. At the B4452 junction turn **left** towards Harbury. After crossing over the train tracks turn slight **right** on Butt Ln. When the road ends at a junction turn **right** towards Chesterton, then keep **left**. Stay **straight** at the B4455, then at the B4087 junction turn **right** towards Whitnash (use the crossings and shared-use path). Keep **straight** on, then turn **left** on Old Warwick Rd to return to the station.

Bike shops

John Atkin's Cycles Ltd
CV31 2DN Tel: 01926 430211

Broadribb Cycles
CV32 5DT Tel: 01926 421428

Evans Cycles
CV32 4QY Tel: 01926 372090

Giant Bicycle Store
CV32 4PW Tel: 01926 460089

Trillion Cycles
CV31 3SF Tel: 01926 359632

Eat & drink

The Stag at Offchurch
CV33 9AQ Tel: 01926 425801

The Two Boats Inn
CV47 9QZ Tel: 01926 812640

Blue Lias Inn
CV47 8LD Tel: 01926 812249

The King's Head
CV47 8NG Tel: 01926 812202

The Folly
CV47 8NZ Tel: 01926 815185

Various in Southam

The Fox & Hen
CV47 2DN Tel: 01926 812498

The Crown Inn Harbury
CV33 9HE Tel: 01926 614995

The Heathcote Inn
CV31 3DG Tel: 01926 887000

The Windmill Inn
CV31 3DD Tel: 01926 831214

The Moorings at Myton
CV31 3NY Tel: 01926 425043

Various in Leamington Spa

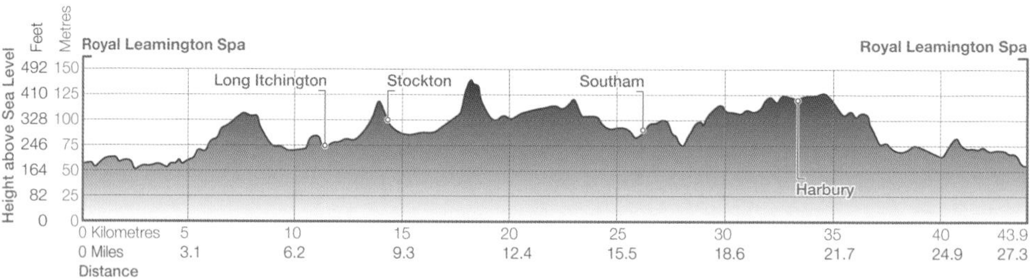

Royal Leamington Spa
Milverton
Lillington
Myton
Leamington Spa
Start
Sydenham
Heathcote
Whitnash
Bishop's Tachbrook
Tach Brook
Hunningham
River Leam
Offchurch
Radford Semele
Birdingbury
Debdale Wood
River Itchen
Long Itchington
Bascote
Bascote Heath
Long Itchington Wood
Ufton Wood
Ufton
Harbury
Chesterton
Chesterton Wood
Wiggerland Wood
Oakley Wood
Southam
Stockton
Leamington Hastings
Kites Hardwick
Hill
Broadwell
Calcutt Spinney
Napton on the Hill
Marston Doles
Ladbroke
Ladbroke Fox Covert
Bishop's Itchington
A452
A445
B4453
B4455
A423
A426
A425
B4087
B4452
B4451
B4100
M40
41
48

From Bicester North Station turn **left** on Buckingham Rd, 2nd exit **left** on North St, **left** on Sheep St and **left** on Bell Ln to join Route 51. Follow Route 51 all the way to Winslow. There turn **right** at the roundabout on Burleys Rd, leaving Route 51. Continue to North Marston, then turn hard **right** on Quainton Rd. Turn **right** towards Hogshaw, then **left** towards Quainton. When you reach Edgcott turn **left** towards Grendon Underwood and then go slight **right** towards Bicester and Marsh Gibbon. At the T-junction turn **right** towards Marsh Gibbon and Bicester. When Whales Ln ends turn **left** on West Edge. At the A41 **jink right left** to cross, then turn **right** on Weir Lane and **right** again to cross straight back over the A41. Continue **straight** and re-join Route 51 at Launton. Turn **right** on Sheep St, **right** on North St and 3rd exit **right** on Buckingham Rd to return to the station.

Bike shops

Broadribb Cycles Bicester
OX26 6JS Tel: 01869 253170

Sports Direct
OX26 6HY Tel: 03443 325004

Halfords
OX26 4JQ Tel: 01869 324723

Eat & drink

The Sow & Pigs
OX27 9BA Tel: 01869 277728

The Crown Inn
MK18 4EG Tel: 01296 730216

The Fountain
MK18 2NT Tel: 01296 730286

Phoenix
MK18 2PZ Tel: 01296 738864

Nag's Head
MK18 3HL Tel: 01296 712037

The Crown
MK18 3NJ Tel: 01296 670216

The Pilgrim
MK18 3PD Tel: 01296 670969

The Greyhound Inn
OX27 0HA Tel: 01869 277365

The Bull Inn
OX26 5DQ Tel: 01869 248158

Various in Bicester

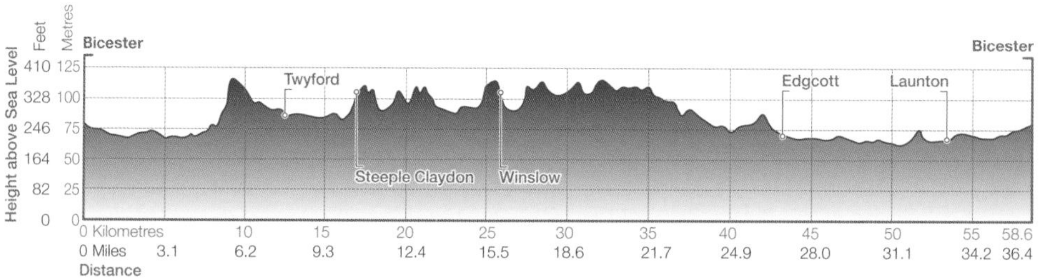

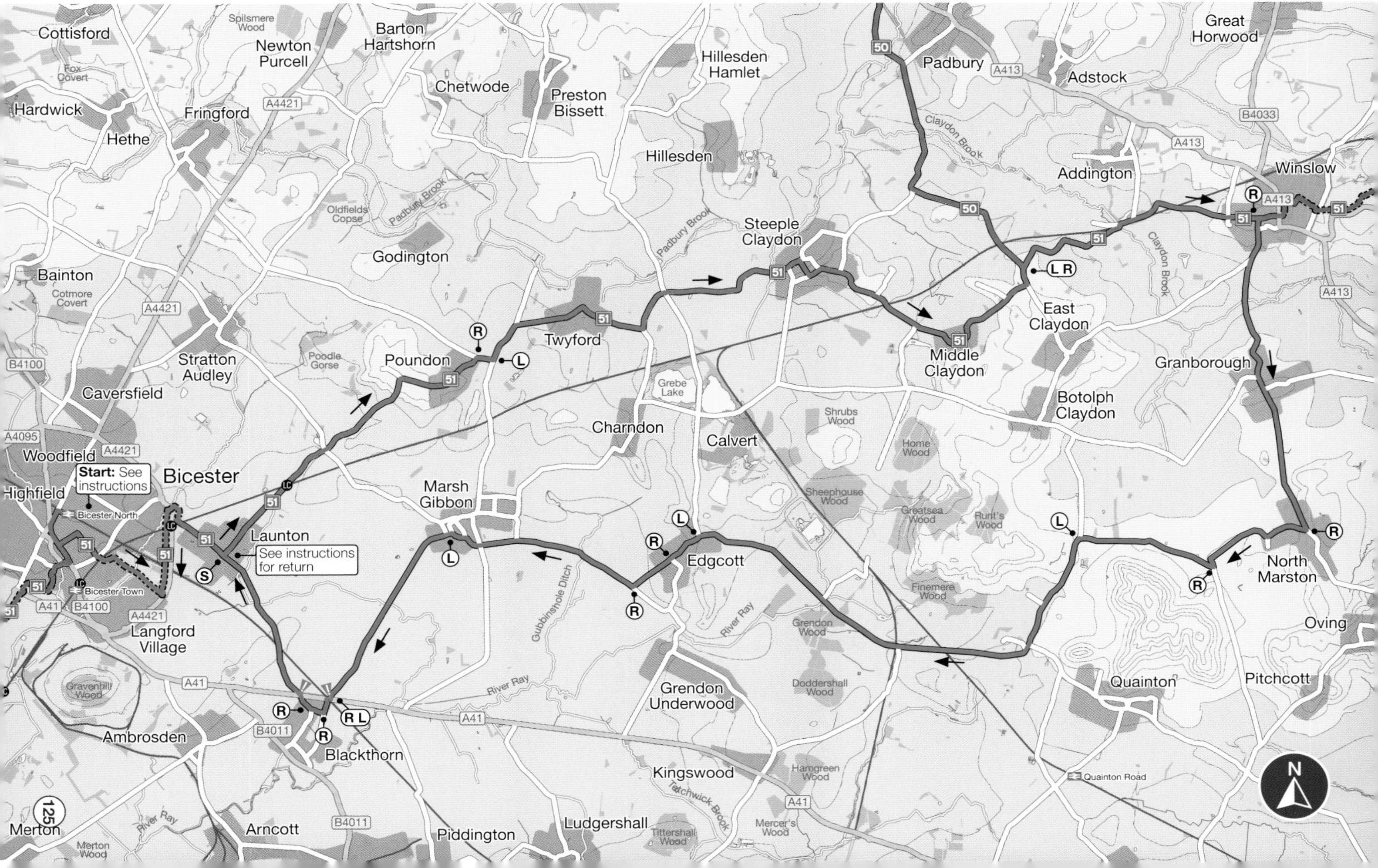

Cottisford
Fox Covert
Hardwick
Hethe
Fringford
Spilsmere Wood
Newton Purcell
A4421
Barton Hartshorn
Chetwode
Preston Bissett
Hillesden Hamlet
Hillesden
Padbury
A413
Adstock
Great Horwood
B4033
Claydon Brook
Addington
Winslow
Oldfields Copse
Padbury Brook
Godington
Steeple Claydon
East Claydon
Bainton
Cotmore Covert
Stratton Audley
Poodle Gorse
Poundon
Twyford
Middle Claydon
Granborough
B4100
Caversfield
Grebe Lake
Botolph Claydon
Shrubs Wood
Home Wood
A4095
Woodfield
Charndon
Calvert
Start: See instructions
Bicester
Highfield
Bicester North
Marsh Gibbon
Sheephouse Wood
Greatsea Wood
Runt's Wood
Launton
See instructions for return
Edgcott
North Marston
Bicester Town
A41
B4011
Langford Village
Gubbinshole Ditch
River Ray
Finemere Wood
Grendon Wood
Oving
Gravenhill Wood
Doddershall Wood
Quainton
Pitchcott
Grendon Underwood
Ambrosden
Blackthorn
Kingswood
Hamgreen Wood
Quainton Road
Tetchwick Brook
Merton
Merton Wood
Arncott
Piddington
Ludgershall
Tittershall Wood
Mercer's Wood
50
51
LC
R
L
S
N

From Tutbury & Hatton Station take the first **left** on Scropton Rd. At the A515 turn **right** and then first **left** on Main Rd. You will pass National Trust property Sudbury Hall and the Museum of Childhood. At the roundabout take the 1st exit **left** towards Doveridge. Turn **right** towards Somersal Herbert. Turn **right** towards Sudbury and Marston. At the T-junction turn **left**, then bear **right**. At the T-junction turn **right**. At the A515 **jink right left** to cross. Turn **left** on The Square. Turn **right** on an unsigned road, then turn **right** and **left** towards Longford. At the stop sign turn **right**. Turn **left** towards Hollington. Turn **right** at the Yew Tree Inn. Turn **right** towards Derby and then **left** on Mill Ln. At the T-junction go **left** then **right**. Stay **straight** and then turn **right** on Lodge Ln towards Kirk Langley, or stay straight to visit National Trust property Kedleston Hall. Turn **left** on Flagshaw Ln. Turn **right** on Radbourne Common, then take next **left**. Turn **right** towards Dalbury. Turn **left** off the road onto the Great Northern Greenway / Route 54 and then go **right** on the path to go south. Go **right** on Route 549 and follow back to the station. After the ride you have the option to visit Tutbury Castle. Pass the station and follow the road south. Turn right on Monk St, right on Castle St, and the entrance will be on your right.

Bike shops

Birkin's Cycles
DE65 5PT Tel: 07875 370296

Tutbury Cycles
DE13 9NG Tel: 01283 815441

Eat & drink

The Vernon Arms
DE6 5HS Tel: 01283 585329

The Coach House Tea Room at Sudbury Hall
DE6 5HT Tel: 01283 585337

Cavendish Arms
DE6 5JR Tel: 01889 564107

The Lighthouse
DE6 5AA Tel: 01335 330658

The Ostrich Inn
DE6 3AH Tel: 01335 330440

The Red Lion
DE6 3AG Tel: 01335 360138

Yew Tree Inn
DE6 3AE Tel: 01335 360433

Old Kitchen Restaurant at Kedleston Hall
DE22 5JH Tel: 01332 842191

The Blue Bell Inn
DE6 4LW Tel: 01332 824423

The Castle Hotel
DE65 5DW Tel: 01283 813396

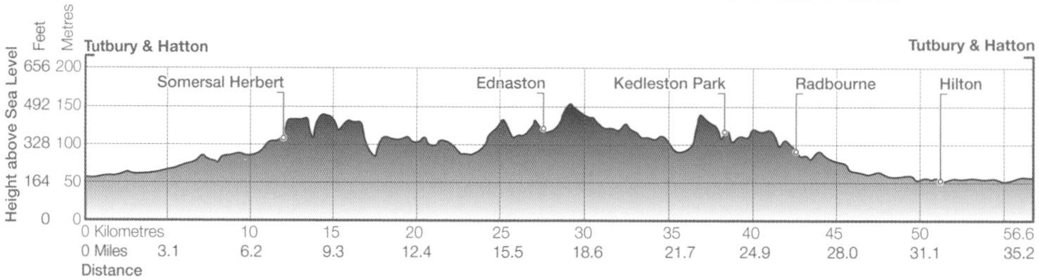

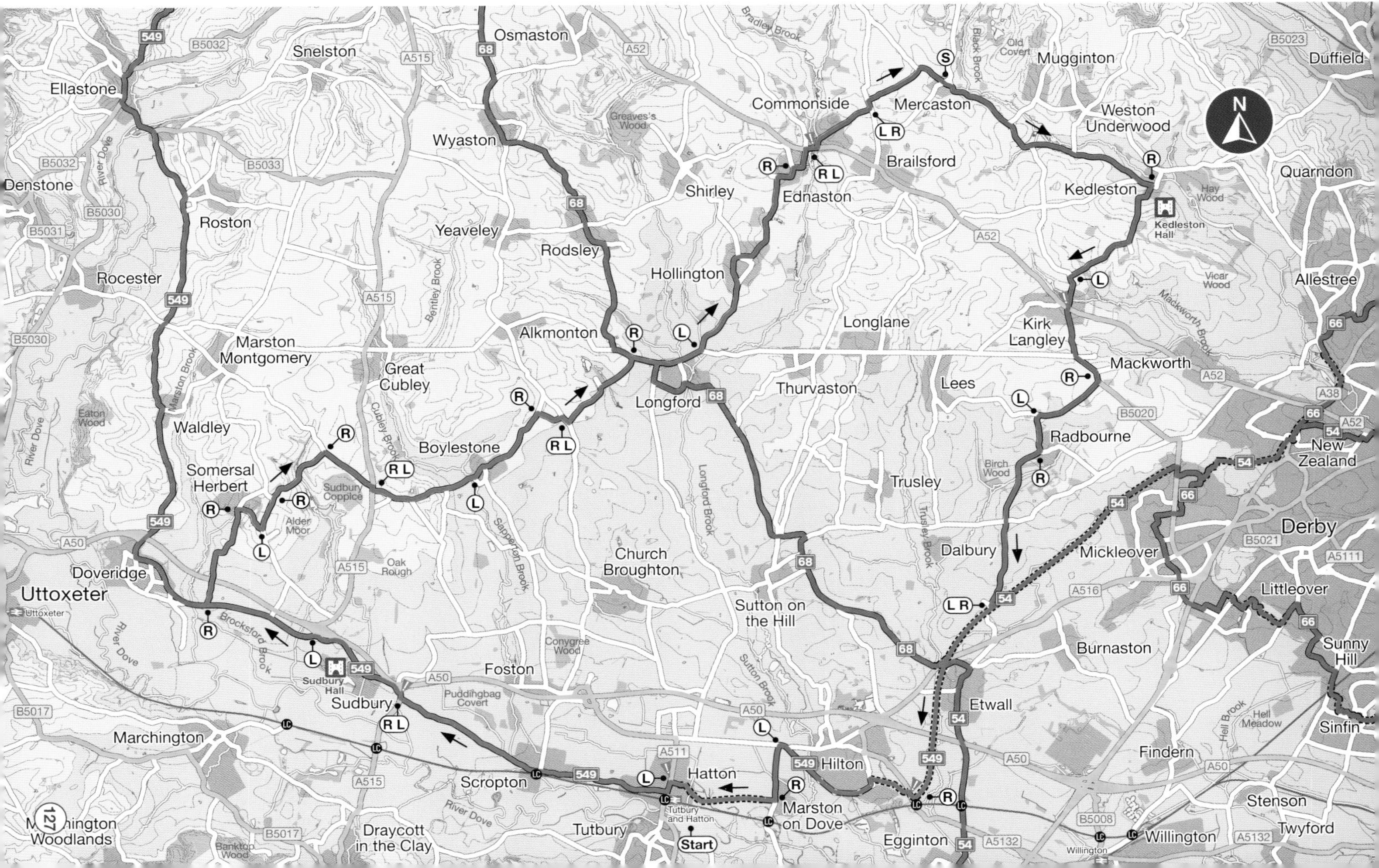
Ellastone
Snelston
Osmaston
Commonside
Mercaston
Mugginton
Duffield
Weston
Underwood
Quarndon
Wyaston
Brailsford
Denstone
Roston
Shirley
Ednaston
Kedleston
Kedleston Hall
Yeaveley
Rodsley
Rocester
Hollington
Allestree
Longlane
Kirk
Langley
Marston
Montgomery
Alkmonton
Great
Cubley
Mackworth
Lees
Thurvaston
Longford
Waldley
Boylestone
Radbourne
Somersal
Herbert
Sudbury Coppice
Alder Moor
Trusley
New
Zealand
Derby
Church
Broughton
Dalbury
Mickleover
Doveridge
Uttoxeter
Sutton on
the Hill
Littleover
Burnaston
Sunny
Hill
Sudbury Hall
Foston
Etwall
Sudbury
Sinfin
Marchington
Hilton
Findern
Scropton
Hatton
Marston
on Dove
Stenson
Draycott
in the Clay
Tutbury
Start
Egginton
Willington
Twyford
Woodlands
Tutbury and Hatton
Uttoxeter
Willington
Greaves's Wood
Old Covert
Hay Wood
Vicar Wood
Birch Wood
Eaton Wood
Oak Rough
Conygree Wood
Puddihgbag Covert
Hell Meadow
Banktop Wood
Bradley Brook
Black Brook
Bentley Brook
Mackworth Brook
Marston Brook
Cubley Brook
Sapperton Brook
Longford Brook
Trusley Brook
Sutton Brook
Brocksford Brook
Hell Brook
River Dove
549
68
54
66
A52
A515
A50
A511
A38
A516
A5111
A5132
B5032
B5033
B5030
B5031
B5017
B5020
B5021
B5023
B5008
N
S
R
L
L R
R L
LC

From Oakham Station follow the tourist information sign **left** and then turn **right** across the tracks on Cold Overton Rd / Route 63. Follow the road to Knossington and turn **right** towards Somerby. Turn **left** towards Somerby – the road becomes Route 64. After Pickwell turn **left** towards Little Dalby. Continue to follow Route 64. Just outside Melton Mowbray turn **right** onto the lane with barriers, leaving Route 64 (or stay straight to go into the town). At the T-junction turn **right** and then first **left**. Continue **straight** on. At Stapleford Rd turn **right** towards Whissendine and then **left** towards Teigh. Stay **right** towards Teigh. At the T-junction turn **right**. Turn **right** on Langham Rd. Turn **right** towards Melton Mowbray then go **left** to join the shared-use path along the A606. Follow the path until it ends and rejoin the road to continue **straight** on back to the station.

To visit Rutland Water Nature Reserve, don't turn left into the station but continue straight after crossing the tracks. Turn right on New St, then left at the mini roundabout, joining route 63. At Catmos St join the shared-use path left and follow Route 63 / Stamford Rd. Go straight at the roundabout. When you see the sign for the Bird Watching Centre leave the path and turn right on the road. Take the next right on Church Road. Pass through Egleton and then turn left on Hambleton Rd.

Bike shops

Oakham Cycle Centre	LE15 6NR	Tel: 01572 757058
Halfords	LE13 1JE	Tel: 01664 566923
Cycle Craft Ltd	LE14 2SQ	Tel: 01664 490443
Windmill Wheels	LE14 2BU	Tel: 01572 787720
Rutland Cycling Whitwell	LE15 8BL	Tel: 01780 460705

Eat & drink

The Fox & Hounds	LE15 8LY	Tel: 01664 452129
The Stilton Cheese Inn	LE14 2QB	Tel: 01664 454394
The Royal Oak	LE14 2ET	Tel: 01664 563147
Various in Melton Mowbray		
The Black Bull Inn	LE15 7PW	Tel: 01572 767677
The Wheatsheaf	LE15 7HY	Tel: 01572 869105
The Noel Arms	LE15 7HU	Tel: 01572 779804
The Grainstore	LE15 6RA	Tel: 01572 770065
The Railway Inn	LE15 6QU	Tel: 01572 722015
Various in Oakham		

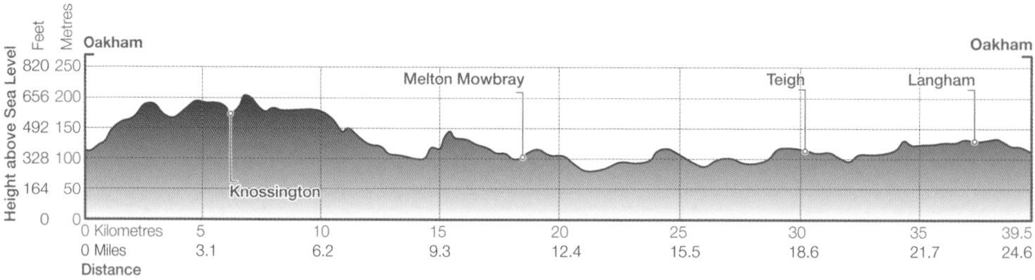

Melton Mowbray
Burton Lazars
Stapleford
Cottage Plantation
Edmondthorpe
Woodwell Head
Teigh
Market Overton
Barrow
Ashwell
Whissendine
Whissendine Brook
Laxton's Covert
Long Spinney
Burton Brook
River Eye
Great Dalby
Little Dalby
Gartree Hill Covert
Leesthorpe
Landfield Spinney
Debdale Spinney
Burrough Hill Covert
Thorpe Satchville
Pickwell
Burrough on the Hill
Somerby
Cold Overton
Cold Overton Park Wood
Knossington
Owston
Twyford
John O'Gaunt
Marefield
Gaddesby Brook
Langham
Barleythorpe
Oakham
Start: See instructions
Burley
Burley Wood
Brick Kiln Covert
Dog Kennel Spinney
A606
A607
B6047
B640
B641
A6003
B668
63
64
N

From Market Harborough Station head north on Route 64 / Great Bowden Rd. In Great Bowden stay **straight** on Sutton Rd, then bear **right** then **left** onto Welham Ln. Follow the route to Welham. After the church turn **right** towards Weston, leaving Route 64. At the B664 turn **left**. Turn **right** on Medbourne Rd. Stay **left** into Ashley. At the fork go **right** towards East Carlton. At the A427 go **left** then **right** towards Pipewell. Stay **left** towards Pipewell. Turn **right** at the T-junction and continue towards Desborough. After crossing the tracks turn **right** and then **left** at the roundabout. Turn **right** on High St and then **jink right left** to cross the B576. Turn **left** on Arthingworth Rd. In Arthingworth turn **right** on Oxendon Rd and follow as it becomes a dirt road. Turn **right** on shared-use path Route 6 and follow back to Market Harborough. Turn **right** on Route 64 and follow back to the station.

Bike shops

Mega Bike UK
LE16 7DT Tel: 07710 409420

George Halls' Cycle Centre
LE16 9HE Tel: 01858 465507

Halfords
LE16 7QE Tel: 01858 412130

Wizbiz
NN18 9NX Tel: 01536 761119

Brampton Valley Cycle Surgery Mobile Repair
LE16 8JZ Tel: 07703 755699

Eat & drink

Shoulder of Mutton
LE16 7EU Tel: 01858 465142

The Old Red Lion
LE16 7UJ Tel: 01858 565253

The Wheel & Compass
LE16 8HZ Tel: 01858 565864

The George
LE16 8HF Tel: 01858 565411

The Red Lion Middleton
LE16 8YX Tel: 01536 771034

The George
NN14 2NB Tel: 01536 760271

The Bull's Head
LE16 8JZ Tel: 01858 525637

The George at Great Oxendon
LE16 8NA Tel: 01858 452286

The Oat Hill
LE16 8AN Tel: 01858 462324

Various in Market Harborough

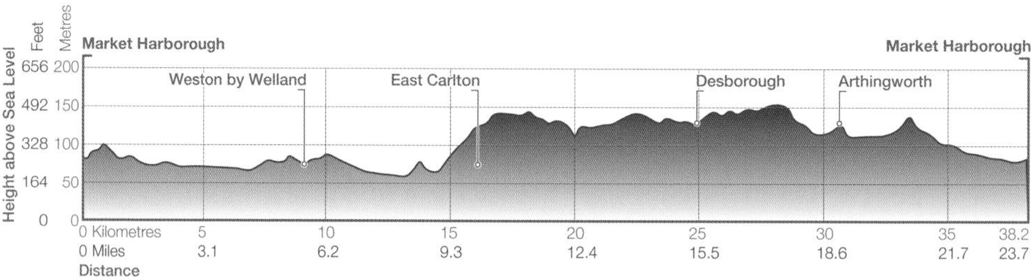

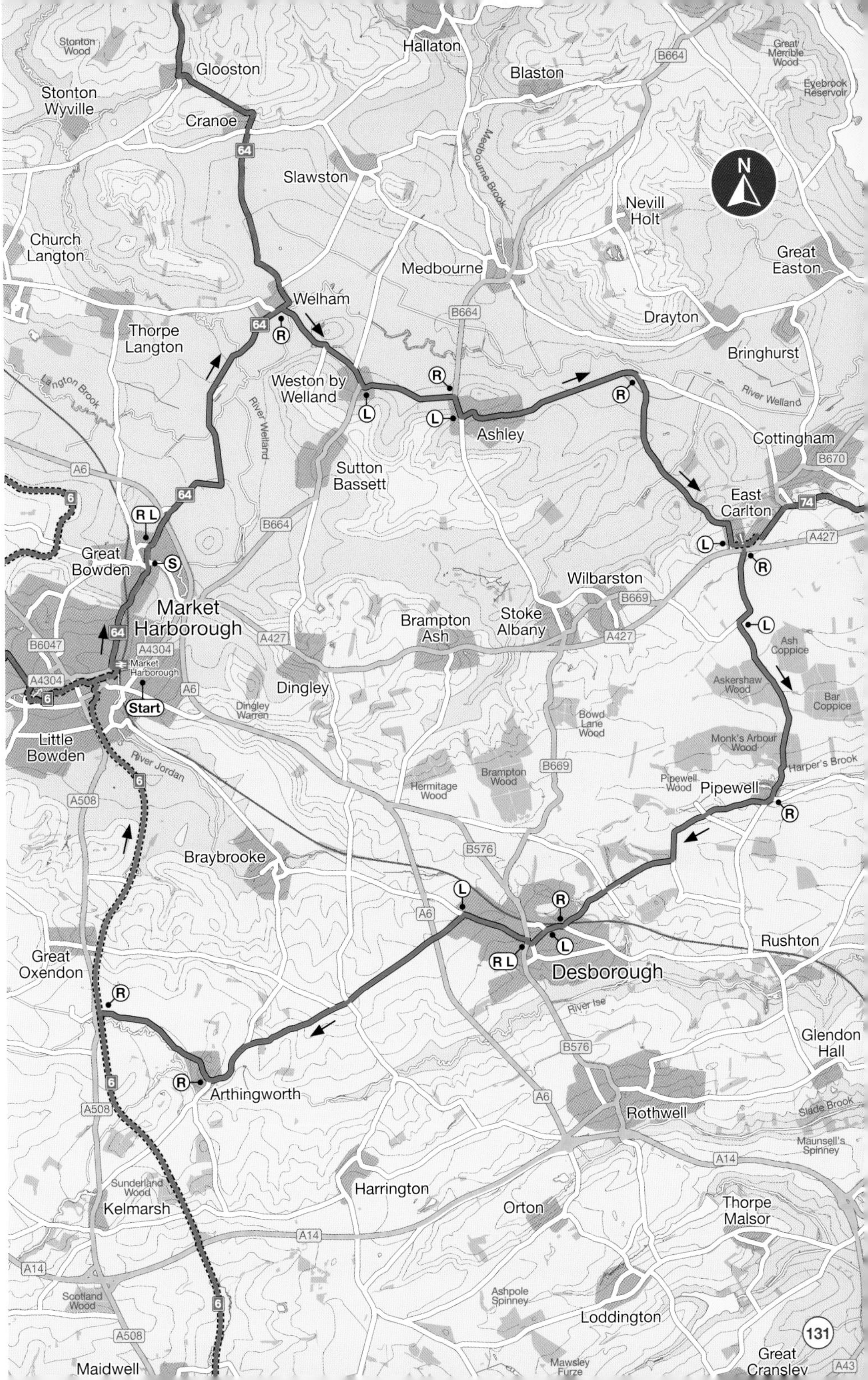
Stonton Wood
Glooston
Hallaton
Blaston
B664
Great Merrible Wood
Eyebrook Reservoir
Stonton Wyville
Cranoe
64
Slawston
Medbourne Brook
N
Nevill Holt
Church Langton
Medbourne
Great Easton
Welham
B664
Drayton
Thorpe Langton
64
R
Bringhurst
Weston by Welland
R
R
Langton Brook
L
L
Ashley
River Welland
River Welland
Cottingham
B670
A6
Sutton Bassett
64
East Carlton
74
6
R L
B664
L
A427
R
Great Bowden
S
Wilbarston
B669
Market Harborough
Brampton Ash
Stoke Albany
L
64
A427
A427
B6047
A4304
Ash Coppice
Market Harborough
A4304
A6
Askershaw Wood
Dingley
Bar Coppice
6
Start
Dingley Warren
Bowd Lane Wood
Little Bowden
Monk's Arbour Wood
River Jordan
Harper's Brook
Brampton Wood
B669
Pipewell Wood
Pipewell
Hermitage Wood
6
A508
R
B576
Braybrooke
L
R
A6
L
Rushton
R L
Desborough
Great Oxendon
R
River Ise
Glendon Hall
B576
R
Arthingworth
6
A6
A508
Rothwell
Slade Brook
Maunsell's Spinney
A14
Sunderland Wood
Harrington
Kelmarsh
Orton
Thorpe Malsor
A14
A14
Scotland Wood
Ashpole Spinney
6
Loddington
A508
Maidwell
Mawsley Furze
Great Cransley
A43

From Wellington Station turn **left** and curve **right** on Market St, then turn **right** at the lights. Take the **2nd exit** at the roundabout on Route 81. At Wrockwardine go **right**, **left**, **left**, **left** to follow Route 81. Turn **right** on Bluebell Ln. Turn **left** and **left** towards Withington. Stay **left** towards Upton Magna. Turn **right** and **right** onto Route 45 towards Whitchurch. Follow Route 45 to Moreton Corbet. Here you can visit the ruins of Moreton Corbet Castle. At Moreton View turn **right** and follow the road through Stanton upon Hine Heath, leaving Route 45. Carefully cross the A53 and continue towards Market Drayton and Great Bolas. At the fork go **left**. At the A442 turn **left** and then carefully take first **right**. At the T-junction turn **right**. Turn **right** at the next T-junction towards Waters Upton. Turn **left** towards Meeson. Stay **left** and **left** towards Cherrington. Turn **right** towards Cherrington. Stay **right** in Kynnersley. Stay **left** in Preston upon the Weald Moors, and then turn **right** towards Horton and Hadley. At the roundabout take the **2nd exit** and then first **right** on Hadley Park Rd. At Leegate Ave cross to the path and go **right** to follow Route 81. When the path ends continue **straight** on Sutherland Rd, then **right** and immediately **left** at the roundabout. Follow Victoria Rd straight through two roundabouts, then turn **right** on Market St back to the station.

To visit National Trust property Sunnycroft, turn right (south) on Tan Bank. At Victoria Rd cross, go around metal fence and continue straight. Turn left on Roseway. Turn right on Rosthwaite. Go right and right onto the B5061 and the entrance will be on your right.

Bike shops

Perry's Cycles
TF1 1HJ Tel: 01952 244802

Plush Hill Cycles
TF3 5BZ Tel: 01952 763274

Eat & drink

Grove Inn
TF6 5EN
Tel: 01952 740814

Hare & Hounds
SY4 4PY
Tel: 01743 709446

Haughmond
SY4 4TZ
Tel: 01743 709918

The Elephant & Castle
SY4 4HP
Tel: 01939 250205

Stanton Arms
SY4 4LR
Tel: 01939 250221

The Tiddly
TF6 6RL
Tel: 01939 250300

The Queens at Horton
TF6 6DW
Tel: 01952 228828

Malt Shovel Inn
TF1 6QG
Tel: 01952 242963

The Plough Inn
TF1 3AW
Tel: 01952 255981

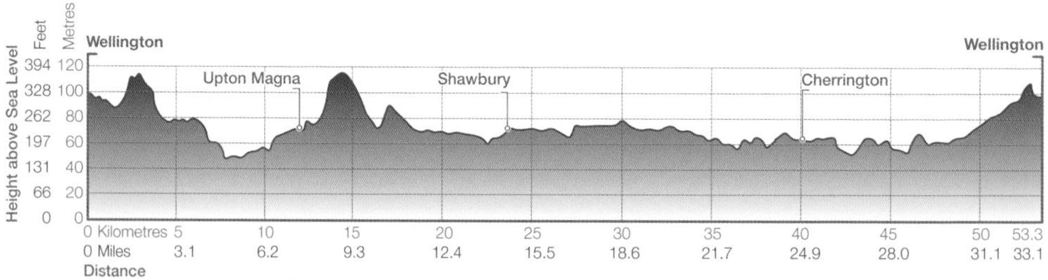

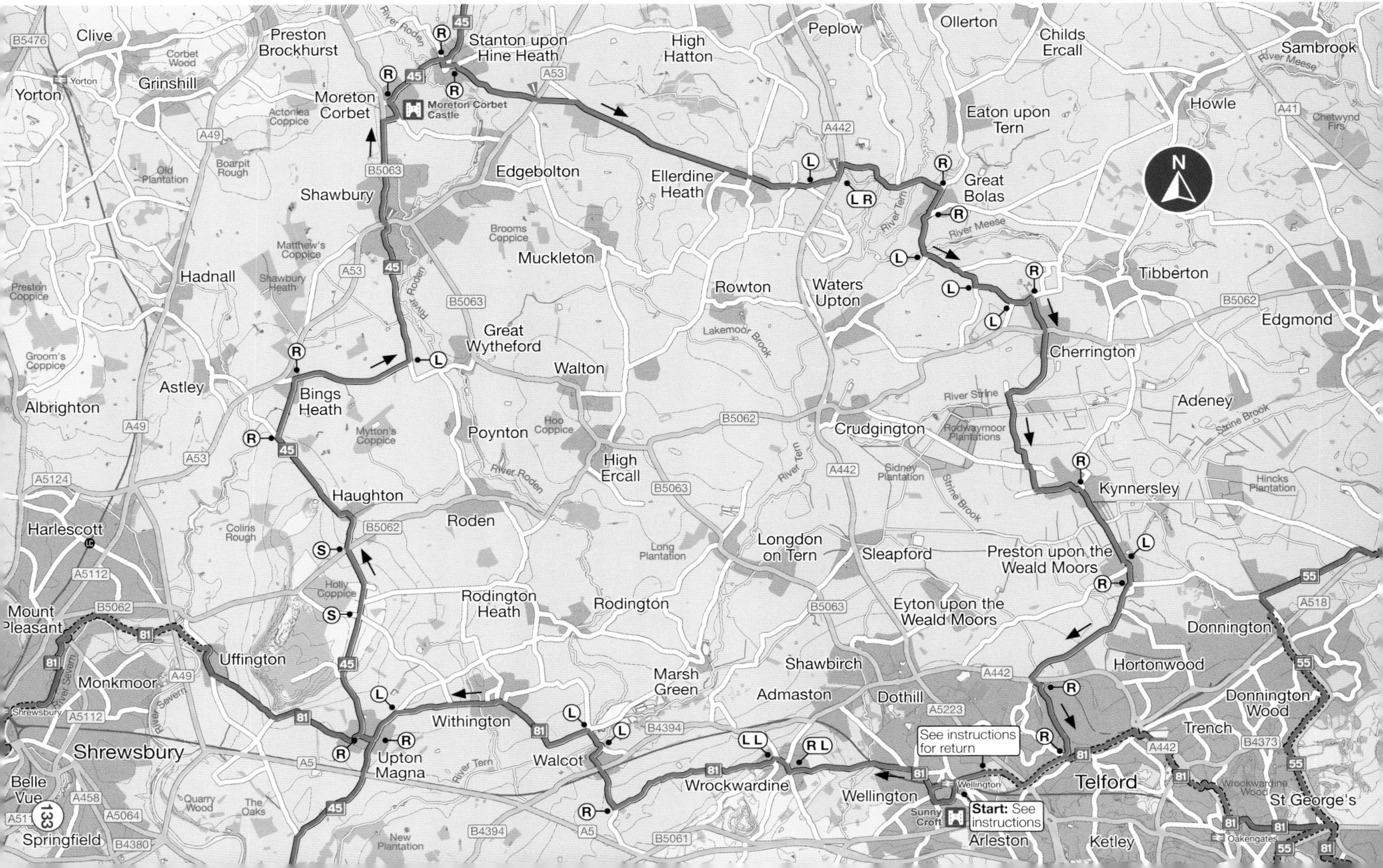
Start: See instructions
See instructions for return
Telford
Wellington
Shrewsbury
Sambrook
Howle
Edgmond
Tibberton
Adeney
Kynnersley
Donnington
Donnington Wood
St George's
Trench
Hortonwood
Ketley
Arleston
Sunny Croft
Childs Ercall
Eaton upon Tern
Great Bolas
Cherrington
Ollerton
Peplow
Waters Upton
Crudgington
Preston upon the Weald Moors
Eyton upon the Weald Moors
Sleapford
Dothill
Shawbirch
Admaston
Longdon on Tern
Rowton
High Hatton
Ellerdine Heath
Edgebolton
Muckleton
Walton
High Ercall
Rodington
Marsh Green
Wrockwardine
Walcot
Withington
Rodington Heath
Roden
Poynton
Great Wytheford
Stanton upon Hine Heath
Moreton Corbet Castle
Moreton Corbet
Preston Brockhurst
Shawbury
Bings Heath
Haughton
Upton Magna
Uffington
Hadnall
Astley
Grinshill
Clive
Yorton
Albrighton
Harlescott
Mount Pleasant
Monkmoor
Belle Vue
Springfield
River Meese
River Tern
River Roden
River Strine
Strine Brook
River Severn
Lakemoor Brook
Chetwynd Firs
Hincks Plantation
Rodwaymoor Plantations
Sidney Plantation
Long Plantation
Brooms Coppice
Hoo Coppice
Mytton's Coppice
Holly Coppice
Matthew's Coppice
Shawbury Heath
Actonlea Coppice
Boarpit Rough
Corbet Wood
Old Plantation
Groom's Coppice
Preston Coppice
Colins Rough
New Plantation
The Oaks
Quarry Wood
Wrockwardine Wood
Oakengates
A41
A442
A518
A53
A49
A5
A5064
A5112
A5124
A458
A5223
A511
B5062
B5063
B5061
B4394
B4373
B4380
B5476
55
81
45

Stafford & Stone

31.1 miles / 50.5 km

From Stafford Station go **left**, **right** at the roundabout, then **left** on South St. Join the Route 5 path along the river. Follow the path north until it ends at the A513, then continue north on Marston Ln. At the fork go **right** towards Sandon. Turn **left** towards Stone. Turn **right** on the path along the A34. Turn **right** towards Aston Marina. Join the towpath going under the bridge. Follow the towpath, then after passing The Star pub exit the towpath at the next bridge and go **left** on Newcastle St. Pass under the tracks and turn **left** on Trent Rd. At the T-junction carefully **jink left right** to cross the busy road. After Yarnfield turn **right** towards Swynnerton, then **left** towards Eccleshall. At the A519 turn **left** towards Eccleshall. Turn **right** at the roundabout. Turn **left** towards Garmelow. Turn **left** on Park Ln, then next **left**. Stay **straight** through Woodseaves and at the B5405 **jink left right** to continue. At the third crossroads turn **right** towards Gnosall. Turn **right** on Audmore Rd. Stay **straight** at the roundabout then turn **left** onto the Route 55 path – follow back to Stafford. Immediately after you cross over the train tracks turn hard **right** on Railway St and follow to the station.

Bike shops

Henry Burton Cycles
ST16 2AJ Tel: 01785 242346

Specialized Concept Store
ST16 2LZ Tel: 01785 220060

Halfords
ST16 2DL Tel: 01785 279810

The Velo Store
ST15 0SR Tel: 01785 818055

The Bike Shack
ST15 8DA Tel: 01785 816924

Eat & drink

The Star
ST15 8QW Tel: 01785 813096

The Wayfarer
ST15 0NB Tel: 01785 811023

The Labour in Vain
ST15 0NJ Tel: 01785 760072

Bell Inn
ST21 6BZ Tel: 01785 850378

The Royal Oak
ST21 6BW Tel: 01785 859065

The Cock Inn
ST20 0NP Tel: 01785 284343

The Horns Inn
ST20 0EX Tel: 01785 747304

George & the Dragon
ST20 0EX Tel: 01785 822905

The Railway Inn
ST16 2EB Tel: 01785 601237

Various in Stafford

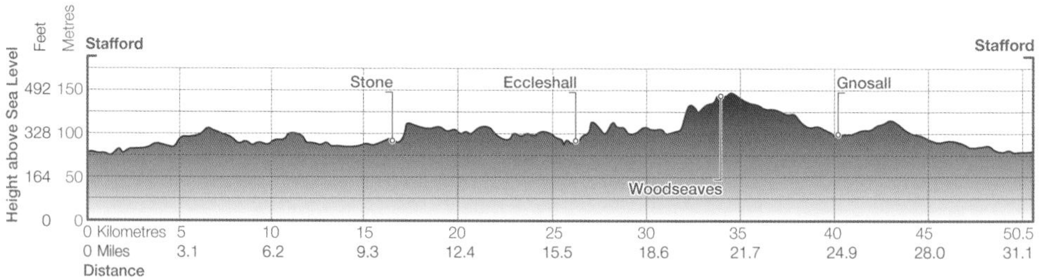

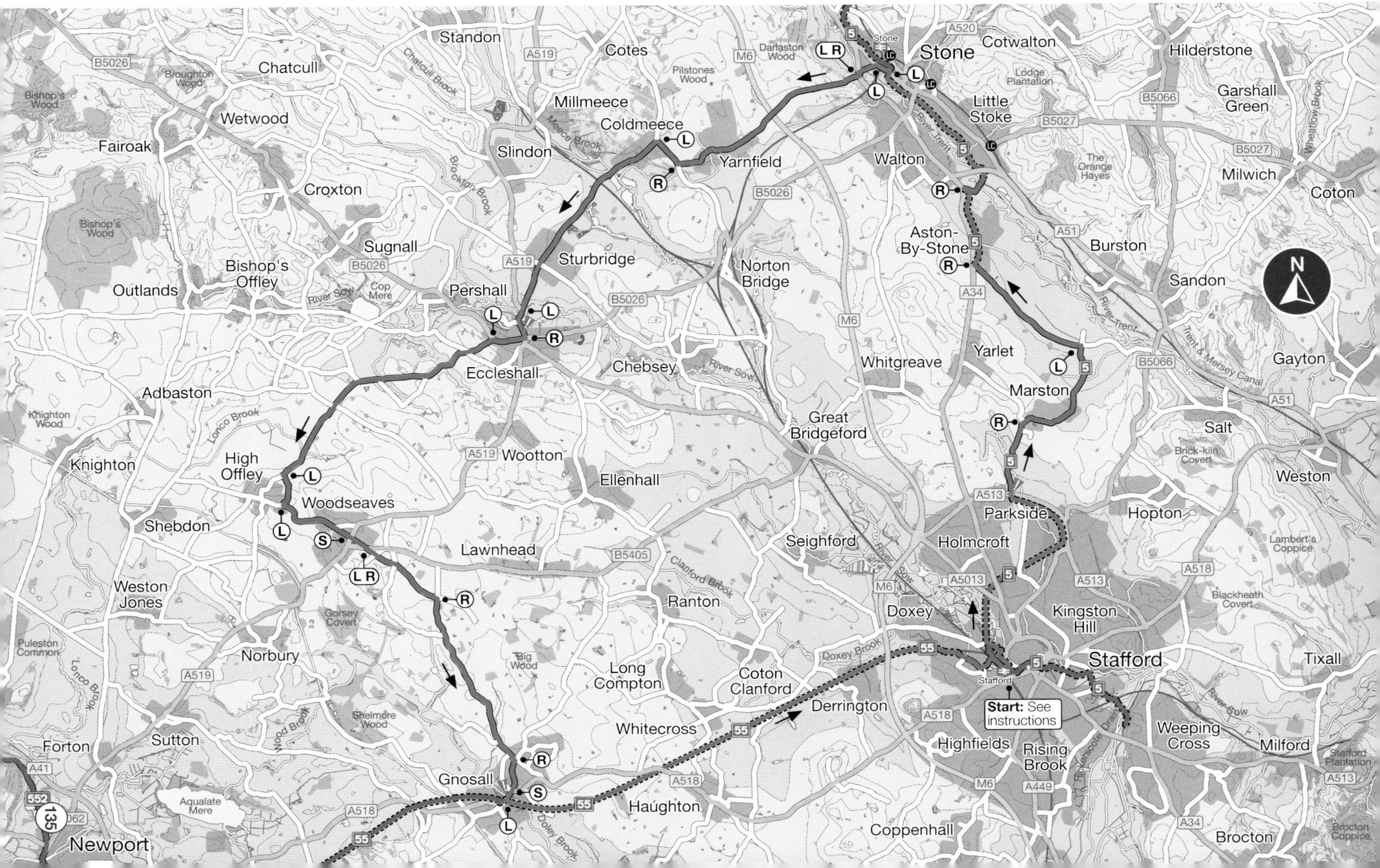
Stone
Cotwalton
Hilderstone
Garshall Green
Little Stoke
Walton
Milwich
Coton
The Orange Hayes
Lodge Plantation
Aston-By-Stone
Burston
Sandon
Yarlet
Marston
Gayton
Whitgreave
Salt
Brick-kiln Covert
Weston
Great Bridgeford
Norton Bridge
Parkside
Hopton
Holmcroft
Lambert's Coppice
Seighford
Doxey
Kingston Hill
Blackheath Covert
Stafford
Tixall
Start: See instructions
Weeping Cross
Milford
Stafford Plantation
Highfields
Rising Brook
Brocton
Brocton Coppice
Coppenhall
Derrington
Coton Clanford
Long Compton
Whitecross
Haughton
Ranton
Ellenhall
Lawnhead
Chebsey
Wootton
Eccleshall
Pershall
Sturbridge
Yarnfield
Coldmeece
Millmeece
Cotes
Pilstones Wood
Darlaston Wood
Standon
Slindon
Chatcull
Broughton Wood
Wetwood
Fairoak
Bishop's Wood
Croxton
Sugnall
Bishop's Offley
Cop Mere
Outlands
Adbaston
Knighton Wood
Knighton
High Offley
Woodseaves
Shebdon
Weston Jones
Gorsey Covert
Norbury
Big Wood
Puleston Common
Shelmore Wood
Forton
Sutton
Aqualate Mere
Gnosall
Newport
River Trent
River Sow
Trent & Mersey Canal
Wheatlow Brook
Chatcull Brook
Meece Brook
Brockton Brook
Lonco Brook
Clanford Brook
Doxey Brook
Wood Brook
Doley Brook
Rickerscote Drain
A520
A519
A51
A34
A513
A5013
A518
A449
A41
B5026
B5027
B5066
B5405
M6
5
55
552
N

From Gobowen Station go **left** on Route 31 / 455. Turn **right** towards Hengoed. Turn **left** towards Pentre then **right**. Turn **left** at the roundabout, then **right**. Turn **right** on Gobowen Rd using the shared-use path. Turn **left** on Black Gate St. Turn **left** on the B4579. Turn **right** towards the recycling centre using the shared-use path. Carefully cross the A483. Continue south towards Woolston. Turn **left** towards Sandford and West Felton then stay **left**. Cross over the A5. Turn **right** on Oak Farm Ln. Turn **left** towards Eardiston. Keep following the signs towards Eardiston. Turn **left** towards Stanwardine. Turn **right** at the T-junction, then next **left**. Turn **left** towards Weston Lullingfields. Stay **left** at the fork and pass through Bagley, Lower Hordley and Hordley. Go **right** at the canal parking sign. Turn **left** then **right** at the A495. Turn **left** at the T-junction then keep **right** at the gate. Turn **left** towards Hindford. Turn **right** towards Iron Mills on Route 31 / 455. Turn **left** towards Gobowen. Turn **right** on the B5009. Turn **left** at the Post Office and return to the station.

Bike shops

BikeWorks
SY11 1HL Tel: 01691 654407

Mike's Bikes
SY11 1AW Tel: 01691 680004

Stuart Barkley Cycles
SY11 2NR Tel: 01691 658705

Halfords
SY11 2RL Tel: 01691 677920

Eat & drink

Various in Oswestry

The Navigation Inn
SY10 8JB Tel: 01691 672958

The Admiral Duncan
SY4 2AY Tel: 01939 262521

The Jack Mytton Inn
SY11 4NL Tel: 01691 679861

Cross Foxes
SY11 3JR Tel: 01691 679474

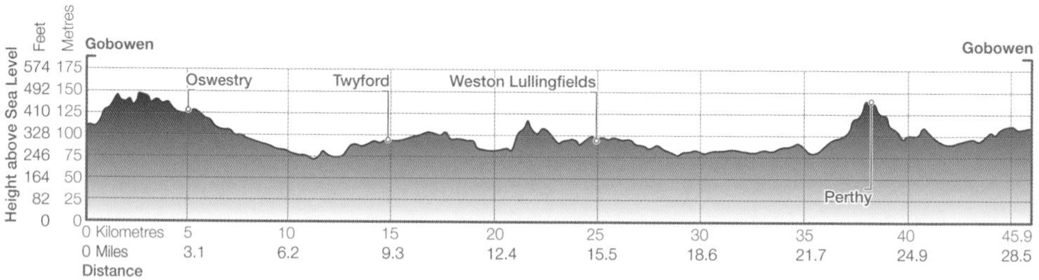

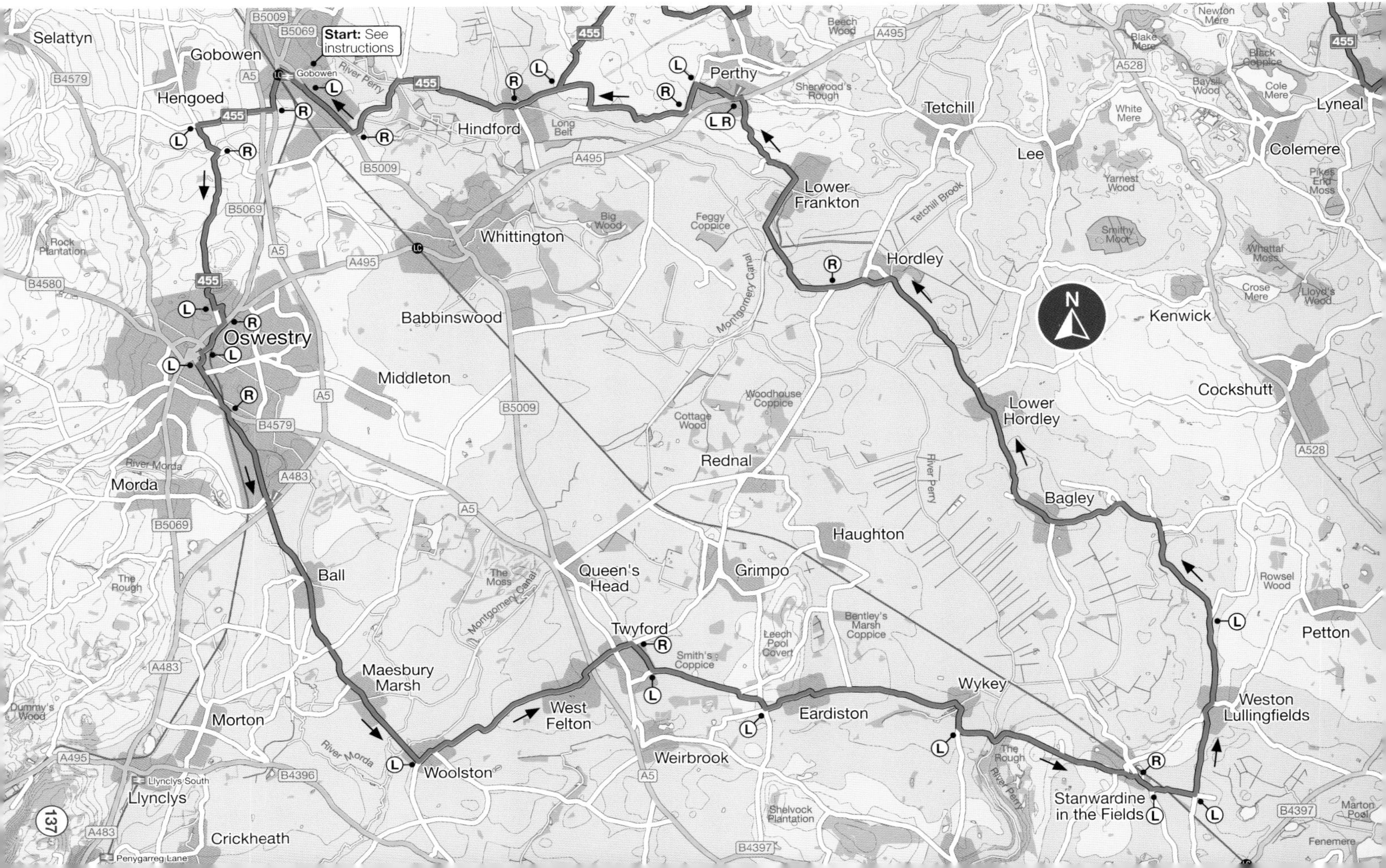
Start: See instructions
Selattyn
Gobowen
Hengoed
Hindford
Perthy
Tetchill
Lee
Lyneal
Colemere
Oswestry
Babbinswood
Whittington
Middleton
Lower Frankton
Hordley
Kenwick
Cockshutt
Lower Hordley
Bagley
Rednal
Haughton
Morda
Ball
Queen's Head
Grimpo
Twyford
Maesbury Marsh
West Felton
Eardiston
Wykey
Weston Lullingfields
Petton
Morton
Woolston
Weirbrook
Stanwardine in the Fields
Llynclys
Crickheath
Montgomery Canal
River Perry
River Morda
Tetchill Brook

From Whitchurch Station head **straight** on Wayland Rd / Route 45. Follow Route 45 through Alkington, Welsh End and Prees. Turn **left** at the B5065 towards Whitchurch, leaving Route 45. Turn **right** towards Calverhall. Turn **left** towards Ightfield. Turn **right** and then stay **left** towards Burleydam. Turn **right** towards Wilkesley then next **left**. Turn **left** towards Wrenbury. After passing the train station turn **left** and **left** on New Rd to rejoin Route 45 back to Whitchurch. Turn **left** under the railway. Turn **left** on Ossmere Ln. Turn **left** towards Whitchurch. Turn **left** on Salisbury Rd then **right**. Turn **left** on Station Rd to return to the station.

Bike shops

Wheelbase
SY13 1DP Tel: 01948 663323

Eat & drink

Bull & Dog
SY13 2RA Tel: 01948 880559

The Old Jack Inn
SY13 4PA Tel: 01948 890235

The Combermere Arms
SY13 4AT Tel: 01948 871223

The Bhurtpore Inn
CW5 8DQ Tel: 01270 780917

The Dusty Miller
CW5 8HG Tel: 01270 780537

The Cotton Arms
CW5 8HG Tel: 01270 780377

Wheatsheaf
SY13 1AD Tel: 01948 666653

Various in Whitchurch

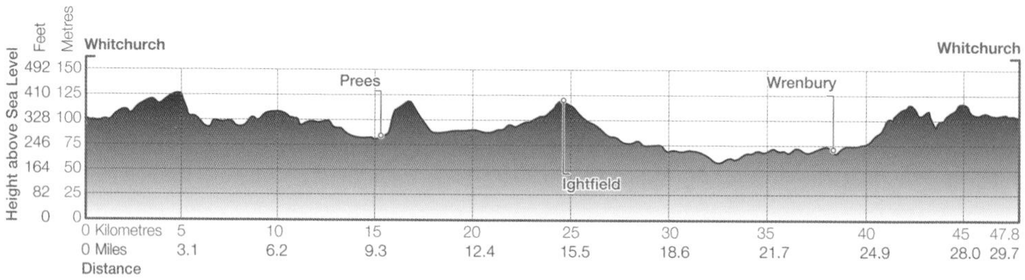

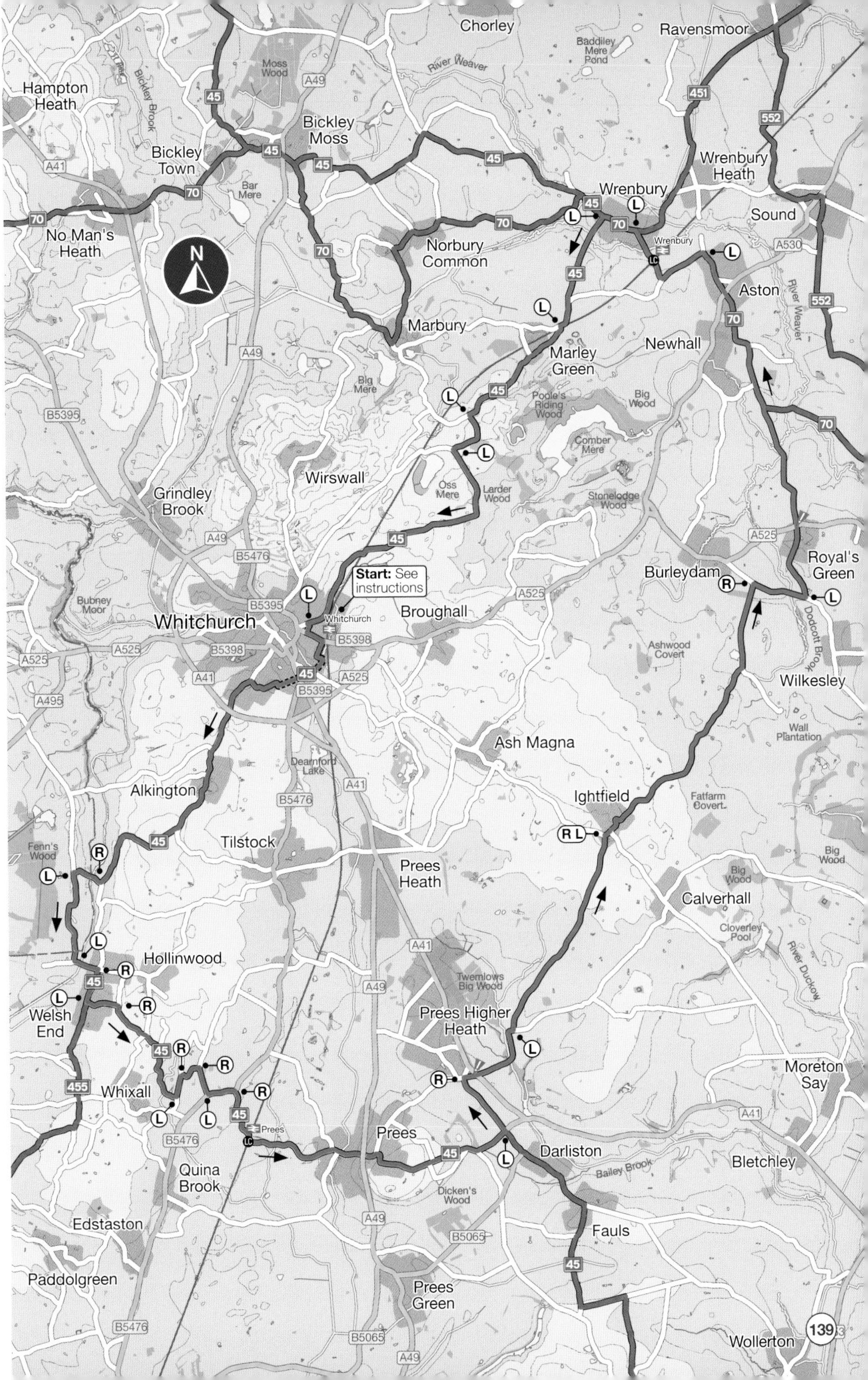
Chorley
Ravensmoor
Baddiley Mere Pond
River Weaver
Moss Wood
Hampton Heath
Bickley Brook
Bickley Moss
Bickley Town
Bar Mere
Wrenbury Heath
Wrenbury
Sound
No Man's Heath
Norbury Common
Aston
Marbury
Newhall
Marley Green
Big Mere
Poole's Riding Wood
Big Wood
Comber Mere
Wirswall
Grindley Brook
Oss Mere
Larder Wood
Stonelodge Wood
Royal's Green
Burleydam
Start: See instructions
Whitchurch
Broughall
Bubney Moor
Dodcott Brook
Wilkesley
Ashwood Covert
Ash Magna
Wall Plantation
Dearnford Lake
Alkington
Ightfield
Fatfarm Covert
Tilstock
Fenn's Wood
Prees Heath
Big Wood
Calverhall
Cloverley Pool
Hollinwood
Twemlows Big Wood
River Duckow
Welsh End
Prees Higher Heath
Moreton Say
Whixall
Prees
Darliston
Bailey Brook
Bletchley
Quina Brook
Dicken's Wood
Edstaston
Fauls
Paddolgreen
Prees Green
Wollerton

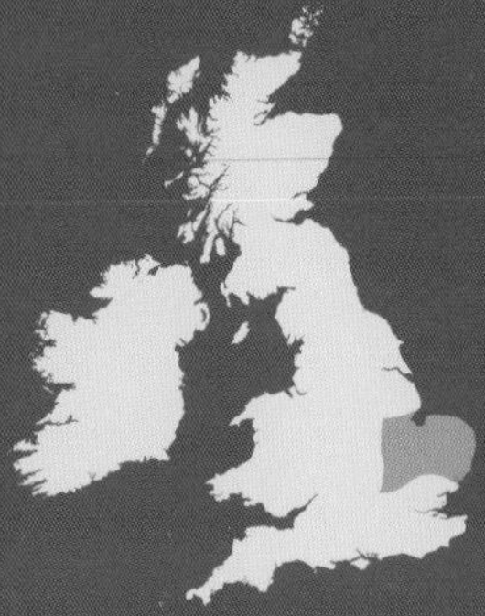

East of England

N
Lincoln
Nottingham
10
11
12
13
Leicester
Peterborough
Corby
King's Lynn
Norwich
07
05
06
04
09
01
02
03
Northampton
Cambridge
Bedford
Ipswich
08
Luton
Chelmsford
Oxford
Southend-on-Sea
London
Reading
Canterbury
Aldershot
Maidstone
Ashford
Crawley
Folkestone
Southampton
Brighton
Portsmouth
Eastbourne

01 Lanes East of Bury St Edmunds

34.9 miles / 52.6 km

From Bury St Edmunds Station turn **right** on the A1101, go **straight** at the roundabout, then turn **left** on Mustow St. Turn **right** onto the shared-use path in the park. Follow Route 51 all the way to Borley Green. There turn **left** towards Elmswell, leaving Route 51. Continue **straight** until you come to a **right** turn for Long Thurlow, then turn **left** for Badwell Ash. There turn **right** towards Four Ashes then **left** towards Langham. At the T-junction turn **left** towards Ixworth and continue straight on. At the A143 roundabout fork **left** onto the off-road path which becomes a road. Turn **left** onto Bardwell Rd, then turn **right** at The Greyhound. At the A1088 turn **left** towards Thetford then almost immediately **left** on Heath Rd. At Troston turn **left** at The Bull – you are now on Route 13. After crossing the B1106 turn **left** on Conyers Way and **right** on School Rd. Keep **straight** on East Barton Rd, then turn **right** on Green Ln. Follow to T-junction and then turn **right** on the shared-use path. Follow the path to Eastgate St and turn **left**, leaving Route 13. It's worth visiting the Abbey Gardens and St Edmundsbury Cathedral on your left. To return to the station, turn **right** on Northgate St, keep **straight** at the roundabout, and it will be on your left.

Bike shops

Cycle King Bury
IP33 1UZ Tel: 01284 769902

Revel Outdoors
IP33 1EB Tel: 01284 761954

Mick's Cycle Centre
IP33 1SJ Tel: 01284 753946

Eat & drink

The Fox & Hounds
IP31 3QT Tel: 01359 232228

The Gardener's Arms
IP30 9PA Tel: 01359 270460

The Swan Inn
IP30 9QN Tel: 01359 240482

The Elmswell Fox
IP30 9HD Tel: 01359 242908

The White Horse Inn
IP31 3DP Tel: 01359 259909

The Greyhound
IP31 2HJ Tel: 01359 230887

The Bull
IP31 1EW Tel: 01359 269646

The Fox Inn
IP33 1XX Tel: 01284 705562

The One Bull
IP33 1UZ Tel: 01284 848220

Various in Bury St Edmunds

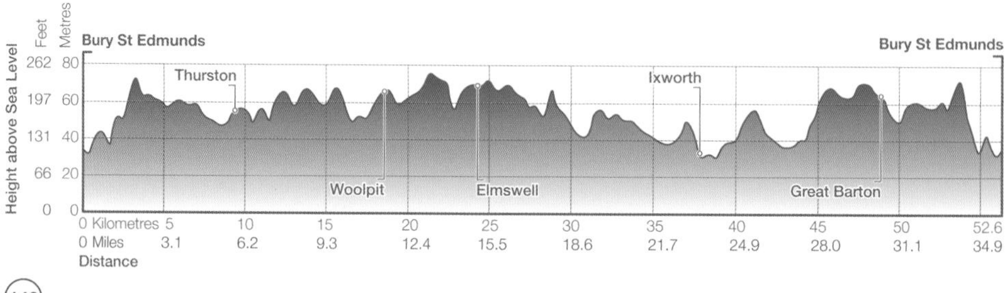

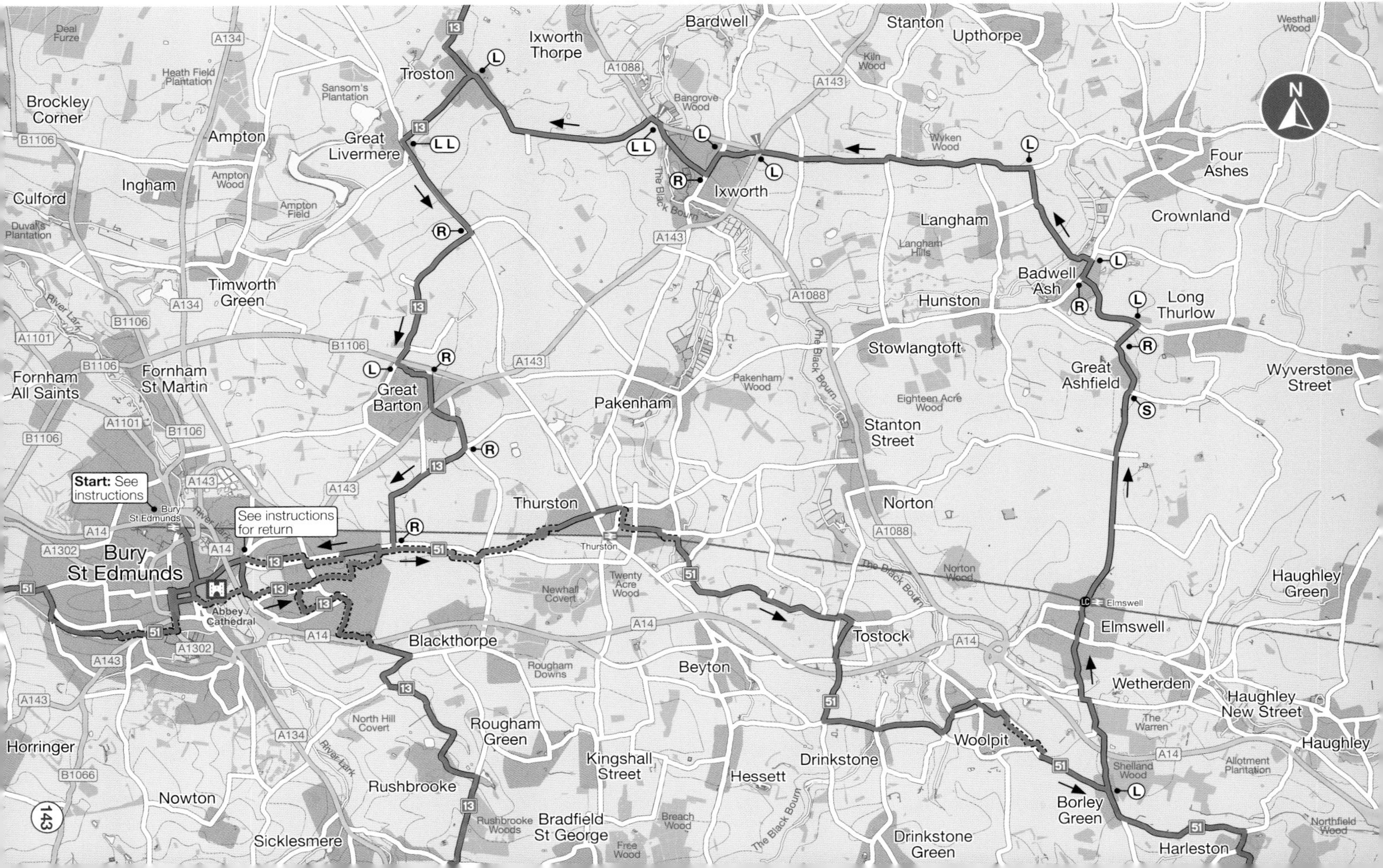

Start: See instructions
See instructions for return
Bury St Edmunds
Abbey / Cathedral
Bury St Edmunds
Thurston
Elmswell
Brockley Corner
Culford
Duval's Plantation
Deal Furze
Heath Field Plantation
Ingham
Ampton
Ampton Wood
Ampton Field
Sansom's Plantation
Great Livermere
Troston
Ixworth Thorpe
Bardwell
Bangrove Wood
Ixworth
The Black Bourn
Stanton
Upthorpe
Kiln Wood
Wyken Wood
Westhall Wood
Four Ashes
Crownland
Langham
Langham Hills
Badwell Ash
Long Thurlow
Hunston
Stowlangtoft
Great Ashfield
Wyverstone Street
Eighteen Acre Wood
Stanton Street
Pakenham
Pakenham Wood
Norton
Norton Wood
Haughley Green
Timworth Green
Fornham All Saints
Fornham St Martin
Great Barton
River Lark
Twenty Acre Wood
Newhall Covert
Blackthorpe
Rougham Downs
Beyton
Tostock
Woolpit
Wetherden
Haughley New Street
Haughley
The Warren
Shelland Wood
Allotment Plantation
Borley Green
Harleston
Northfield Wood
Drinkstone
Drinkstone Green
Hessett
Kingshall Street
Rougham Green
Breach Wood
Free Wood
Bradfield St George
Rushbrooke Woods
Rushbrooke
North Hill Covert
Sicklesmere
Nowton
Horringer
A134
A1088
A143
A1101
A14
A1302
B1106
B1066
13
51
L
LL
R
S
N

From Darsham Station go north on the shared-use path along the A12. Turn **left** on Willow Marsh Ln signed Heveningham. At the T-junction turn **right** and **right** to join Route 1. At the next T-junction turn **right** on the Suffolk Coast Cycle Route 42 towards Bramfield. Take the next **left**, then **right** when the road ends. Continue **straight** to Blackheath then turn **right** towards Blythburgh. Take the next **right** towards Yoxford. Turn **left** and cross the B1125 towards Dunwich. Follow the road **left** in Dunwich, then turn **left** towards Minsmere. If you'd like to visit Minsmere Nature Reserve, look out for the signed left turn. At Eastbridge stay **right** at the first fork and **left** at the second. At the T-junction turn **left** towards Kelsale. At the B1121 turn **right** then **left** towards Peasenhall. Cross the A12 and continue **straight** on towards Peasenhall. At the T-junction go **right** then **left** signed 'All Routes'. Take the next **right** onto Route 1 towards Peasenhall. For an optional excursion turn left on Route 1 which will take you to Framlingham Castle. Follow Route 1 signs through Peasenhall and then turn **right** towards Darsham. Follow the signs for Darsham and the station. At the A12 turn **right** to take the path back to the station.

Bike shops

Sax Velo
IP17 1AG Tel: 07484 805507

Eat & drink

The Queen's Head
IP19 9HT Tel: 01986 784214

The Star Inn
IP19 9HF Tel: 01502 478240

Dingle Hill Tearooms
IP17 3DZ Tel: 01728 648872

The Ship at Dunwich
IP17 3DT Tel: 01728 648219

The Eels Foot Inn
IP16 4SN Tel: 01728 830154

The Poacher's Pocket
IP17 2QS Tel: 01728 602174

Sibton White Horse
IP17 2JJ Tel: 01728 660337

The Fox Inn
IP17 3QE Tel: 01728 668436

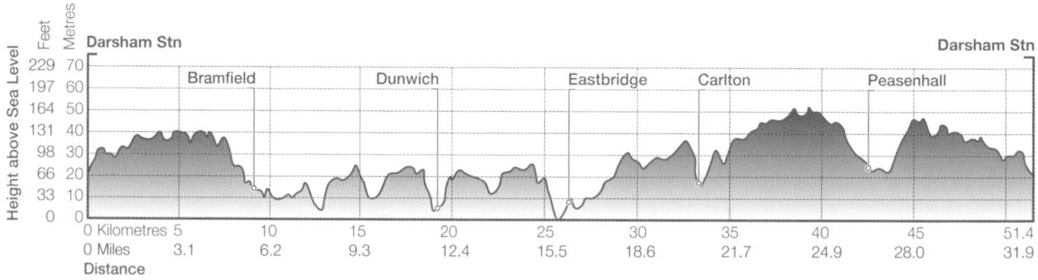

Cookley
Cratfield
Walpole
Huntingfield
Ubbeston
Heveningham
Ubbeston Green
Wenhaston
Blythburgh
Walberswick
Thorington
Bramfield
Darsham
Start
Dunwich
Peasenhall
Yoxford
Westleton
Middleton
Theberton
Eastbridge
Bruisyard
Curlew Green
Kelsale
Carlton
Saxmundham
Rendham
Cransford
Sizewell
Minsmere Haven
Minsmeare Nature Reserve
River Blyth
River Yox
River Aide
Minsmere River
Dunwich River
Minsmere New Cut
Dunwich Forest
Theberton Woods
Willowmarsh Wood
Bramfieldhall Wood
Kingstall Wood
Cats Covert
Thomas's Covert
Bruisyard Wood
Coe Wood
Lonely Wood
Frederick's Wood
Hog's Grove
Scheiller's Grove
Fen Covert
Big Wood
Old Covert
Hoist Covert
Hill Covert
Scottshall Coverts
Island Mere
West Scrape
Ash Wood
Nursery Covert
Broom Covert
Broomgreen Covert
Simple Corner Covert
The Wilderness
A12
A144
A1120
B1117
B1119
B1121
B1122
B1125
B1387

03 North East of Sudbury (South Suffolk Route) 34.8 miles / 56.0 km

From Sudbury Station go **left** to pass the leisure centre and Waitrose to join the path along the river. Follow Route 13 north. When the path ends turn **left**. Turn **right** towards Liston. Turn **right** towards Long Melford. At the B1064 turn **left**, then turn **right** on Bull Ln at The Bull. Cross the A134 and take the first **left** towards Lavenham. At Sudbury Rd turn **left**. Turn **left** on Potland Ln in front of the Church of St Peter and Paul. When Hall Rd ends **jink left right** on Market Ln. At the end of the road turn **left**. Turn **right** towards Brettenham. Keep **right** leaving Route 13. Turn **right** on The Street. At Whelp St keep **right**. Turn **left** towards Monks Eleigh. At the town sign turn **left**. Stay **left** on the B1115 towards Stowmarket. Turn **right** at the Peacock Inn. Turn **right** towards Lindsey. Turn **left** after the Lindsey Rose. At the T-junction turn **right**. Turn **right** towards Kersey. Turn **right** towards Boxford. Turn **right** towards Edwardstone. Turn **right** following South Suffolk Route and **left** signed 'By Road'. Turn **left** towards Edwardstone. At the fork stay **right** towards Waldingfield, at the second fork stay **left**. Turn **left** towards Melford and Sudbury. At the fork stay **right** towards Upsher Green. At the B1115 turn **left** then **right** towards Melford. In Acton turn **left** on Sudbury Rd. Turn **right** towards Melford. Carefully cross the A134. Turn **left** on the off-road path Route 13 back to the station.

Bike shops

Torque Bikes
CO10 2DJ Tel: 01787 379406

Halfords
CO10 2XQ Tel: 01787 378908

Eat & drink

Cock & Bell
CO10 9JR
Tel: 01787 379807

The Bull
CO10 9JG
Tel: 01787 378494

The Cock Horse Inn
CO10 9SA
Tel: 01787 827330

Lavenham Greyhound
CO10 9PZ
Tel: 01787 249553

Six Bells
CO10 9NG
Tel: 01787 247440

The Swan Inn
IP7 7AU
Tel: 01449 763163

The Peacock Inn
IP7 7HU
Tel: 01449 743952

The Lindsey Rose
IP7 6PP
Tel: 01449 741424

The Bell Inn
IP7 6DY
Tel: 01473 823229

The Edwardstone White Horse Inn
CO10 5PX
Tel: 01787 211211

The Crown
CO10 0AT
Tel: 01787 377204

Various in Sudbury

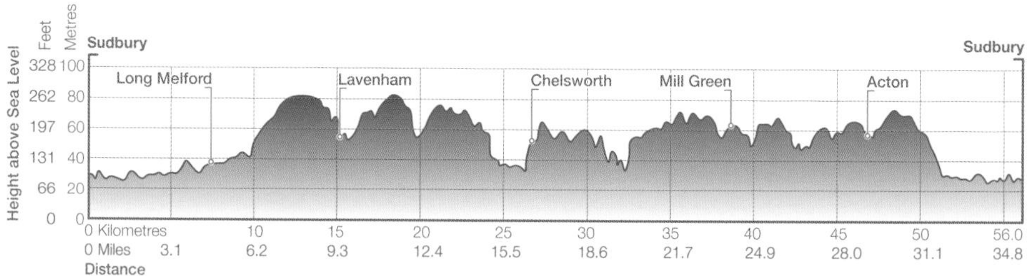

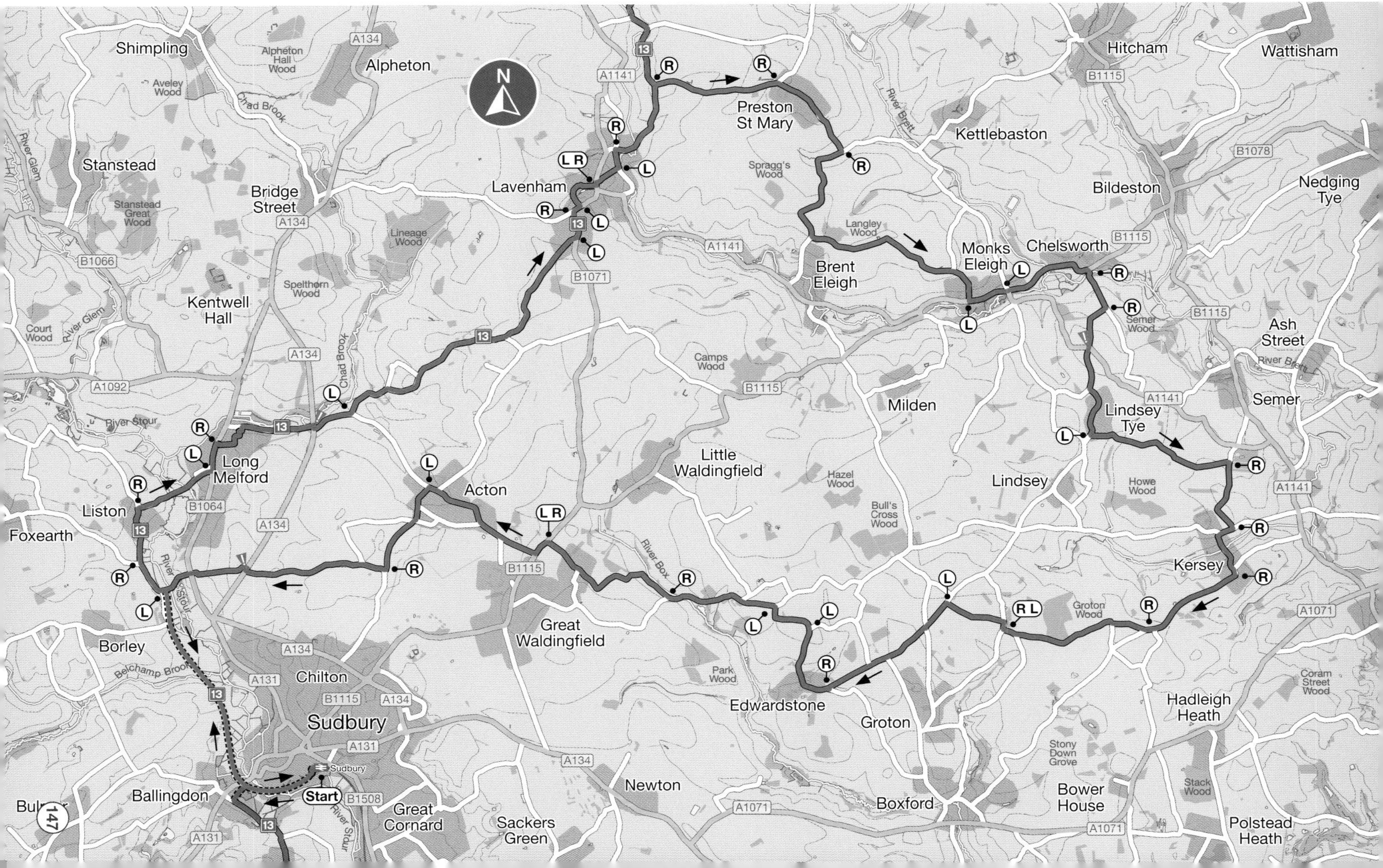
Shimpling
Alpheton Hall Wood
Alpheton
Aveley Wood
Chad Brook
Stanstead
Stanstead Great Wood
Bridge Street
Lavenham
Preston St Mary
Spragg's Wood
Kettlebaston
Hitcham
Wattisham
Bildeston
Nedging Tye
River Brett
Lineage Wood
Langley Wood
Kentwell Hall
Spelthorn Wood
Brent Eleigh
Monks Eleigh
Chelsworth
Semer Wood
Ash Street
Court Wood
River Glem
Camps Wood
Milden
Semer
Lindsey Tye
River Stour
Long Melford
Little Waldingfield
Hazel Wood
Lindsey
Howe Wood
Bull's Cross Wood
Liston
Acton
Foxearth
River Box
Kersey
Groton Wood
Borley
Great Waldingfield
Belchamp Brook
Chilton
Park Wood
Edwardstone
Groton
Hadleigh Heath
Coram Street Wood
Sudbury
Stony Down Grove
Stack Wood
Ballingdon
Start
Newton
Great Cornard
Sackers Green
Boxford
Bower House
Polstead Heath
Bulmer

The route starts in the charming market town of Beccles. From Beccles Station head west on Station Rd. Turn **right** on Smallgate, then **left** on Old Market. Turn **right** on Northgate / Route 1. Turn **left** towards Gillingham. Follow Route 1 until just before reaching the A143 – you will see a left turn signed Two Rivers Cycle Route 30 towards Bungay. Turn **left** and follow Route 30 on the path along the A143. When the path ends turn **left** off the path and **right** onto Pirnhow St (not the A143). Follow Route 30 to the centre of Bungay, then turn **left** on Trinity St and stay **left** to join Route 40. Turn **right** on Annis Hill Ln, then **jink left right** to continue. Follow the brown route signs towards St Andrew. When the route curves east towards Ringsfield Corner it becomes Route 1. At Ringsfield Corner follow Route 1 **left**, then **right** towards Beccles. Route 1 takes you all the way back to the centre. Before the bell tower, turn **right** down a narrow alley (next to the Beccles map) and continue **straight** on the road back to the station. If you are visiting during spring or summer, consider a visit to the heated Beccles Lido for a post-cycle dip.

Bike shops

Michael's Cycles
NR34 9AB Tel: 01502 717413

M G Cycles
NR35 1AG Tel: 01986 892985

Eat & drink

Bear & Bells
NR34 9AP Tel: 01502 712291

The Wherry Inn
NR34 0LB Tel: 01508 518371

Locks Inn
NR34 0HS Tel: 01508 518414

The Castle Inn
NR35 1AF Tel: 01986 892283

The Tally Ho Tearooms
NR35 1TL Tel: 01986 897818

The Ringsfield Horseshoes Inn
NR34 8LR Tel: 01502 713114

Various in Beccles

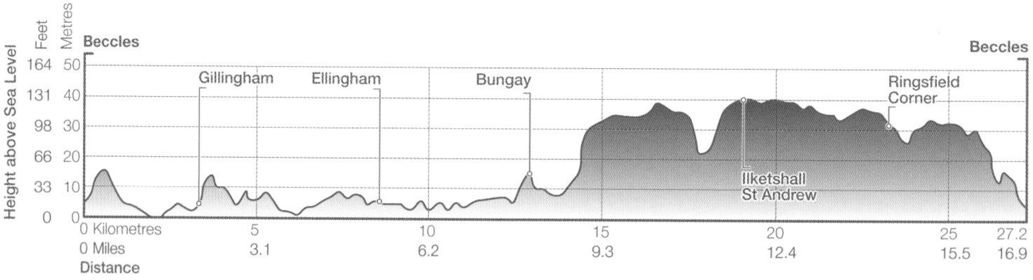

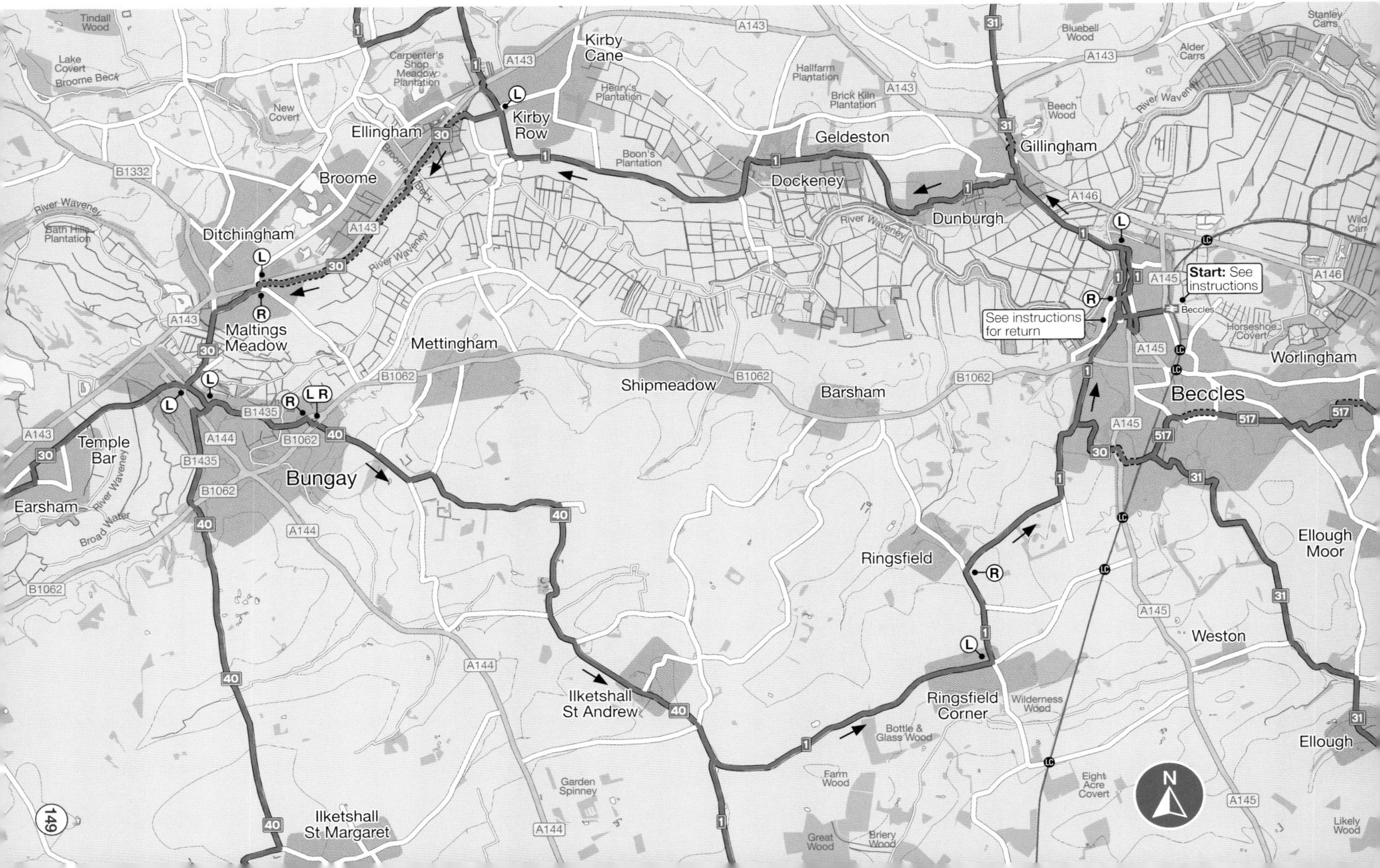
Start: See instructions
See instructions for return
Beccles
Worlingham
Horseshoe Covert
Wild Carr
Stanley Carrs
Alder Carrs
Bluebell Wood
Beech Wood
River Waveney
Gillingham
Dunburgh
Dockeney
Geldeston
Hallfarm Plantation
Brick Kiln Plantation
Boon's Plantation
Henry's Plantation
Kirby Cane
Kirby Row
Carpenter's Shop Meadow Plantation
Ellingham
Broome Beck
Broome
New Covert
Tindall Wood
Lake Covert
Ditchingham
Bath Hills Plantation
Maltings Meadow
Mettingham
Shipmeadow
Barsham
Bungay
Temple Bar
Earsham
Broad Water
Ringsfield
Ringsfield Corner
Wilderness Wood
Bottle & Glass Wood
Farm Wood
Great Wood
Briery Wood
Garden Spinney
Ilketshall St Andrew
Ilketshall St Margaret
Ellough Moor
Ellough
Likely Wood
Weston
Eight Acre Covert
A143
A145
A146
A144
B1062
B1332
B1435
1
30
31
40
517
L
R
LC
N

Worstead & Happisburgh Figure of 8

20.7 miles / 33.2 km

From Worstead Station turn **left** on Station Rd. Turn **right** on Westwick Rd. Continue **straight** on until the road ends in a T-junction – turn **left**. At Honing **jink left right** towards Crostwight. At the second crossroads **jink right left**. Stay **right** and join Route 30 / Norfolk Coast Cycleway. Turn **right** towards Ridlington. Turn **right** then **left** on The Street. Turn **left** on Old Lane. **Jink left right** at the B1159, then **right left** again. Turn **right** at the pond. At the T-junction turn **left**, leaving Route 30. Turn **right** and follow the road around right. You can make an optional stop off at the beach and see the lighthouse. Turn **right** on Coronation Rd, then **right** towards East Ruston. Turn **left** towards Stalham. At the T-junction turn **left** then **right** on Long Common. At the crossroads turn **right** and keep following signs towards Honing. Pass through Honing and then turn **left** on Station Rd and carry **straight** on towards Worstead. At the church turn **right** on Westwick Rd, then turn **left** on Station Rd to return to the station.

Bike shops

No bike shops

Eat & drink

Cross Keys Inn
NR28 9PS Tel: 01692 536398

The Lighthouse Inn
NR12 0PE Tel: 01692 650371

The Hill House
NR12 0PW Tel: 01692 650004

Smallsticks Café
NR12 0QL Tel: 01692 583368

Butcher's Arms
NR12 9JG Tel: 01692 650237

The White Lady
NR28 9RW Tel: 01692 535391

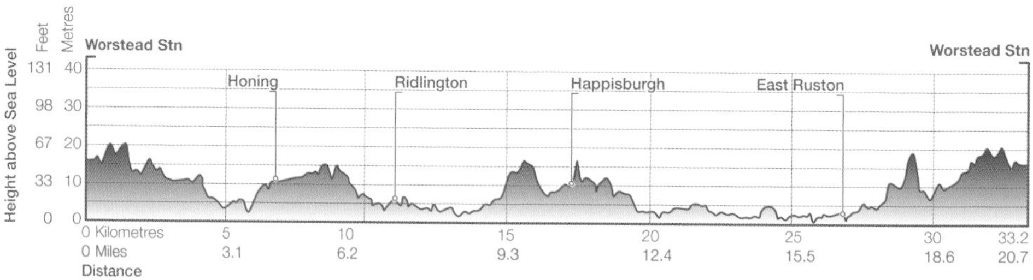

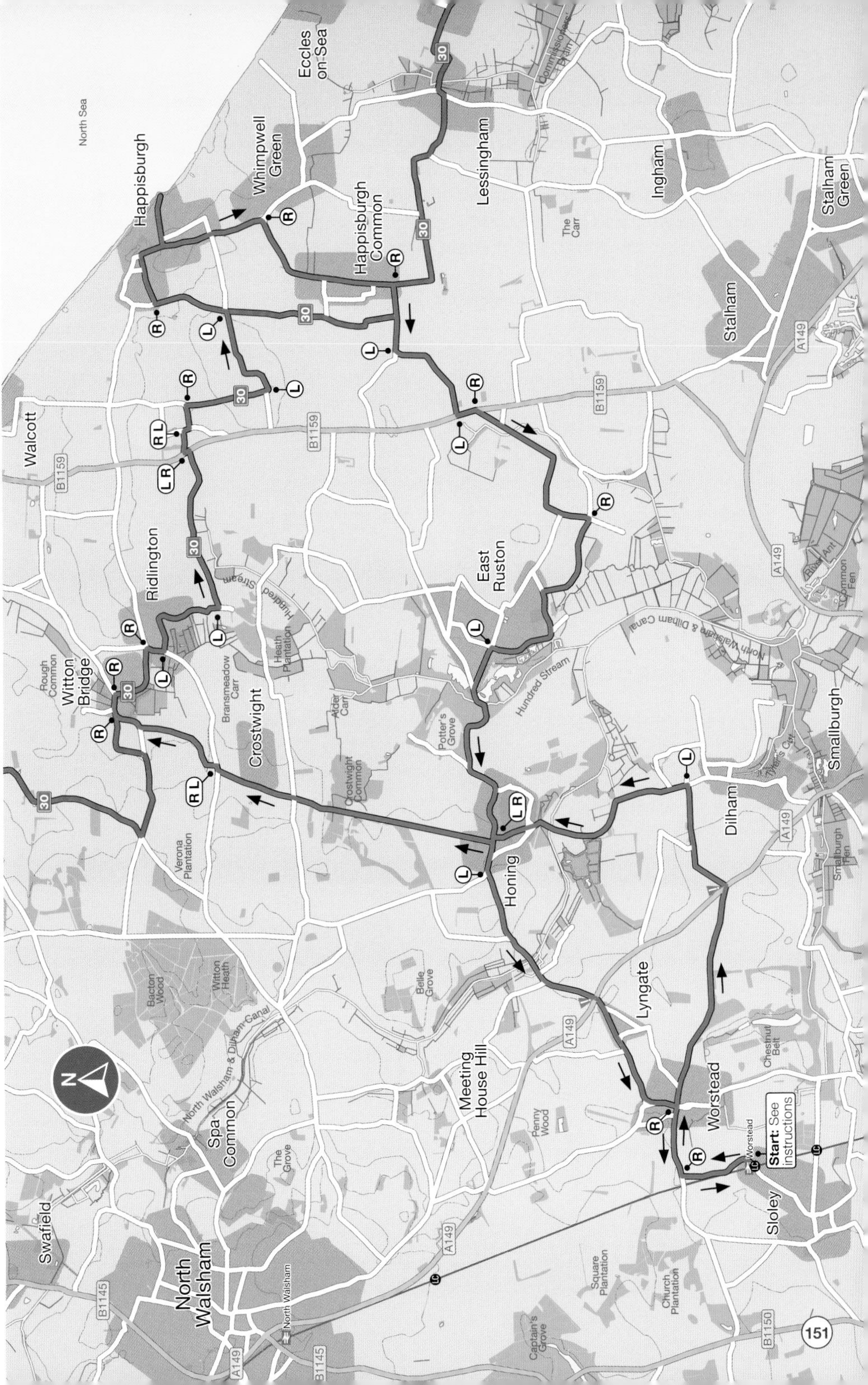
North Sea
Happisburgh
Eccles on-Sea
Whimpwell Green
Happisburgh Common
Lessingham
Ingham
Stalham Green
The Carr
Stalham
Walcott
Ridlington
East Ruston
Witton Bridge
Rough Common
Bransmeadow Carr
Heath Plantation
Crostwight
Alder Carr
Crostwight Common
Potter's Grove
Hundred Stream
North Walsham & Dilham Canal
River Ant
Common Fen
Smallburgh
Tyler's Cut
Smallburgh Fen
Dilham
Honing
Verona Plantation
Bacton Wood
Witton Heath
Belle Grove
Lyngate
Chestnut Belt
Worstead
Start: See instructions
Meeting House Hill
Penny Wood
Spa Common
The Grove
Sloley
Swafield
North Walsham
Square Plantation
Church Plantation
Captain's Grove
B1159
B1145
B1150
A149
30

From Thetford Station turn **left** on Station Rd. When the road ends turn **left** and **left** to join Route 13 / 30. Cross the A1066 via the path and continue north. After Croxton turn **right** to continue on Route 13 towards Wretham. At East Wretham continue **straight** leaving Route 13. At the A1075 **jink right left**. At the A11 go **left** and **right** to cross under the road, then turn immediate **left** and immediate **right** towards the Angel Inn. Follow the road to cross back over the A11 and continue north. At the yellow and terracotta semi-detached houses turn hard **right** on Chalk Ln. Go **straight** through the double roundabouts over the A11. After the recycling centre turn **right** on Heath Rd. At T-junction turn **right** on Quidenham Rd. At East Harling turn **right** and then take the first **left** on West Harling Rd. At the T-junction turn **right** towards Brettenham – you are now back on Route 13. Follow the route **right** towards Bridgham. Before reaching the A1075 turn **left** onto the off-road path. When the path ends, cross the A1066 and continue **straight**. Turn **right** on Castle St towards the town centre. At the church turn **right** on Whitehart St. When it ends use the crossing to cross the busy road and continue on Station Rd back to the station.

Bike shops

Halfords
IP24 2BU Tel: 01842 752443

Eat & drink

The Norfolk Terrier
IP24 1TA Tel: 01842 754965

Dog & Partridge
IP24 1QS Tel: 01953 497014

The Angel Inn
NR16 2QU Tel: 01953 717963

The George & Dragon
NR16 2AD Tel: 01953 717918

The Albion
IP24 2DN Tel: 01842 338208

The Green Dragon
IP24 2AJ Tel: 01842 753111

Bell Inn
IP24 2AZ Tel: 01842 754455

The Railway Tavern
IP24 1AH Tel: 01842 824663

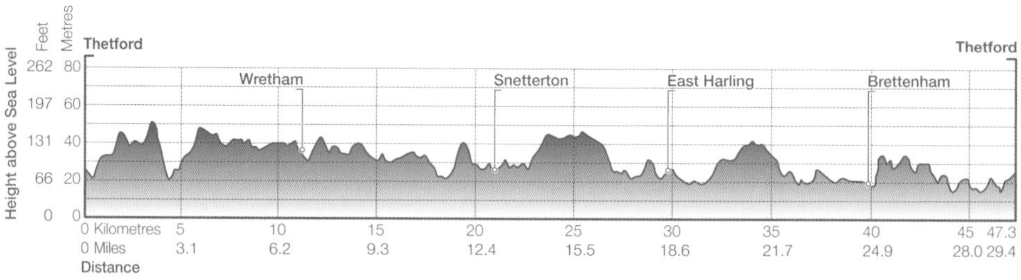

Great Hockham
Shropham
North End
Snetterton
Eccles Road
Eccles Wood
River Wittle
East Harling Fen
East Harling
Middle Harling
Garboldisham
Garboldisham Belt
Ten Acre Plantation
West Harlinghill Plantation
Big Wood
Hatchet Plantation
West Harling Common
West Harling Heath
Carter Belt
Long Belt
Bridgham
Bridgham Belt
Roudham Hall
River Thet
Larling
Larling Fen
Harling Road
Fen Carr
Hills and Holes
Illington
Roudham Heath
Scotch Plantation
Black Plantation
Brettenham
Kilverstone Belt
Kilverstone Hall
Snarehill Wood
The Forest
Oak Wood
Rushford
Wretham
Stonebridge
Sails Plantation
Bragmere Belt
Square Covert
Forest Covert
Brickkiln Covert
Gregson's Plantation
Cornnell's Plantation
Corkmere Plantation
Thorpe Belt
Croxton Heath
Cross Strips
Heath Coverts
Jubilee Wood
Box Strip
Croxton
Reed Fen
Little Ouse River
Abbey Heath
Thetford
Start
Redcastle Furze
Newtown
153

From North Walsham Station turn **right** on the B1150 and **left** on the A149. Turn **left** then first **right**, taking care turning across the busy road. At the T-junction turn **right**, then **jink left right** towards Bradfield. Keep **right** towards Bradfield. At the forks go **right** then **left**. The road becomes Regional Route 30. Follow the signs through Southrepps. Go **left** then **right** through Northrepps, then follow Route 30 and signs for Cromer. In Cromer go **right** at the double mini roundabout, then turn **right** on Church St and **left** on Mount St. Turn right if you'd like to visit the beach and Cromer Pier, otherwise turn **left** and then **left** on Hall Rd. Follow the road south, then stay **right** on Route 33 towards Felbrigg Hall. Route 33 passes through the grounds of National Trust property Felbrigg Hall and Gardens, which is worth a visit if you have time. When you exit the grounds turn **left**. At the T-junction turn **left** to follow Route 33, then take the next **right**. At the T-junction turn **right** and then take the next **left**. At Thurgarton stay **left** towards Erpingham. At Thwaite Hill **jink right left** leaving Route 33. Stay **left** towards Erpingham, then stay **left** towards Aylsham. Cross the A140 and then turn **left** at Long Ln. Turn **left** towards Antingham. At the A149 **jink right left** to cross. After crossing the tracks turn **right**, then go **right** and then **left** towards Walsham. Follow the road **left** then **right**. Turn **left** on Bradfield Rd. At the T-junction join the road **left**. Turn **right** on the A149, then turn **right** on the B1150 and the station will be on your left.

Bike shops

Doctor Wheelgood
NR28 0DA Tel: 01692 405033

Halfords
NR27 9ST Tel: 01263 510420

Eat & drink

Vernon Arms
NR11 8NP Tel: 01263 833355

Foundry Arms
NR27 0AA Tel: 01263 579256

Various in Cromer

Felbrigg Hall Tearoom
NR11 8PR Tel: 01263 837444

The Black Boys
NR11 7NX Tel: 01263 761649

Erpingham Arms
NR11 7QA Tel: 01263 761591

Various in North Walsham

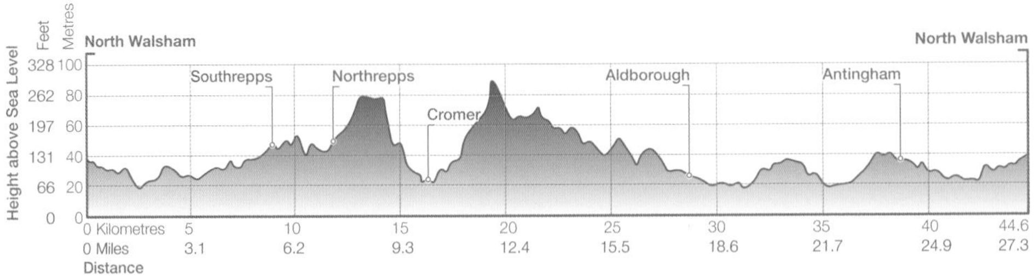

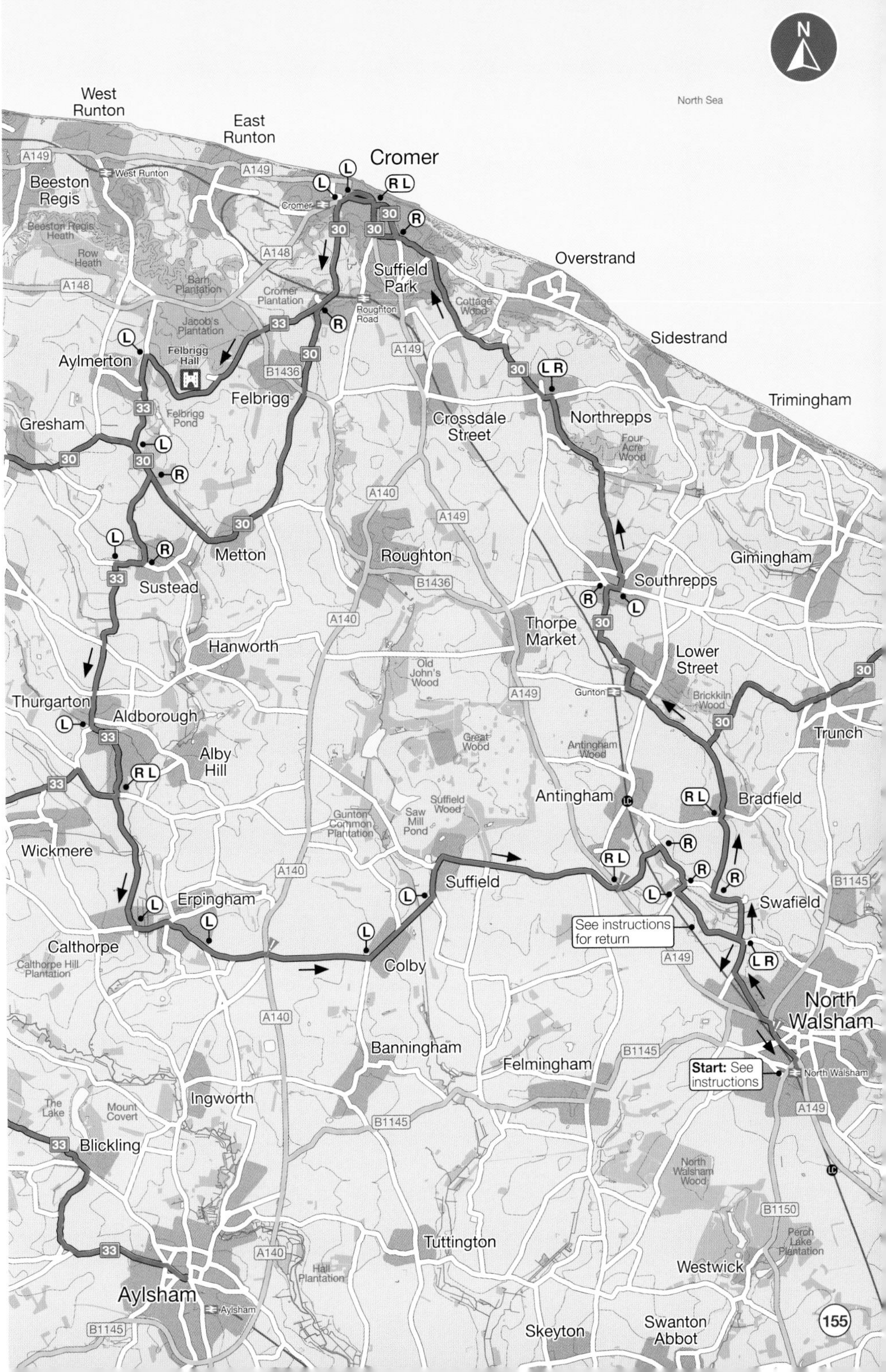
N
North Sea
West Runton
East Runton
Cromer
Beeston Regis
Beeston Regis Heath
Row Heath
A149
A148
West Runton
Cromer
Barn Plantation
Cromer Plantation
Jacob's Plantation
Felbrigg Hall
Suffield Park
Roughton Road
Cottage Wood
Overstrand
Sidestrand
Trimingham
Aylmerton
Felbrigg
Felbrigg Pond
B1436
Gresham
Crossdale Street
Northrepps
Four Acre Wood
A140
Metton
Roughton
Gimingham
Sustead
Southrepps
Thorpe Market
Hanworth
Lower Street
Old John's Wood
Gunton
Brickkiln Wood
Thurgarton
Aldborough
Trunch
Alby Hill
Great Wood
Antingham Wood
Antingham
Bradfield
Wickmere
Gunton Common Plantation
Suffield Wood
Saw Mill Pond
Suffield
Swafield
B1145
Erpingham
See instructions for return
Calthorpe
Calthorpe Hill Plantation
Colby
North Walsham
Banningham
Felmingham
Start: See instructions
North Walsham
Ingworth
The Lake
Mount Covert
Blickling
North Walsham Wood
B1150
Tuttington
Perch Lake Plantation
Hall Plantation
Westwick
Aylsham
Aylsham
Skeyton
Swanton Abbot
30
33
L
R
RL
LR
LC

Southwest of Stevenage

26.8 miles / 43.2 km

From Stevenage Station go **right** to follow the Route 12 path south. When the path ends turn **right** under the railway tracks. After passing under the motorway turn **right** to continue on Route 12. Follow the route until you reach Ayot St Peter Rd – here stay **straight** leaving Route 12. Take the next **right** on Hill Farm Ln. Turn **left** towards Shaw's Corner. Turn **right** towards National Trust property Shaw's Corner - stop for a visit if you have time. Turn **left** towards Wheathampstead. Turn **right** on Holly Ln. Turn **right** at the end of the lane, then turn **left**. Turn **right** on Plummers Ln. Stay **left** towards Chiltern Green. Turn **right** on Chiltern Green Rd. Turn **right** towards Breachwood Green and stay straight on the road. At the T-junction turn **left** then first **right**. Stay **right**, then stay **left** towards Preston. Turn **right** to go through Preston. At the T-junction turn **left**. Turn **right** towards Lt Almshoe. Turn **right** towards Titmore Green. Stay **right**, then **right** at the Todds Green mini roundabout. After crossing over the A1(M), turn **left** on Fishers Green and then **left** on Julians Rd. At the A602 join the shared-use path **right** and follow the path back to the station.

Bike shops

Scuffwheels
SG1 1DB Tel: 01438 723298

Decathlon Stevenage
SG1 1LA Tel: 01438 369870

Stevenage Cycles
SG2 0DJ Tel: 01438 340004

Edd's Bikes
SG2 0LQ Tel: 01438 220401

Contour Cycles Ltd
SG2 8EE Tel: 01438 748104

Eat & drink

Robin Hood & Little John
AL6 9UB Tel: 01438 812361

The Globe
SG4 8UA Tel: 01438 821947

The Brocket Arms
AL6 9BT Tel: 01438 820250

Cross Keys
AL4 8LA Tel: 01582 832165

The Bright Star
LU2 9QP Tel: 01438 832351

The Red Lion
SG4 8NU Tel: 01438 833123

The Plough
SG4 8LA Tel: 01438 871394

The Red Lion
SG4 7UD Tel: 01462 459585

The Rusty Gun
SG4 7PG Tel: 01462 432653

Hermit of Redcoats
SG4 7JR Tel: 01438 747333

Various in Stevenage

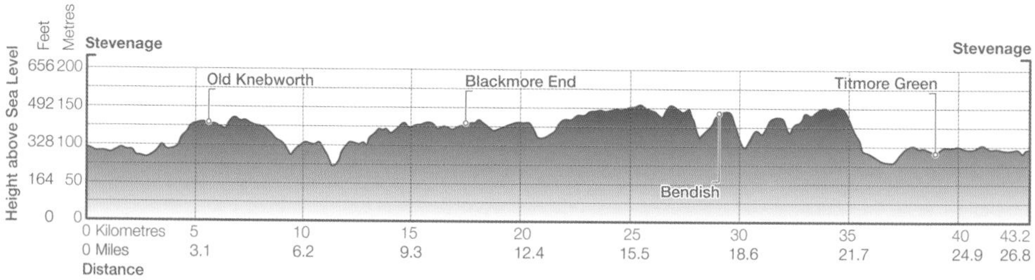

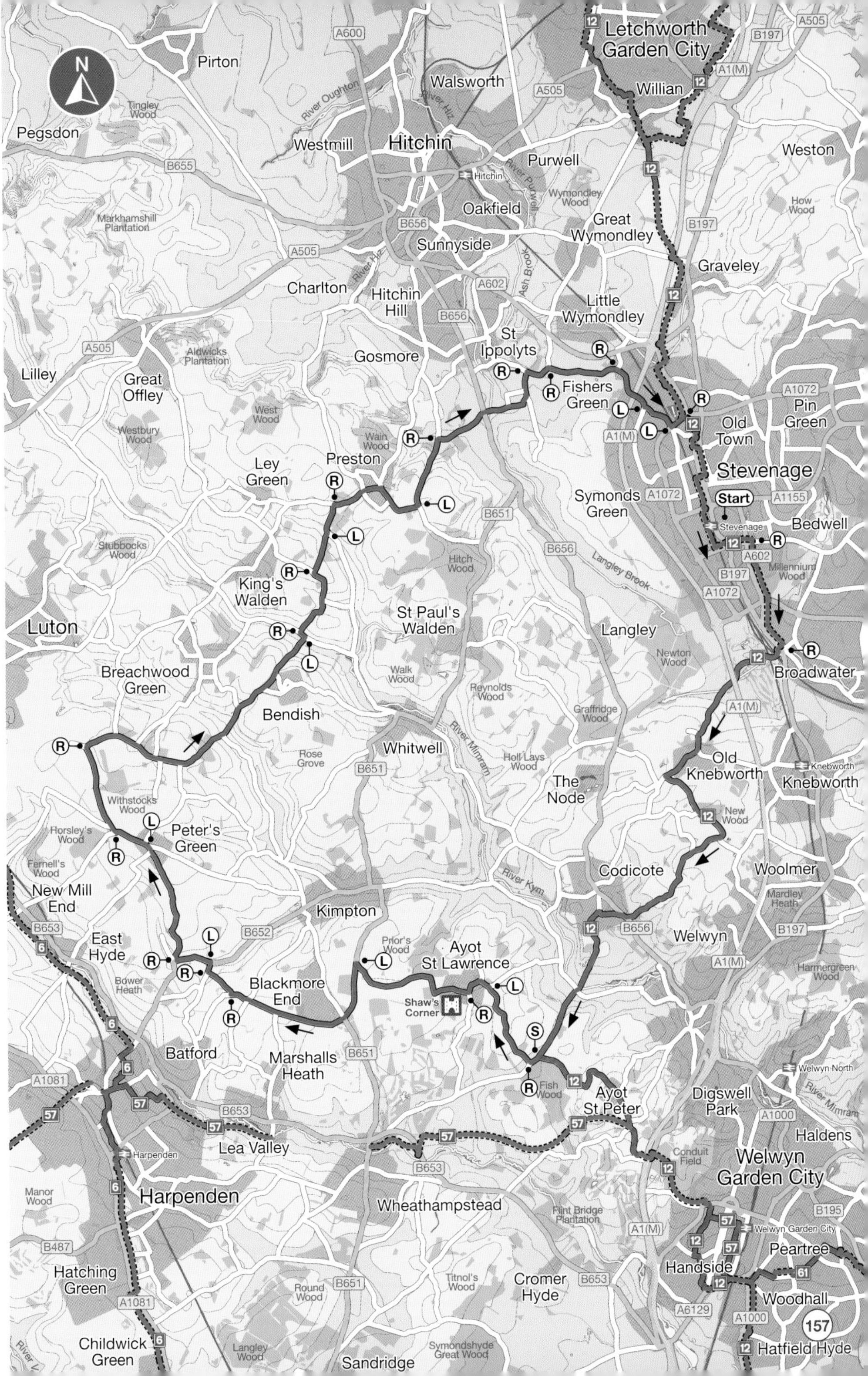

N
Letchworth Garden City
Pirton
A600
A505
B197
A1(M)
Walsworth
River Oughton
River Hiz
Willian
Tingley Wood
Pegsdon
Westmill
Hitchin
Purwell
Weston
B655
Hitchin
River Purwell
Wymondley Wood
How Wood
Markhamshill Plantation
Oakfield
B656
Great Wymondley
B197
Sunnyside
A505
Ash Brook
Graveley
Charlton
Hitchin Hill
A602
B656
Little Wymondley
St Ippolyts
A505
Aldwicks Plantation
Gosmore
Lilley
Great Offley
Fishers Green
A1072
West Wood
Pin Green
Westbury Wood
Wain Wood
Old Town
A1(M)
Ley Green
Preston
Stevenage
Symonds Green
A1072
Start
A1155
B651
Stevenage
Bedwell
Stubbocks Wood
B656
A602
Hitch Wood
Langley Brook
Millennium Wood
B197
King's Walden
A1072
Luton
St Paul's Walden
Langley
Newton Wood
Broadwater
Breachwood Green
Walk Wood
Reynolds Wood
Graffridge Wood
A1(M)
Bendish
Whitwell
River Mimram
Rose Grove
B651
Holl Lays Wood
Old Knebworth
Knebworth
Knebworth
The Node
Withstocks Wood
Peter's Green
Horsley's Wood
New Wood
Fernell's Wood
River Kym
Codicote
Woolmer
New Mill End
Mardley Heath
Kimpton
B653
B656
B197
East Hyde
B652
Welwyn
Prior's Wood
Ayot St Lawrence
A1(M)
Harmergreen Wood
Bower Heath
Blackmore End
Shaw's Corner
Batford
Marshalls Heath
B651
A1081
Fish Wood
Ayot St Peter
Welwyn North
Digswell Park
River Mimram
B653
A1000
Lea Valley
Haldens
Harpenden
Conduit Field
Welwyn Garden City
B653
Manor Wood
Harpenden
Wheathampstead
Flint Bridge Plantation
B195
A1(M)
Welwyn Garden City
B487
Peartree
Hatching Green
Handside
Round Wood
B651
Titnol's Wood
Cromer Hyde
B653
Woodhall
A1081
A6129
A1000
Childwick Green
River Ver
Langley Wood
Sandridge
Symondshyde Great Wood
Hatfield Hyde

From Cambridge Station go **left** on Station Place. Turn **right** on Brookgate and stay **straight** at the junction. At the A1134 junction cross the road and join the shared-use path Route 11. Follow Route 11 through central Cambridge and then east along the River Cam. After passing the old industrial chimney, go **left** over the bridge to continue on Route 11. At the roundabout on Green End Rd join the shared-use path Route 51. At New Rd turn **left** off Route 51 and follow the shared-use path. At the end of the road turn **right** onto Route 24 and follow through Longstanton. At the B1050 roundabout take the 1st exit **left** (take care on this busy road). Stay **straight** through the next roundabout and then turn **right** towards Norman Way. Turn **right** on Glover St, then **right** on Willingham Rd. The road bends left then right, then at the T-junction turn **left**. At the library turn **right** and **right** on Priest Ln. Follow the road to Rampton and turn **left** at the T-junction. At Cottenham turn **left** at the roundabout towards Histon, then **left** at the fork and **left** at the mini roundabout. At the war memorial bear **right**, then follow the road to the right. At the T-junction turn **right** towards Landbeach. At the A10 use the shared-use path to cross and then turn **right** on Landbeach Rd. **Jink right left** onto Fen Rd. The road dead ends at Route 11 – turn **right**. When the path ends go **left** on Water St, stay straight through the barrier posts, then opposite the Green Dragon pub go **left** over the pedestrian bridge (please dismount). Continue **right** along the river and follow Route 11 back to the A1134 junction. Turn **left** on Brooklands Ave and then **left** on Station Place to return to the station.

Bike shops

Rutland Cycling (shop & hire)
CB1 2JW Tel: 01223 352728

Cam Cycles
CB1 2BD Tel: 01223 500988

The Bike Shed
CB1 2AD Tel: 01223 360028

S & G Cycles
CB2 1SD Tel: 01223 311134

City Cycle Hire
CB3 9EY Tel: 01223 365629

Cambridge Cycles
CB5 8JE Tel: 07778 484280

More in central Cambridge

Eat & drink

The Haymakers
CB4 1NG
Tel: 01223 311077

The White Horse
CB24 3AB
Tel: 01223 232417

The Black Bull
CB24 3BS
Tel: 01954 789589

The Admiral Vernon
CB24 5NB
Tel: 01954 232357

The Porterhouse Pub
CB24 5HF
Tel: 01954 488080

The Black Horse
CB24 8QE
Tel: 01954 251867

The Chequers
CB24 8QP
Tel: 01954 488201

Jolly Brewers
CB24 6AD
Tel: 01223 863895

The Green Dragon
CB4 1NZ
Tel: 01223 505035

Fort St George
CB4 1HA
Tel: 01223 354327

Various in central Cambridge

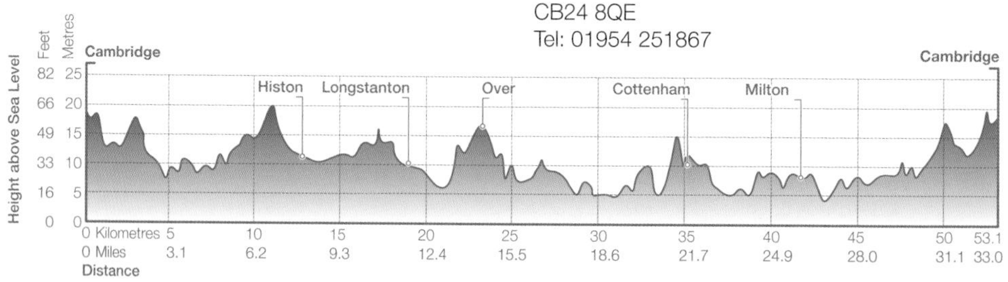

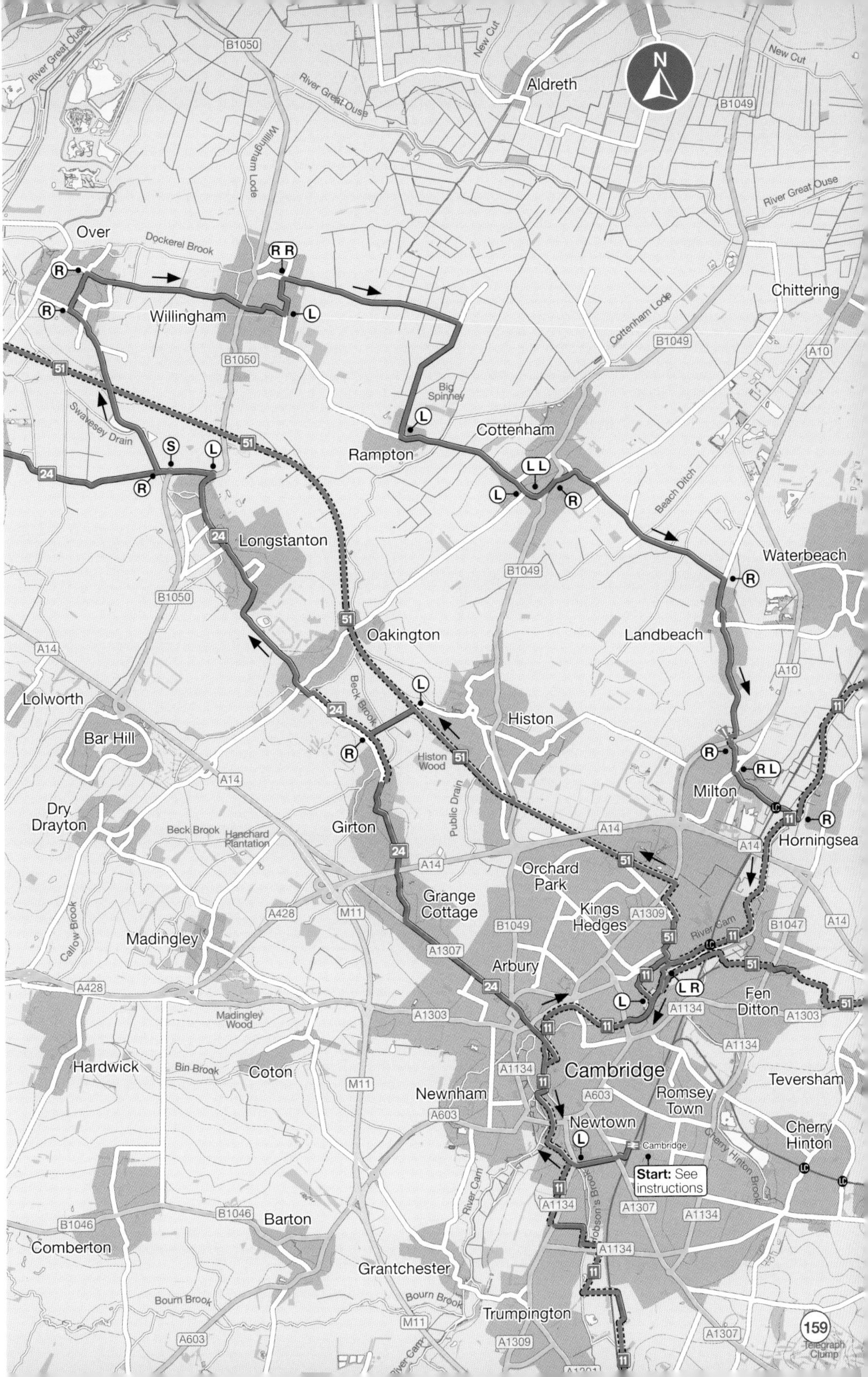

N
River Great Ouse
B1050
River Great Ouse
New Cut
Aldreth
New Cut
B1049
River Great Ouse
Willingham Lode
Over
Dockerel Brook
R R
R
R
L
Willingham
Chittering
Cottenham Lode
B1049
B1050
A10
51
Swavesey Drain
Big Spinney
L
Cottenham
S
L
51
Rampton
24
R
L L
L
R
Beach Ditch
24
Longstanton
Waterbeach
B1049
R
B1050
51
Oakington
Landbeach
A14
A10
L
Beck Brook
Lolworth
24
11
Bar Hill
R
Histon Wood
51
Histon
R
R L
A14
Dry Drayton
Beck Brook
Hanchard Plantation
Girton
Public Drain
Milton
11
R
Horningsea
A14
24
A14
51
A14
Orchard Park
Grange Cottage
Kings Hedges
A1309
A428
M11
B1049
51
River Cam
11
B1047
A14
Callow Brook
Madingley
A1307
Arbury
51
11
L R
Fen Ditton
A428
24
L
A1134
A1303
51
A1303
Madingley Wood
11
11
A1134
Hardwick
Bin Brook
Coton
A1134
Cambridge
Teversham
M11
11
Newnham
A603
Romsey Town
A603
Newtown
Cherry Hinton
L
Cambridge
Start: See instructions
Cherry Hinton Brook
River Cam
11
A1134
Hobson's Brook
A1307
A1134
B1046
B1046
Barton
Comberton
A1134
11
Grantchester
Bourn Brook
Bourn Brook
Trumpington
M11
A603
A1309
A1307
Telegraph Clump
11

Boston Circular & Frampton Marsh

18.0 miles / 29.0 km

From Boston Station turn **left** on West St. Turn **left** on High St, cross the bridge and turn immediate **right**. Join the cycle lane and turn **right** over the bridge, then immediate **left** on High St – you are on Route 1. Cross the bridge and turn **left** following Route 1. At Slippery Gowt Ln turn **left**, leaving Route 1. Turn **right** on Closshill Ln. Turn **left** at the T-junction. Turn **left** at the next T-junction. Turn **right** towards Frampton Marsh. Turn **left** towards Frampton Marsh. Turn left for an optional detour to Frampton Marsh Nature Reserve, otherwise turn **right** towards Frampton. Continue **straight** on this road through Frampton. Before the A16 turn **left** on Horseshoe Ln. Stay **straight** at the roundabout. Turn **left** at the B1397, **right** at the church, then **left** on Church Ln. At the end of the lane turn **right**, **left**, **right** along the drainage creek. Continue **straight** on to Kirton Holme. Turn **right** on Beck Bank. Stay **straight** towards Westgate Wood. **Jink right left** to continue straight. At the T-junction of Wyberton West Rd turn **right** and stay straight on this road. At the end of the road get on the path to the roundabout and carefully cross to London Rd. Follow the road across the bridge and follow Route 1 back the way you came. Turn **left** on West St to return to the station.

To extend the route, you can ride along the River Witham on Route 1 to Langrick Bridge and back.

Bike shops

Noel Craft Cycles
PE21 8TS Tel: 01205 311888

Halfords
PE21 8XZ Tel: 01205 362110

Eat & drink

Spirit of Endeavour
PE21 7QS Tel: 01205 356678

The Black Bull Inn
PE20 1JE Tel: 01205 722530

The Merry Monk
PE20 1EH Tel: 01205 724723

The Poacher's Hotel
PE20 1SQ Tel: 01205 290310

Black Sluice Riverside Café
PE21 7RA Tel: 01205 310006

Robin Hood Inn
PE21 8TA Tel: 01205 356696

Golden Lion
PE21 8SP Tel: 01205 359410

Moon Under Water
PE21 8SH Tel: 01205 311911

Various in Boston

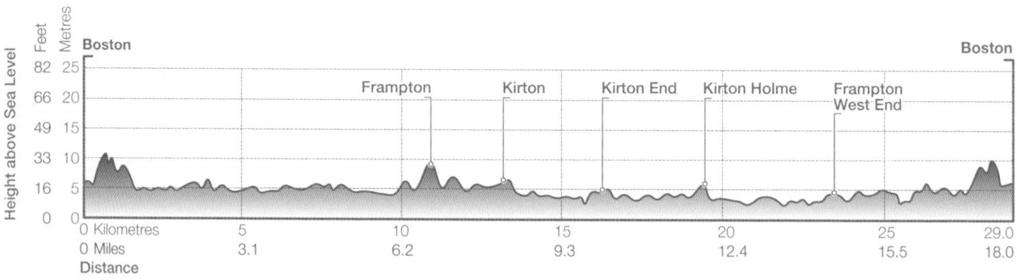

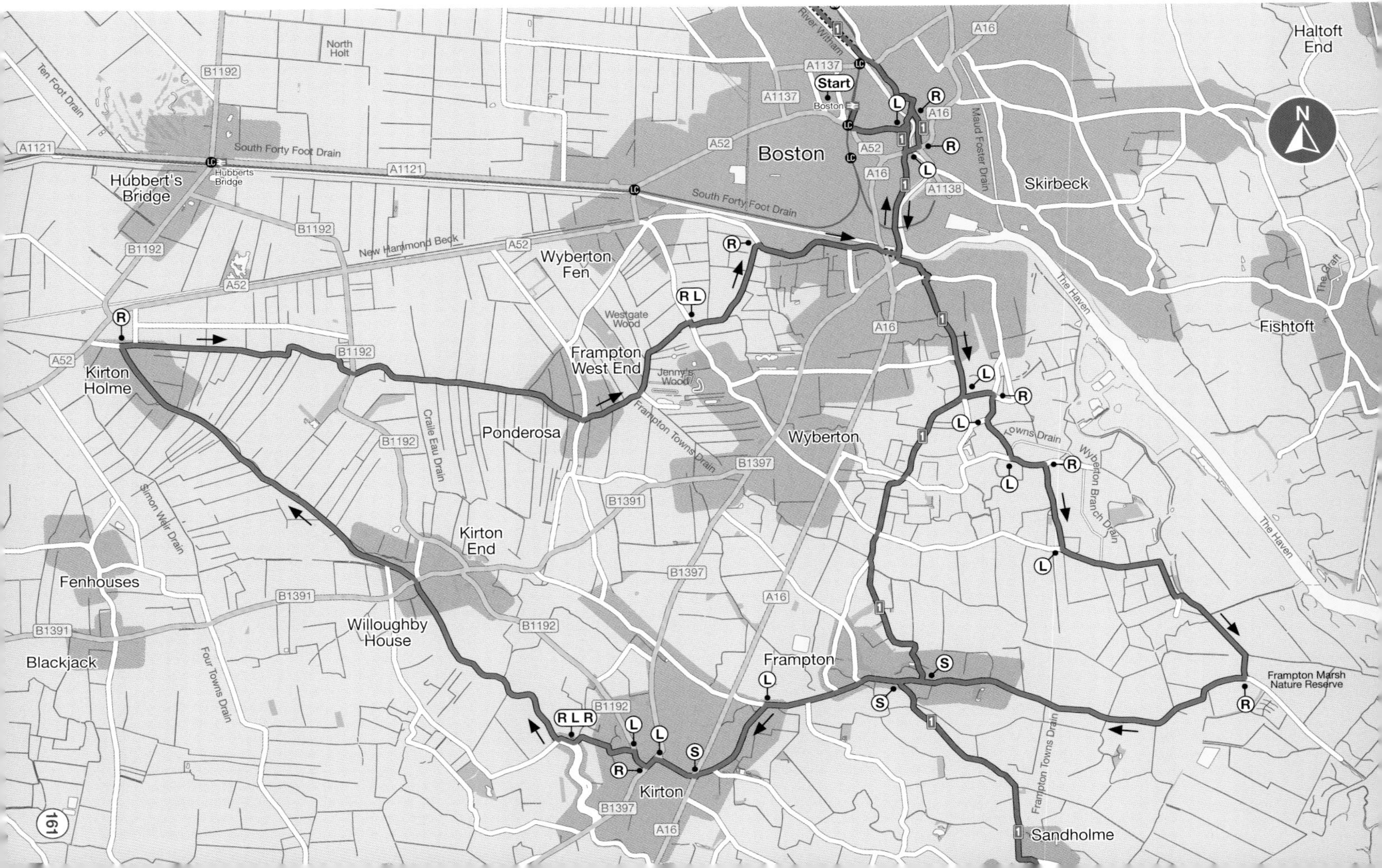
Haltoft End
N
Start
Boston
River Witham
A1137
A1137
A16
A16
A16
A16
A16
A16
A52
A52
A52
A52
A1138
A1121
A1121
Maud Foster Drain
Skirbeck
Fishtoft
The Graft
The Haven
The Haven
Hubbert's Bridge
Hubberts Bridge
South Forty Foot Drain
South Forty Foot Drain
Ten Foot Drain
North Holt
B1192
B1192
B1192
B1192
B1192
B1192
B1192
New Hammond Beck
Wyberton Fen
Westgate Wood
Frampton West End
Jenny's Wood
Frampton Towns Drain
Frampton Towns Drain
Wyberton
Towns Drain
Wyberton Branch Drain
Kirton Holme
Ponderosa
Craile Eau Drain
B1397
B1397
B1397
B1391
B1391
B1391
Kirton End
Simon Weir Drain
Four Towns Drain
Fenhouses
Willoughby House
Blackjack
Frampton
Frampton Marsh Nature Reserve
Kirton
Sandholme

Grantham Circular

28.3 miles / 45.6 km

With your back to Grantham Station go **right**. At the T-junction turn **left**. Turn **right** after the museum. Turn left on Castlegate to visit National Trust property Grantham House. At the river turn **left** onto the signed shared-use path Route 15. When the Route 15 path ends go **right** on the path and then **left** on Belton Ln shared-use path. Follow the path **right** along Sunningdale. At the mini roundabout go **left**, then turn **right**. At the T-junction turn **left**. At the B6403 turn **left** and then carefully take first **right** towards Welby. At the crossroads turn **right** towards Ropsley. Turn **left** towards Folkingham and stay **left**. Turn **right** towards Humby. Stay **left** at the fork then follow the road around south towards Ingoldsby and Bitchfield. At the B1176 go **right** and then **left**. Turn **left** towards Great Ponton. At the B6403 go **left** and **right** to cross. At the T-junction turn **left**. Use the stepped bridge to cross the A1 and continue towards Hungerton. Stay **right** and then at the T-junction turn **right** towards Grantham. Turn **left** towards Harlaxton. Turn **right** on High St. After the bridge turn **right** on the Route 15 canal path and follow back to Grantham. After crossing under the tracks, leave the path and turn **right** along Station Rd to return to the station.

Bike shops

Cyclesport
NG31 6EX Tel: 01476 574268

Pedal Pushers
NG31 6HN Tel: 01476 569508

Halfords
NG31 6HS Tel: 01476 591434

Chris O'Connor Cycles
NG31 6PR Tel: 01476 560877

Eat & drink

The Royal Queen
NG31 9PH Tel: 01476 564410

The Crown & Anchor
NG32 3LP Tel: 01400 230307

The Green Man
NG33 4BE Tel: 01476 585897

The Gregory Arms
NG32 1AD Tel: 01476 577076

Various in Grantham

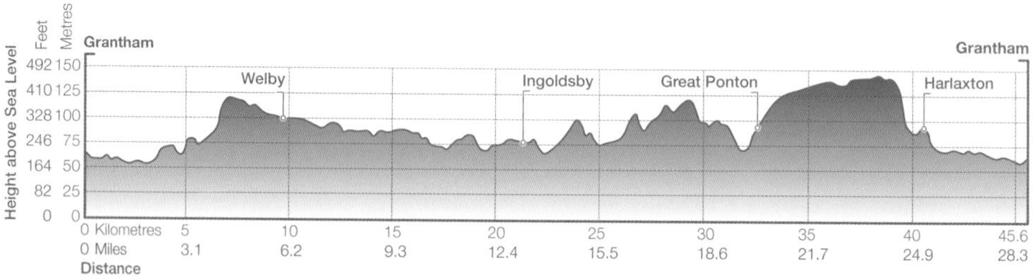

Heydour
Aisby
Oasby
Aunsby
Dembleby
Heydour Southings
Newton
Haceby Great Wood
Haceby
Braceby
Sapperton South Wood
Pickworth Wood
Pickworth
Sapperton
Ropsley
Humby
Lenton
East Glen River
Ingoldsby
Keisby
Hawthorpe
Ingoldsby Wood
Osgodby Coppice
Far Old Park Wood
Hurn Wood
Kirton Wood
Bitchfield
B1176
West Glen River
Boothby Little Wood
Boothby Pagnell
Westby
Welby
Ropsley Rise Wood
Londonthorpe
Bellmount Plantation
B6403
A52
Old Somerby
Boothby Great Wood
Bassingthorpe
Bassingthorpe New Plantation
Stoke Park Wood
Belton
Old Wood
Cherry Orchard
Harrowby
Spittlegate
Ponton Park Wood
Little Ponton
River Witham
A607
Manthorpe
Grantham House
Grantham
Start: See instructions
B1174
A1
Great Ponton
Cringle Brook
Walk Plantation
Farm Plantation
Stoke Rochford
Gonerby Hill Foot
Great Gonerby
Beeden Park
Barrowby Stream
Earlesfield
Mow Beck
Stroxton
Harlaxton Wood
Harlaxton
Gonerby
Barrowby Thorns
Barrowby
Stoke Pasture
Wyville
Weaaldmore Covert
Casthorpe Covert
Sedgebrook
Allington
Old Beck
Denton
Black Fir Plantation
Cooper's Plantation
15
R
L

From Spalding Station go **right**, then turn **right** and **left** onto St Thomas Rd. At the end of the road turn **left** then **right** along the river – this is Route 12. Follow the route south along the river towards Crowland. Follow the route **left** over the bridge, then **left** again towards Crowland. Stay **straight** on Kemp St leaving Route 12. Turn **left** on Postland Rd and **left** on Cloot Drove. Follow the road towards Moulton Chapel. Take the **left** curve towards Moulton Chapel and Spalding. Turn **right** on Oxcroft Bank. At the crossroads turn **right**. At the B1165 turn **left**. Go slight **right** towards Whaplode. Turn **left** on Little Ln. Turn **right** on Hogs Gate. Turn **left** towards Moulton. At the T-junction turn **left** and then stay **right** at the fork on West Cob Gate. Turn **left** on Broad Gate towards Weston Hills. Turn **right** on Austendyke Rd. Turn **right** on Mallard Rd. When the road ends turn **right**. Turn **right** on the B1165 and use the path to cross **straight** at the A16 roundabout. Take the 1st exit **left** at the mini roundabout. Stay **right** on Church St. Cross the river and turn **left** then **right** on Vine St. Follow the road through the centre, then at the A151 junction turn **right** to return to the station.

Bike shops

Gibbons' Cycles & Sports
PE11 1HA Tel: 01775 722050

Halfords
PE11 1RQ Tel: 01775 714498

J R Cycles
PE12 6TJ Tel: 01406 373030

Eat & drink

The Drayman's Arms
PE11 2UE Tel: 01775 723755

Ye Old Bridge Inn
PE6 0HJ Tel: 01733 688232

George & Angel
PE6 0EF Tel: 01733 210550

The Wheatsheaf
PE12 0XL Tel: 01406 380525

The Swan
PE12 6QB Tel: 01406 370349

The Chequers of Weston
PE12 6RA Tel: 01406 370407

The Bell Inn
PE12 6BX Tel: 01406 371306

Ye Olde White Horse
PE11 2RA Tel: 01775 766740

Various in Spalding

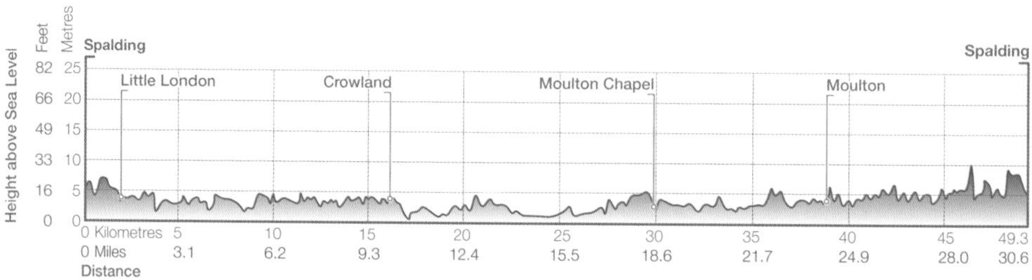

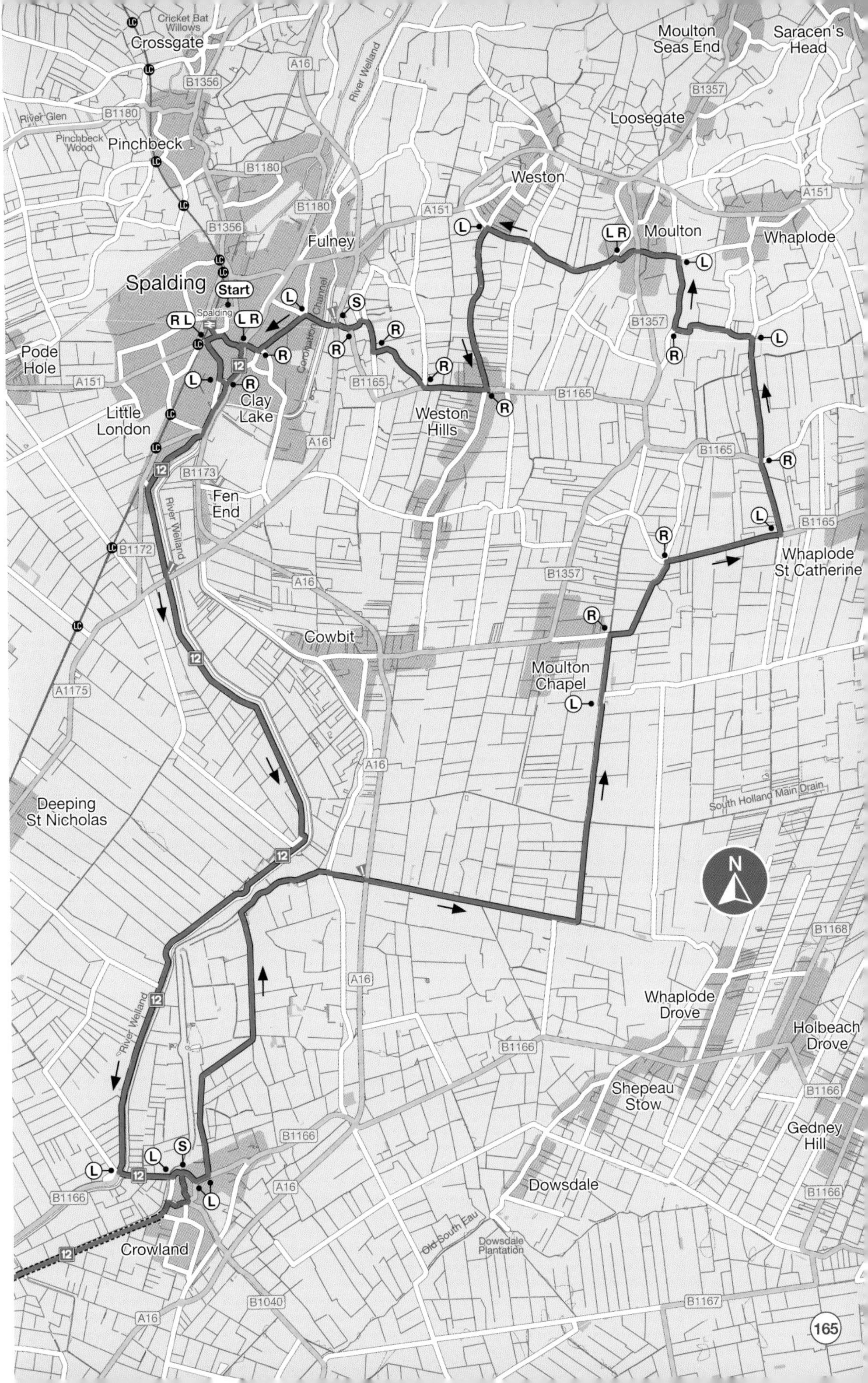

Cricket Bat Willows
Crossgate
A16
B1356
River Welland
Moulton Seas End
Saracen's Head
B1357
River Glen
B1180
Loosegate
Pinchbeck Wood
Pinchbeck
B1180
Weston
A151
B1180
A151
B1356
Fulney
L
L R
Moulton
Whaplode
L
Spalding
Start
Coronation Channel
S
L
Spalding
R L
L R
B1357
R
R
R
L
R
Pode Hole
R
R
A151
L
R
B1165
B1165
Clay Lake
R
Weston Hills
Little London
A16
B1165
R
B1173
Fen End
River Welland
L
B1165
R
B1172
Whaplode St Catherine
B1357
A16
R
Cowbit
Moulton Chapel
L
A1175
A16
South Holland Main Drain
Deeping St Nicholas
N
B1168
A16
Whaplode Drove
River Welland
Holbeach Drove
B1166
Shepeau Stow
B1166
Gedney Hill
L
S
L
L
B1166
A16
Dowsdale
B1166
Crowland
Old South Eau
Dowsdale Plantation
B1040
B1167
A16
12
LC

13 Stamford to Rutland Water

27.8 miles / 44.8 km

At the end of the Stamford Station approach road turn **left** and cross through the park on Route 63. Follow the route around **left** and continue **straight**. Don't follow Route 1 right on Roman Bank but continue **straight** on the A6121 to Ketton. Turn **right** on Empingham Rd towards Empingham. When the road ends at a T-junction, cross and go through the gate then turn **left** on the river ring road / Circuit of Rutland Water. Follow the road to the Lyndon Visitor Centre where you can enjoy the self-guided bird-watching trail. Keep following the circuit and turn **right** on St Mary's Rd - this will take you to the Rutland Water Nature Reserve. To continue, follow Hambleton Rd towards Egleton and turn **right**. When the road ends at a T-junction, turn right to do the optional circuit around Hambleton Peninsula, otherwise turn **left** and then first **right** onto the Route 63 path. After you pass Rutland Fly Fishing Adventures, stay **straight** at the mini roundabout, leaving the circuit. At the A606 use the path to cross and turn **left** towards the Falconry Centre. Stay straight if you want to visit Barnsdale Gardens, otherwise follow Route 63 **right** towards Empingham. The route will take you all the way back to where you started. Turn **right** on Gresley Dr to return to the station.

Bike shops

Richardson's Direct Cycles
PE9 2YN Tel: 01780 480455

Giant
LE15 8HD Tel: 01780 720888

Oakham Cycle Centre
LE15 6NR Tel: 01572 757058

Rutland Cycling Whitwell
LE15 8BL Tel: 01780 460705

Eat & drink

The Northwick Arms
PE9 3TA
Tel: 01780 720238

The Railway Inn Ketton
PE9 3RD
Tel: 01780 721050

Wheatsheaf
LE15 8EZ
Tel: 01780 720083

The Horse & Jockey
LE15 8SU
Tel: 01572 737335

Finch's Arms Hambleton
LE15 8TL
Tel: 01572 756575

The Harbour Café
LE15 8BL
Tel: 01780 461288

Barnsdale Gardens Tea Room
LE15 8AH
Tel: 01572 813200

Fox & Hounds Exton
LE15 8AP
Tel: 01572 812403

The Crown
PE9 4AP
Tel: 01780 753838

The Stampford Post
PE9 2QZ
Tel: 01780 753832

Various in Stamford

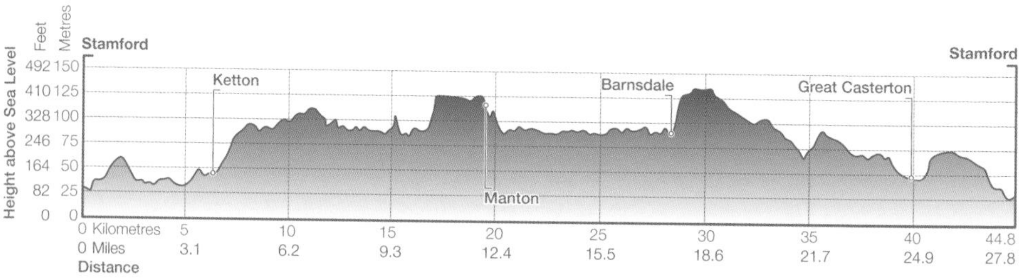

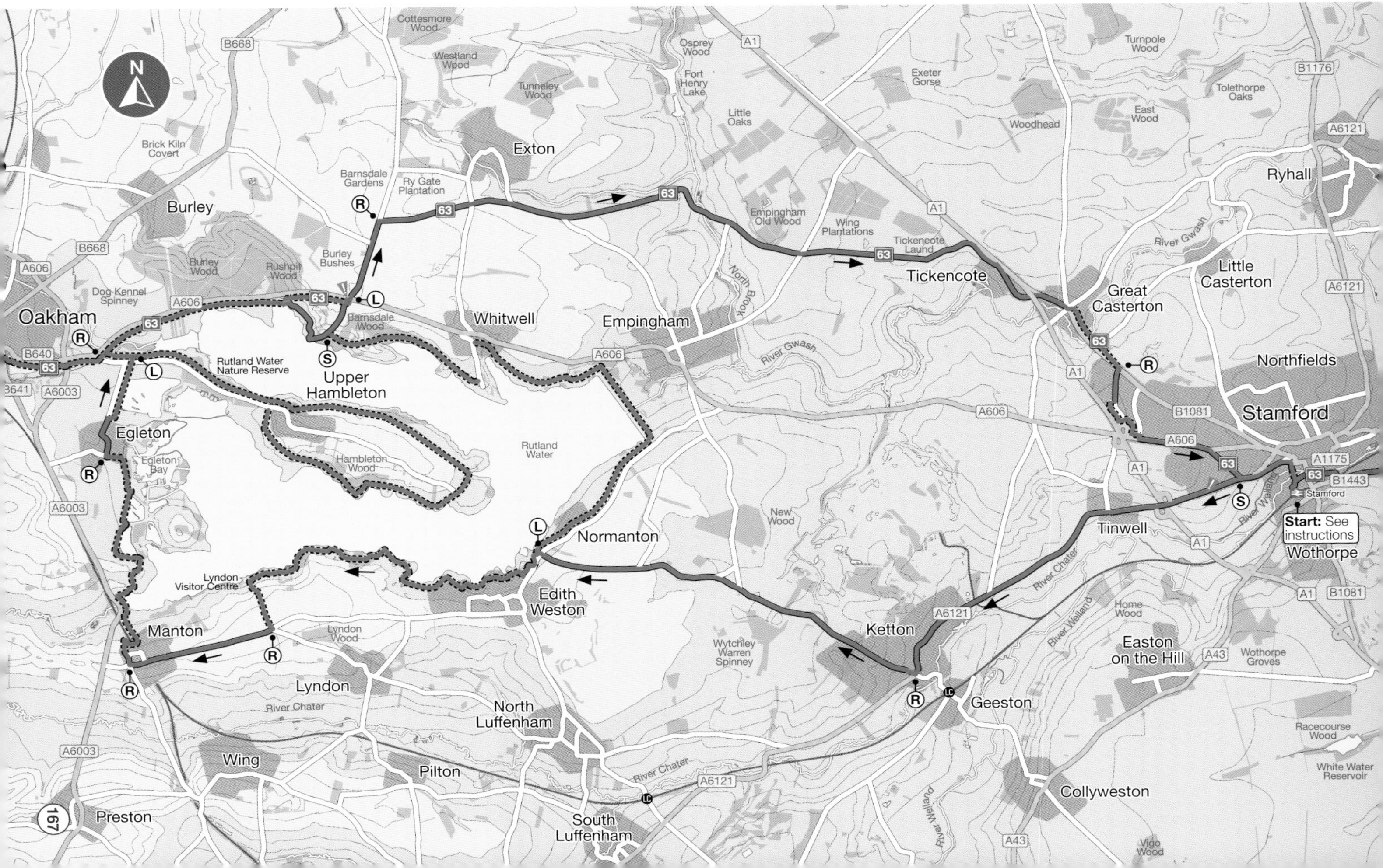
N
Oakham
Burley
Brick Kiln Covert
Dog Kennel Spinney
Burley Wood
Rushpit Wood
Burley Bushes
Barnsdale Gardens
Ry Gate Plantation
Barnsdale Wood
Cottesmore Wood
Westland Wood
Tunneley Wood
Exton
Whitwell
Upper Hambleton
Rutland Water Nature Reserve
Egleton
Egleton Bay
Hambleton Wood
Rutland Water
Lyndon Visitor Centre
Manton
Lyndon Wood
Lyndon
River Chater
Wing
Pilton
Preston
North Luffenham
South Luffenham
Edith Weston
Normanton
Empingham
North Brook
River Gwash
Osprey Wood
Fort Henry Lake
Little Oaks
Empingham Old Wood
Wing Plantations
Tickencote Laund
Tickencote
Exeter Gorse
Woodhead
Turnpole Wood
East Wood
Tolethorpe Oaks
Ryhall
Little Casterton
Great Casterton
Northfields
Stamford
Tinwell
River Welland
Start: See instructions
Wothorpe
New Wood
Wytchley Warren Spinney
Ketton
Geeston
Home Wood
Easton on the Hill
Wothorpe Groves
Racecourse Wood
White Water Reservoir
Collyweston
Vigo Wood
A606
A6003
A1
A6121
A1175
B1443
B1081
B1176
B668
B640
A43
63

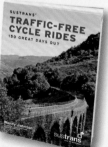

Photo credits

Front cover: © Jonathan Bewley 'Torridge Viaduct on the Tarka Trail'

Page 1: © Shirley Acreman 'Camel Trail, National Route 3'

Page 6: © Jonathan Bewley 'Tarka Trail, National Route 3'

Page 7: © Jonathan Bewley 'Bristol and Bath Railway Path, National Route 4'

Back Cover: © FourPoint Mapping 'Colliers Way outside of Frome'